JEWISH

IN

MUSLIM LIBYA

JEWISH LIFE

IN

MUSLIM LIBYA

Rivals & Relatives

HARVEY E. GOLDBERG

The University of Chicago Press
Chicago and London

Harvey E. Goldberg is professor in the Department of
Sociology and Social Anthropology at the Hebrew
University of Jerusalem. He is the author of *Cave
Dwellers and Citrus Growers*, editor of *Judaism Viewed
from Within and from Without*, and translator and editor
of Mordechai Ha-Cohen's *The Book of Mordechai: A
Study of the Jews of Libya*.

The University of Chicago Press, Chicago 60637
The University of Chicago Press, Ltd., London
© 1990 by Harvey E. Goldberg
All rights reserved. Published 1990
Printed in the United States of America
99 98 97 96 95 94 93 92 91 90   54321

Library of Congress Cataloging-in Publication Data

Goldberg, Harvey, E.
    Jewish life in Muslim Libya : rivals & relatives / Harvey
E. Goldberg.
      p. cm.
    Includes bibliographical references.
    ISBN 0-226-30091-9 (cloth).—ISBN 0-226-30092-7
(paper)
      1. Jews—Libya—History.   2. Jews—Libya—Social
life and customs.
      3. Libya—Ethnic relations.   I. Title.
DS135.L44G65   1990
961.2'004924—dc20   89-20593
                                    CIP

For Judy

Nature has but little clay
Like that of which she moulded you

—VIRGINIA WOOLF,
To the Lighthouse

Contents

Preface   ix

1 Introduction   1

2 Jewish Life in Muslim Tripoli
  in the Late Qaramanli Period   18

3 The Ottoman Period: Political Change
  and Traditional Rhetoric   35

4 Jewish Weddings in Tripolitania:
  A Study in Cultural Sources   52

5 Itinerant Jewish Peddlers in Tripolitania
  at the End of the Ottoman Period
  and under Italian Rule   68

6 Jewish-Muslim Religious Rivalry
  in Tripolitania   82

7 The Anti-Jewish Riots of 1945:
  A Cultural Analysis   97

8 History and Cultural Process:
  Change and Stability in the Meaning
  of Jews in Libyan Society   123

Notes   139

References 159

Index 172

Photographs following page 34

Preface

My first contact with the Jews of Libya took place thirty years ago, when I was an American student in Israel. Barely knowing the meaning of the term *anthropology* at the time, I could hardly suspect that four years later I would embark on a field trip to an Israeli village of Libyan Jews to write a dissertation on the subject. On one of my early trips to locate a moshav of Tripolitanian Jews I drove into the village of Ben Zakkai, and the first person I spoke to spontaneously brought up the subject of the 1945 anti-Jewish riots in Tripoli. I remember chiding myself at the time not to get involved with the topic because I was doing anthropology and not political science.

Since then, anthropologists' claims regarding the scope of their concerns have been expanded, and my desire to understand the former cultural milieu of Libyan Jews has made the topic of Muslim-Jewish relations central in my research. My hope is that the present study will contribute to an understanding of Jewish life as part of Libyan society and culture, and will prove the merit of the peculiar combination of field study and library research that this endeavor represents.

The field data were collected in various projects supported, at different stages, by the Hebrew University, the Israel Academy of Sciences, the Memorial Foundation for Jewish Culture, and the United States National Endowment for the Humanities and National Science Foundation. The United States–Israel Binational Science Foundation supported field research undertaken jointly with Claudio Segrè. I am also grateful to New Hall in Cambridge and the Annenberg Institute of Judaic Studies for fellowship opportunities that allowed this work to reach its final form.

I owe an immeasurable debt to many Libyan Jewish families who, over the years, accepted me into their homes. Particular mention must be made of several friends whose assistance has been essential in expanding both my field of contacts and horizons of understanding. Raffaello Fellah, of Rome, has been a keen challenge to my work by his interest in all aspects of Libyan Jewish life and his tireless effort to ensure that a record of that life survives. His constant support is deeply appreciated. Benzion Rubin, in his readiness to encourage work on the subject, implicitly reinforces the position that concern with one's history does not have to be antithetical to a deep involvement with today's society. Moshe Ji'an's own inquisitiveness about the community of his birth was a source of inspiration to my efforts, and if some anthropological principles have filtered into his pursuit of the past, I can only be gratified at the opportunity for mutuality.

Selecting a few photographs to represent a complex historical topic is always risky. The present selection was guided by several criteria. First, I stress pictures that have not previously been published. Second, most of the pictures depict the focus of this study which is the traditional life of Jews in interaction with Muslims, rather than internal Jewish life as it developed in the period of Italian influence. Thanks are due to those who made photographs available, and to Amos Lighziel for several of the reproductions.

Parts of this work have appeared before, but in every instance have been revised. Thanks are due to the several journals where some material appeared in an early form: "Rites and Riots: The Tripolitanian Pogrom of 1945," *Plural Societies* 8 (Spring 1977):35–56; "The Jewish Wedding in Tripolitania," Maghreb Review 3, no. 9 (1978): 1–6; "Religious Rivalry in Tripolitania," *International Journal of Middle East Studies* 12 (1980):152–70; and "Jewish Life in Muslim Tripoli," *Urban Anthropology* 13 (1984): 65–90. Material also appeared in an earlier form in the following books: Mordechai Ha-Cohen, *Higgid Mordecaï* (in Hebrew), ed. H. Goldberg (Jerusalem: Ben-Zvi, 1978); H. Goldberg, ed. and trans., *The Book of Mordechai* (Philadelphia: ISHI, 1980); J.-L Miège, ed., *Les relations entre Juifs et Musulmans en Afrique du nord; XIXe–XXe siècles* (Paris: CNRS, 1980), 143–59; E. G. H. Joffe and K. S. Mclachilan, eds., *Studies in the Social and Economic History of Libya: The Colonial Period* (Wisbech, Cambridgeshire: MENAS Press, 1982), 161–72; and, in collaboration with Rachel (Rosen) Wasserfall, M. Abitbol, ec., *Communautés juives des marges du Maghreb* (Jerusalem: Ben-Zvi, 1982), 303–20.

It was also thirty years ago that I met my wife, Judy. Everything I have done since then has been shared with her. To her, this work is dedicated.

1 Introduction

At midcentury there were about two million Jews living in the Middle Eastern countries (Chouraqui 1952:135). Today their number stands at less than seventy thousand, and in several countries, such as Algeria or Iraq, which formerly had large Jewish communities, Jews are all but absent.[1] This has led some historians, such as Bernard Lewis (1984:191), to speak unequivocally about the end of Judeo-Islamic symbiosis and has also spurred researchers, including several anthropologists, to document the remnants of Jewish life, while describing ongoing Muslim-Jewish interaction, in settings that seemed to be on the verge of disappearing.

A number of these studies have been carried out in North Africa. On the eve of Algerian independence (in 1962), Briggs and Guède (1964) conducted a rapid ethnographic investigation in the community of Ghardaia in the Mzab, which had been under French military administration and had therefore preserved many traditional features, in comparison to the majority of the Algerian Jews in the north who were French citizens. In their study of the Moroccan town of Sefrou, Geertz, Geertz, and Rosen (1979) have shown the Jews' importance in the local economy, and Rosen (1972, 1984) has provided a fine-grained analysis of Jewish-Muslim relations viewed from the perspective of interpersonal ties within Moroccan culture at large. Most recently, Udovitch and Valensi (1984) produced a field study of the "Last Arab Jews," based on fieldwork on the island of Jerba in southern Tunisia. Add to these the volume by Stillman (1979), which (like Lewis's 1984 work) surveys the history of Jews in all Arab lands, providing documents from North Africa and elsewhere, and we find a growing body of systematic information on Jews in Muslim North Africa which is informed by thoughtful analysis.[2]

The present volume seeks to contribute to this field in several ways. Geographically, its focus is on Libya, a country that has benefited from relatively little social research in general[3] and investiga-

1

tion of Jewish life in particular.[4] Second, the emphasis is on aspects of
everyday behavior which, while not ignored in other studies on the
mutual involvement of Muslims and Jews, deserve more penetrating
attention than they have thus far received. The aspects of life with
which we are concerned are found in areas often relegated to the supposedly nonserious realm of "folklore," such as marriage customs or
the rituals of daily contact, but they often reflect the interfaces of
Muslim and Jewish interaction. These practices, therefore, may be
sensitive indicators of the meanings that each group had for the other.
Third, this sudy is based on a methodology that has arisen in response to the materials at hand. The method combines oral history,
namely, the interviewing of Libyan Jews now found in Israel concerning life in their original communities, with written historical sources
viewed in anthropological perspective.[5] While keenly aware of the
limitations of this method, I hope to show that it is capable of il-
luminating systems of meaning that animated the interchanges
between Muslim and Jew in everyday life in Tripoli and Tripolitania.[6]

There is yet a fourth area in which this study hopes to make a
contribution, and that is the exploration of interrelationships between "text and context." This phrase is used by Redfield (1955) to
point out the differences in emphasis in the work of historical and
literary specialists, on the one hand, and that of anthropologists on
the other. Recently there have appeared an increasing number of studies advocating greater textual sensitivity on the part of anthropologists and providing some examples of the fruitfulness of that approach.[7] The relation of community to text is doubly complex in the
case of Judaism and Islam, for not only do sacred texts form what is
viewed as the blueprint for correct action, but they define the very
boundaries of these societies, setting them off from one another. In
several of the chapters that follow, I discuss aspects of everyday life
that cannot be understood without reference to textual-based traditions, while attempting not to compromise the anthropological
insistence on the contextual analysis of cultural forms.

The concern with the importance of the traditional texts, the
Qur'an and the Torah,[8] which clearly point Islam and Judaism in different directions, is the background to the central problematic of this
study, which seeks to document and analyze *cultural* interchange, at
an everyday level, between Jews and Muslims in Libya. The focus on
the question of interchange means that adequate attention must be
paid to both the nature of the dominant Muslim community and the
internal texture of Jewish life. Many studies of North Africa have
been content to focus on Muslims alone, mentioning the formerly
important Jewish communities only in passing, if at all. On the other

hand, some studies of the Jews of North Africa carried out in Israel, where these Jews no longer are found in their original environment, tend to downplay the significance of the Islamic setting within which these communities lived their lives. It is our aim to elucidate some of the mechanisms and dynamics of this no-longer-extant intricate interchange.

By emphasizing questions of cultural dynamics, this study also intends to move "beyond" questions of a strictly sociological or so-cio-legal nature. Thus, it is not my main purpose to evaluate "the status" of the Jews in Libyan Muslim society, or to reach a summary determination about the nature and extent of their participation in general social life. These are crucial topics, to which serious atten-tion will be given, and in dealing with them I lean heavily on earlier works concerned with similar issues in other Muslim societies where Jews have dwelt. The special contribution of this investigation, how-ever, concerns the cultural forms of everyday life, details of behavior often seen as "quaint" or "curious." These cultural details, it is claimed, constitute significant elements in the immediate environ-ment of the individual and of social networks, and thereby are critical in shaping the meanings and experiences that characterized life in those societies. In focusing on everyday life, I do not intend to sepa-rate cultural analysis from the broader political, economic, and social settings in which it must be placed, but to show how the analysis of these larger structures can benefit by attention to ethnographic de-tails describing everyday customs and micro level social processes.

The focus of this study, as stated, is on the Jews of Libya, from the turn of the nineteenth century until the middle of the twentieth, when the vast majority of Libyan Jews decided to emigrate, prior to Libyan independence, and to settle in Israel. Libya, having the small-est general population of all the Maghrib countries, also had the smallest Jewish community, numbering in the vicinity of six or seven thousand at the beginning of the period under consideration, and somewhat over thirty-five thousand in 1949. The question may be rightly asked, therefore, as to the larger relevance of this enterprise. Is it intended as a footnote to a topic already well thrashed over, or can the study of this particular group throw light on the dynamics of Mus-lim-Jewish interchange in other lands and at other periods?

While the present work makes no pretense at revising, in a basic manner, the findings and insights of specialists, mostly historians, who have addressed themselves to the question of understanding non-Muslim groups under Islamic rule, I attempt to refine this under-standing through the use of anthropological tools and perhaps there-by illuminate topics that have not achieved their desired clarity. A general discussion is therefore required as to how anthropological perspectives may be placed in relation to historical work.

In dealing with a civilization such as Islam, historians have insisted, rightly in my estimation, that it must, in the first instance, be viewed in its classic expression. In the Middle Eastern Muslim world this expression occurred in the "high Middle Ages," when Islamic societies were powerful, cultural and religious creativity was at a peak, and Islam self-confidently confronted, in various spheres of life, the other cultures and civilizations with which it had contact. From this vantage point, the challenge of the European Crusades and the invasions from central Asia marked shifts in power which robbed preeminence from Islam and coincided with what is seen by many as the onset of civilizational decline. The emergence of the Ottoman Empire, which rivaled and threatened Europe in the sixteenth and seventeenth centuries, again gave Islam political prominence, but it, in turn, grew weak in the face of the development of modern Europe, as became clear throughout the course of the nineteenth century. The researcher, whether historian or anthropologist, seeking to study a Muslim society in the modern period must obviously relate to contemporary factors that impinge on that society, yet also must maintain an awareness of the nature and form that classical cultural conceptions assume in the more recent eras. In this work we are faced with the task of appreciating time-honored notions such as that of *dhimmi*, the governing Islamic legal concept dealing with protected non-Muslims under Muslim rule, while assessing the specific forces that shaped the place and perception of Jews in Libyan society during the period under question.

The notion of dhimmi, as is well known, is applied to several "peoples of the book"—groups that had had the benefit of a revealed religion, but had not recognized the truth—that Muhammad was the "seal of the prophets." This status initially referred mainly to Christians and Jews, and was extended by jurists in early Islam to include Zoroastrians. The term *dhimmi* carries the meaning of "contract," but it clearly is not a contract of equals. Lewis (1984, chap. 1) surveys various interpretations of the term, and their legal implications, that have been highlighted at different times and in different circumstances. Whatever the more technical meanings of the term may have been, it both reflects and helped shape a broad cultural conception in which weaker non-Muslim groups are seen as agreeing to accept certain conditions, such as special financial obligations and restricted participation in social life, thereby acknowledging, implicitly, the supremacy of Islam while acquiring the right to be protected by the Muslim power under which they reside.

The term *dhimmi* took on a special meaning, referring only to Jews, in the context of North African society, because Almohad rule in the area (twelfth century) resulted in the disappearance of native Christian communities. Nevertheless, it should not be forgotten that the term refers to a general legal-religious category, and, in the classical period, rivalry with Christianity and concern with Christians in the Islamic world were of much greater salience than the corresponding concerns with Jews and Judaism. As for religious polemics, much more energy was devoted by Muslims to challenging and rebutting Christianity as compared to Judaism. According to Perlmann, "For Muslims, Jews and Judaism were an unimportant subject" (1974:126).

There seems to be scholarly consensus that the classic stance of Islam toward Judaism, as recorded in the sources analyzed by Perlmann, Lewis, and others, was one of *ignore*-ance, and that for most Muslims, Judaism was not significant enough to be viewed as a religious threat. Several interpretations have been given for this difference between Islam's positioning vis-à-vis Judaism and Christianity. One is based on political reasoning (cf. Lewis 1984:12; Cohen 1986). Because the Christian world represented a strong political reality which could resist and even threaten Islam, the need was felt to defend the theological underpinnings of Islamic society in respect of Christian claims (no such threat was to be found from Jewish quarters). A second explanation relates more directly to ideological matters, comparing Islam's attitude toward Judaism with Christianity's attitude toward its predecessor. This theory emphasizes the challenge to Christian belief stemming from the very continued existence of Judaism and of Jews, and the demonic view of Jewry which may be seen as its outgrowth. By contrast, Judaism did not present such an ideological problem to Islam. In Lewis's words, "In Islamic society hostility to the Jew is non-theological. . . . For Muslims, it is not part of the birth pangs of their religion, as it is for Christians" (1984:85).

Given these two very different levels of explanation, the social scientist cannot but wonder about the relationship between them. If there had been a powerful Jewish polity in the Middle Ages, could we expect to have found more vigorous Muslim-Jewish polemics? And, continuing this speculation, if such polemics had existed, might not some scholars have hypothesized that the very existence of Judaism and Jews, who were the recipients of early revelations but who did not accept Muhammad, constitute an inherent theological problem for Islam? Obviously, no answer can be given to these "what-if" questions, and a re-reading of medieval sources is far beyond the present researcher's competence. For the time being, I would like to note that a characterization of Islam as basically uninterested in Judaism does not seem altogether appropriate with regard to popular religion in North Africa in recent times. For this reason our exploration of Muslim-Jewish interchange in Libyan society is offered for close examination, and as more than a peripheral addition to a thoroughly understood subject.

Returning momentarily to the medieval period, there is no doubt that one of the central contributions shaping the scholarly view of the place of the non-Muslims in Muslim society has been Goitein's researches on the Cairo geniza material.[9] The fact that Goitein could justifiably name his study *A Mediterranean Society,* while relying on documents primarily written by Jews in a Jewish script (many of the documents are in the Arabic language written in Hebrew characters), underlines his thesis concerning the widespread involvement of Jews (and Christians)[10] in many facets of the social life of medieval Cairo. One of the reviewers of the second volume of Goitein's opus stated: "I felt on finishing this book that I learned more about medieval Islamic society than I had from any other single book" (Bulliet 1976:457). The same reviewer notes the far-reaching similarities between Jewish life and Muslim life at that period, but goes on to point out that Goitein does not provide "a centralized discussion of the evident convergence of Muslim and Jewish social life . . . nowhere is this convergence treated as a *problem* in itself. Did Muslim society evolve institutions on the pattern of earlier Judeo-Christian institutions, or did the minority communities slowly approximate the institutional framework of the dominant religion?" (p. 458). The social anthropologist is not normally in a position to answer questions of long-term historical trends, but can help refine the discourse within which such questions are stated. Whether Jews and Christians influenced Muslims, or whether the opposite trend predominated (obviously both processes must have been at work), there is room for a detailed examination of the nature of daily contact and the mechanisms of cultural give-and-take. Here is one of the points at which the anthropologist, attuned to the subtleties of daily interaction, can form a useful partnership with the historian.

The exploration of such a partnership may begin by considering the title of another of Goitein's (1955) books concerned with our topic: *Jews and Arabs: Their Contacts through the Ages.* In the main title no mention is made of Christians, but the issue is stated in bipolar terms: Jews on one side and Arabs on the other. This juxtaposition is surprising from several points of view. Not only are the Jews taken out of the general category of dhimmi and presented, in the title, as an issue in their own right (the book itself, of course, does not ignore Christianity), but scholarly attention is lavished on this very small group which in no Arab country, in recent history, constituted more than 3 percent of the population.

Various reasons make the focus on the specific ties and differences between Jews and Arabs of interest. Lewis (1968) has discussed how the subject of Jews under Islam in "the golden era of Spain" was of special attraction to nineteenth-century European Jewish scholars who utilized this historical construct to criticize the contemporary Christian world, which still hesitated at granting Jews full participation in European society. Goitein (1955:ix–xiii) explicitly motivated the writing of the first edition of his short book in terms of the recent establishment of the state of Israel and the necessity for a clear historical picture of the relations between the two peoples.[11] Both these reasons, however, place the historical interest in Jews qua Jews in Muslim society as growing out of the life situation of researchers, whose definition of the problematics may or may not coincide with concerns as defined internally in traditional Muslim society. It nevertheless is my claim that the contrast of Muslim and Jew had specific importance in North African society in recent times, irrespective of nineteenth-century intellectual currents and independent of the development of Zionism and the establishment of Israel.

Not only, as mentioned, had the term *dhimmi* become synonymous with *Jew* in the context of North Africa, because of the absence of a native Christian population, but, it shall be argued, a close-up, anthropological view of daily life suggests that the Jews took on significance within the woof and warp of daily meanings which was greater than would be expected by their demographic strength, or even by the economic roles in which they tended to specialize. In exploring this claim, it is necessary to go beyond written texts and attempt to appreciate the complex interplay of "official" meanings and those that arose over the course of years of multilayered daily contacts.

For example, normally my interviewing among the Jews of Tripolitania did not concern standard legal notions, but sought descriptions of everyday interactions. In the course of the resulting depictions, spontaneous expressions of attitudes or interpretations of values often were offered. On several occasions, Tripolitanian Jews, wanting to demonstrate the closeness that Muslims felt to them, said that they would call the Jews *dimmi*. The term, as pronounced in the local vernacular, was explained as deriving from the word for blood, the implication being that the Muslim treated the Jew with affection, as being "part of himself." My interlocutors did not relate to the term as part of an official status in Muslim law, but at the

same time, upon further questioning, it became clear that the notion continued to bear some of its classical meanings of weakness
and dependence. One possibility is that this was a Jewish interpretation placed on a Muslim concept, thereby mitigating its severity in
the Jews' eyes. My sense is, however, that my informants reported an
aspect of "folk" culture which was shared by both (some) Jews and
Muslims. In any event, this interpretation, growing out of ongoing
practice, may be seen as a kind of *miscognisance* (Bourdieu 1977)
which upends official doctrines while maintaining them and highlights the need for appreciating popular consciousness in matters
enshrined in written historical sources.

Another topic, that of commensuality, which was surrounded
and indeed constituted by daily ritual, can indicate the kinds of hy-
potheses that are explored in greater depth. Both Judaism and Islam,
in contrast to Christianity, are characterized by detailed dietary restrictions, while the restrictions are more elaborate in Jewish
tradition than in Muslim practice. A part of the dietary laws, in both
cases, concerns forms of slaughtering, and here also the Jewish re-
quirements are more confining than the Muslim ones. This seems to
imply that if food is permitted to Jews, it should also be permitted
under Islamic law, and the Qur'an, in fact, states that it is lawful for
Muslims to eat the "food of those who have been given the Book" (V,
7). Most religious authorities have permitted Muslims to eat the meat
of the Jews (Lewis 1984:85), and throughout North Africa it was common for Muslims to purchase and eat meat slaughtered and sold by
Jews (cf. Deshen 1983:44), although the reverse did not normally occur (cf. Udovitch and Valensi 1984:105). Muslims might also eat meat
meals prepared and served by Jews, although this was less common;
for a Jew, however, the partaking of a nonkosher meal would be a gross
abandonment of his religious and social identity. A situation existed
in which Jews allowed their meat to be eaten by Muslims, but refrained from reciprocity.

In addition to a behavioral account of these well-known social
patterns, different values may be placed on this imbalance in the symbolic logic of everyday life. From the point of view of the Jews, it
seems clear that they regarded their slaughtering as representing a
higher religious level which set them "above" the Muslims. The fact
that Muslims continued to preserve the imbalance may have constituted, in Jewish eyes, an implicit admission of the latter's religious
virtuosity. It may be hypothesized, based on a comparative symbolo-
gical (Turner 1982) perspective which compares such matters in
different cultural contexts, that Muslims often implicitly sensed
such a meaning, which contradicted the status accorded to Jews by

formal Islam, but still continued to collude in its perpetuation. It is possible to offer an alternative symbology, congenial to both the Muslim practice and official ideology, in which Islamic slaughter would be viewed as "too sacred" to be eaten by Jews, but the reverse (Jewish meat is not too sacred for Muslims) would not be true. This explanation, however, is contradicted by the fact that in the Jebel Nefusa, southwest of Tripoli, maraboutic[12] groups possessing an extra degree of sanctity than ordinary Muslims would refrain from eating Jewish slaughter, while rank-and-file Muslims did not observe this restriction. A paradoxical situation appears to have existed. Muslims, who took for granted the weakness and inferiority of Jews, nevertheless, on a daily level, continued to behave in a manner that (mis)recognized the Jews as following a special path which was both comprehensible and valued in terms of Muslim religious sensibilities. Thus the Jews cannot be viewed as an accidental, peripheral variant in the environment of North African Muslims, but, in the words of one historian, their position was "structural" (Wansbrough 1977). It is the nature and dynamics of that structuring, in everyday interchange, which this study hopes to elucidate.

It is not only the Jews' continued interaction with the wider social and cultural environment which shaped the contours of Jewish-Muslim give-and-take, but the Jews' general awareness of being a small minority in a Gentile world. As a Jewish society, they viewed themselves as part of an ancient tradition forged by scripture and the writings of rabbinic sages who strove to maintain that tradition over the generations. It therefore behooves the researcher to take into account the written texts that played a role in shaping local practice, even though many of the less literate and nonliterate (in particular, women) members of society may barely have been aware of the textual aspects of time-honored custom.

For example, Udovitch and Valensi (1984:71–72) describe how the Jews of Jerba, just to the west of Libya, utilize a form of wordplay on the New Year (Rosh ha-Shanah) which refers to the fruits and vegetables that adorn the festive holiday table. Utilizing homonyms and homophones, associations are created between these foods and qualities of the coming New Year that members of the family, and the community at large, wish to invoke. The Arabic word for beans, their Jerban informants explained, evokes the Hebrew stem meaning "growth," and the local term for squash connotes Hebrew "tear apart," with the implication that the consequences of past sins should be destroyed. This practice, taking place at one of the central moments of the ritual year, signals an intricate symbiosis between universal Jewish tradition and the specific reality in which Jews find themselves as expressed in the vernacular and the produce of the market.

This custom, however, not only represents some regional North African trait, but carries with it the weight of rabbinic tradition. Its prototype is outlined in the Talmud, where the spoken language is Aramaic, and is encoded in the standard legal compendium, the *Shul-ḥan 'Arukh*, authored in the sixteenth century by a prominent Sephardic scholar living in the Ottoman Empire. In some North African communities, such as Algeria, this custom is spelled out in the Rosh ha-Shanah *maḥzor* (prayer book), and there the resemblance between some of the current Arabic food terms and the original Aramaic comes into view. In other communities, including Jerba, many versions of the Mahzor do not spell out this practice, so that its immediate impact is that of a tradition carried within the living community which resonates closely with the contemporary spoken language.

The power of the overall, pan-Jewish, written tradition is indicated by the fact that Rosh ha-Shanah food wordplay was also found in Yiddish-speaking regions, and one of the leaders of ultra-orthodoxy in nineteenth-century eastern Europe, in his commentary on the Shul-han 'Arukh, explicitly states that this practice should be extended to every land and adjusted to the local language.[13] It is far from my intention to claim that every detail of local behavior on the part of North African Jews is anchored in a proof-text, but the Rosh ha-Shanah table example should alert us to an important cultural mechanism operating among Jews in the Maghrib and elsewhere. At a quintessential moment in the Jewish ritual year, Jewish tradition, as embodied in Hebrew words (which over the centuries were accentuated primarily in their written rather than spoken forms), expands to impose its own interpretations on the non-Jewish setting to which it normally must accommodate itself. Albeit a moment of mild levity within one of the year's most solemn days (or perhaps precisely because it appears in the form of "play"), this custom, and others that parallel it, shows the ability of the tradition of the minority, linked to the language and books shared with Jews everywhere, to transform the external to one's own, the Arabic to Hebrew, the *realia* of daily existence to a gloss on a hallowed text.

In examining conventional religious interchange and the consciousness of classic texts in everyday life in Libya, this study has continual recourse to the work of Mordechai Ha-Cohen, whose life spanned the period of Ottoman rule in Libya and the early years of the Italian regime. Ha-Cohen was born in Tripoli in 1856 and passed away in Benghazi in 1929. He had no opportunity for an extended education, but his inquisitiveness and intelligence led him to pursue many subjects on his own, including the study of languages. He began his career as a humble teacher and peddler, later learned to fix clocks, and, after that, began to work as a licensee in the rabbinic court and spent many hours in its archives. There he began work on his manuscript, *Highid Mordekhai* (literally, "Mordechai Narrated"), a record of the history, customs, and institutions of the Jews of Tripoli and Tripolitania, written in Hebrew.[14]

Ha-Cohen was born into a traditional society on which European influences, in the form of the Ottoman reforms that were being applied in Libya, were making their first impressions. In terms of technology, he grew up in a land where irrigation was carried out by animal power, and in his life witnessed the introduction of the steamship, the telegraph, and the first use of airplanes in warfare (by the Italians against the Libyans). Although his formal education was limited, as was that of other Jewish children in Tripoli of his day, he constantly strove to learn as much as he could of the world at large. The breadth of his perspective is evident in *Highid Mordekhai*, which shows his interest in topics ranging from detailed accounts of technical processes to a summary of tribal structure in the Jebel Nefusa. His historical account is based on the examination of extant texts (in Hebrew, Arabic, and Italian), as well as on observations of Libyan society of his day and interviews with Muslim and Jewish elders. The question of the position of the Jews in Muslim society was of abiding concern to him, as shown in this lengthy quote from his work, indicating both the centrality of the subject in his eyes and the value of his writings as a historical source:[15]

> Most of the Muslims of Tripoli are eager to argue about matters of religion, but do not do this justly, for the sake of determining the truth. They believe deeply that their religion is the most holy and felicitous, compared to all other religions, and do not accept rational argument. If a Jew bests them in a dispute, they hold deep resentment toward him, especially if their honor is offended in the argument. They are astounded at the Jews and Christians who appear to wear blinders that keep them from seeking and choosing the felicitous Muhammadan religion, which gives its believers great joy and concubines in paradise hereafter. The learned and the notables, however, do not involve themselves in disputes.[16]
>
> The Muhammadans[17] of the district have the hatred of Jews and Christians implanted in their hearts, but the Jews succeed in minimizing it; they humble themselves before the Muhammadans, the lords of the land. The Jews, and the Christians too, bear animosity toward the Muhammadans, and often say: "As in water, face answers face, so the

heart of man to man."[18] During the reign of Yusef Pasha Qaramanli, a marabout from Wadai came to Tripoli and preached vilification of the Jews, sowing hatred, as recorded in section 38.[19]

The Turks are not so given to religious hatred, but after settling here, some of them have learned the ways of the Arabs. In former times, if someone from another religion so much as uttered a word that suggested belief in Muhammad, prophet of the Ishmaelites, he became trapped like a bird in a snare. It was impossible for him to return to the religion of his fathers unless he succeeded in fleeing to another city where he was not recognized. There he could return to his people and to his God.

A person who accepts the Muhammadan religion is viewed as a saint. He will be surrounded by many new friends, who honor the religion and hope to receive blessing through him. They will donate money to him in great and small amounts, each man according to his means. At present, however, the officials of the Turkish government realize that the converts who enter the Muhammadan religion are usually not upright people. It is not that they love the Muslim religion more than the religion into which they were born, but that they wish to use the religion for some reason, and as soon as possible they return to their former faith. Therefore, the officials have decided not to accept converts except after thorough investigation, so that the religion will not be trifled with.

The Muhammadans of the villages do not have religious hatred toward the Jews, but, nevertheless, are very proud. They will not allow a Jew to pass in front of them, mounted on an animal, nor will they permit him to carry a weapon. The Jews lower themselves and accord honor to the Muhammadans, the lords of the land. Even so, when the Muhammadans have the opportunity to rob and oppress, then the wealth of the Jew becomes like ownerless property because he does not believe in the Muhammadan religion and he has no weapon to defend himself against attackers.

The Muhammadans of the villages are unstinting in following one of their customs; they desire to honor guests by preparing them an elegant meal and gladly bring them everything they need with generosity. If something is lacking in the house, they will borrow from another in order to properly honor their guest. In particular, if a mounted warrior comes to their house, or even an ordinary Jew, they earn a good name by greatly honoring him. This is so even if they follow the law of blood vengeance, pursuing a murderer to avenge him, a life for a life, as described in section 11, note 17.[20] If the murderer is in the avenger's home, the avenger will not harm him so long as he is under his protection.

In later chapters I refer to several parts of this quote, along with other passages of Ha-Cohen's work which throw light on our subject. For the time being, it is sufficient to underline his grasp of the local situation that matters of religion, and rivalry between Muslims and non-Muslims, are prominent and enduring features of life in Libya.

Chapter 2 of this volume deals with the late medieval period, focusing on the latter years of the Qaramanli dynasty, which came to an end when Tripoli was placed under direct Ottoman rule in 1835. There is fairly good documentation of everyday life in Tripoli at this time. The Jews had the official status of dhimmi under Islamic law, a definition that, as elsewhere, allowed them to run their internal affairs and permitted wide-ranging participation in economic and social life. During this period, state-supported piracy was being undermined by European powers, a process affecting all of Tripolitan society. A text from the middle of the nineteenth century recalls a weekly sports contest among the Jews, in the Jewish quarter of town—a contest that attracted the attention of many of the town's residents in the late Qaramanli period. Utilizing recent anthropological approaches to the analysis of games and spectacles, I suggest that this intramural Jewish contest became a model for the political and economic struggle then being carried out between Tripoli and the European world bearing down upon it. While the Jews were ostensibly encapsulated within circumscribed spheres of social and cultural life, symbolic linkages bridged the world of the Jews with that of the society at large, while perhaps masking the prominence of a Jewish presence in the town's affairs.

In 1835 the Ottoman Empire established direct rule over Libya, and throughout the remainder of the nineteenth century (and the beginning of the twentieth) took steps to introduce reforms there, parallel to the modernizing efforts elsewhere in the empire (Anderson 1986). This involved, among other things, a change in the civil status of the Jews, so that they became, in principle, subjects of the empire equal to all other subjects. In addition, some of the more energetic governors actively sought the cooperation of the small group of wealthy Jewish merchants in developing the region's economy (Simon 1982). These steps, however, had to take into consideration the reluctance of the population at large to change their perception of the dhimmi. Within the traditional discourse of Muslim life in North Africa, it was common to refer to Jews in rhetoric that took for granted their lowly position. The power of a ruler would be extolled by saying that a woman or a Jew could travel throughout the realm and fear no harm. The logic to this statement was, "How much more so a full member of society!" The developments of the nineteenth century in Libya take an unusual twist, and (early in the twentieth century) this popular logic was utilized by reforming Turkish governors in an attempt to establish the conscription of Libyan Muslims. Two governors pressured the Jews to agree to military service (the ultimate expression of full societal membership), a step that would allow the governors to say to the other Tripolitanians, "If the Jews serve in the army, how much more so the Muslims!" It is only by appreciating time-honored cultural notions that one can comprehend the political tactics of modernizing through the manipulation of traditional rhetoric that continued to be meaningful within the population at large.

Life in Tripolitania, in both the Qaramanli and Ottoman periods, involved a great deal of contact between Muslims and Jews. This was particularly true in the small towns of the hinterland, in which the Jews usually numbered several hundred souls. A situation such as this, which existed over generations, undoubtedly led to extensive cultural borrowing, from the majority to the minority, but perhaps in the other direction as well. Given the length of their coresidence it no doubt would be a futile exercise to try to sort out which cultural "traits" were "Jewish" and which were "Muslim." It is possible, however, to try to appreciate some of the dynamics of this situation, particularly from the point of view of the Jews who were faced with the challenge of remaining distinct in spite of the overwhelming cultural pressures around them. Attachment to normative Jewish tradition, as written in sacred books and as interpreted by specialists who were familiar with these writings, became a major mechanism, and a symbol, of Jewish distinctiveness. This process is examined by a close look at wedding ceremonies, both Jewish and Muslim, as carried out in mountainous regions to the south of Tripoli. While the process of borrowing from the environment is eminently clear, the examination also shows how small communities exhibit the influence of *halakhic* (rabbinic-legal) practice, and how they interpret and reinterpret customs, which "objectively" may be similar to those of the Muslims, in ways that assert and underline their Jewishness and their difference.

The extensive similarity of customs and practices shared by Muslims and Jews indicates prolonged and intimate contact. This was particularly pronounced in the rural areas, where the Jews' daily search for a livelihood brought them into regular and complex contacts with Muslims. Chapter 5 looks in detail at an instance of this interaction—the case of the rural peddlers in the Tripolitanian hinterland. A detailed focus on this "role" reveals that its economic aspects were intricately bound up with social values such as honor and shame, which, in the rural setting, meshed easily with the distinction between Muslim and Jew, and between male and female. While the "official" distinction between Jew and Muslim, anchored in the realm of religion, may be seen as relegated to the spheres of

synagogue or mosque and family, in which members of the two communities were firmly separated, an analysis of the peddlers' activities
shows how the distinction was given cultural expression in mundane,
quotidian activities, and was thereby reinforced and reproduced in
life situations not strictly regulated by specific religious rules.

Neither rural Tripolitanians nor the majority of Muslims or Jews
in the town of Tripoli was very learned in terms of the standard texts
of their respective religions, but the religious concerns and debates of
the classic religions nevertheless had an impact on everyday life.
Given that the principles of both religions are embodied in ritual-
legal dictates concerning everyday life, such as in the realm of food,
and in precisely prescribed practices, such as circumcision, religious
debate is not only a matter of cerebral and verbal skills, but takes
place in concrete actions wherein each group may set itself off from
the other. Religious debate is thereby woven into the threads of daily
praxis of all members of society. This is illustrated in the analysis of a
text presenting the story of a Muslim converting to Judaism in the
city of Tripoli in the seventeenth century. Whether this story is historically accurate is not of as much interest as the fact that the story
was preserved in the oral literature of the Jews up to the end of the
nineteenth century, and that cultural practices similar to those in the
narrative are documented, through ethnographic reconstruction, for
the twentieth century. The popular text in question shows that topics
central to the explicit doctrines of the great traditions receive expression in the lives of illiterate town dwellers. Conversely, various
genre of folk traditions may serve as storehouses wherein major religious themes and conflicts, which often are muted in the main
spheres of economic and social action, are preserved and become
available as the basis of activity under appropriate circumstances.

In October 1911 Tripoli was taken by Italian forces, and in the
treaty of Lausanne (October 1912) the rulers of Turkey ceded Libya to
Italian control. With the revolt of Arab forces in the interior, and the
intervening of World War I, full control of the province was not established until 1922 (only subsequently were the Fezzan and Cyrenaica
brought totally under Italian rule), and it was just over twenty years
later (January 1943) that the British took Tripoli from the Italian and
German forces. This relatively brief period (the shortest colonial rule
in North Africa) was characterized by dramatic and contradictory
shifts in the position of the Jews. Toward the very end of Turkish
(Young Turk) rule, a small number of the Jewish elite began to express
strong pro-Italian sentiments, and the conquering army and new administration immediately turned to the Jews, who often knew Italian
as well as Arabic, as "natural" middlemen in their relationships with

the local Muslim population. The Italian leadership soon realized, however, that it had to win the direct loyalty of the Muslims, and this involved a considered distancing of themselves from the Jews. With the rise of fascism, the official policy of coolness toward the Jews increased, although this did not prevent many Jews from relocating their residence and place of work to the new parts of the city, nor did it squelch their learning Italian and their general tendency to link themselves with the growing European population of the town. When racial laws were introduced in Italy in 1938, Balbo, the governor of Libya, worked to delay their implementation in Libya for various reasons, including the importance of the Jews in the local economy. While the last years of the Italian regime brought hardships such as forced labor and, in the case of Benghazi, the deportation of Jews to a concentration camp in Tripolitania, the Italians are generally remembered as having improved the position of the Jews and as having treated them well.

Throughout this generation of political developments, the majority of the Jews continued to live in the Jewish quarter of the city and to maintain more or less traditional patterns of interaction with the Muslims. I am unaware of a Libyan Jew who did not know Arabic as a first language, although he or she might have spoken Italian as well (and within the last pre-immigration generation might have spoken to age-mates in Italian while conversing with parents in Arabic). Although the education of the Jews was for the most part separate from that of the Libyan Muslims, in the realm of work most Jews had contact with Muslims as customers, suppliers, clients, or employees. As had been the case in earlier periods, the everyday life of the two communities was intensely intertwined, while equally suffused with markers of distinction and difference. Traditional notions concerning the lowly position correctly assigned to the Jews did not disappear, while it seems that the new rights and position accorded the Jews by Italian rule were the basis of enhanced resentment, which during the Italian colonial period was generally not permitted to attain direct expression.

With the establishment of the British military administration and the eventual end of World War II, expectations grew among Libyan Muslims for complete freedom from colonial rule. In the uncertain political atmosphere of late 1945, an anti-Jewish riot broke out in which more than 130 Jews (and one Muslim) were killed in three days of rioting in Tripoli and nearby communities. Older sociological views of violent outbursts have seen them as breakdowns of social organization, but recent studies have pointed to the structure and "rationality" of riotous events in the pursuit of political goals. Relatively little information is available on the social organization of the Tripolitanian pogrom, but analysis of aspects of the outbreak reveals both organization and structuring which allow it to be interpreted as a ritualized and culturally stereotypic event. The contents of this structuring, even while influenced by modern nationalist ideas, grew out of traditional conceptions of believers and nonbelievers in Muslim society. The riot, directed concretely against the Jews, may be viewed as a massive symbolic statement claiming the restoration of the proper order of Muslim sovereignty. This traumatic event, enmeshed in midcentury politics, can only be understood against the background of accepted Muslim ideas that were maintained and reproduced in the context of everyday life in Tripoli throughout the period of European rule. Lewis's (1984:14) suggestion that "mentalities" often become important at times of crisis seems relevant here and implies that anthropological study of everyday custom can be woven into historical research stressing social and political change. For most of the Jews of Libya, the riots constituted what Turner (1957) has called a "social drama" marking the onset of a process in which this ancient population decided to sever its ties with the land that had been its home.

2 Jewish Life in Muslim Tripoli in the Late Qaramanli Period

From 1711 to 1835, Tripolitania was controlled by the Qaramanli dynasty which, nominal allegiance to the Porte notwithstanding, ruled independently, making wars and concluding peace at its own initiative. This chapter considers the Jewish community of Tripoli, and Jewish-Muslim relations in the town, during the latter years of the Qaramanli dynasty, from the end of the eighteenth century through the first third of the nineteenth. Knowledge about the community before that period, both in its internal and external aspects, is scant. It appears that reestablishment of Jewish life in the sixteenth century, after the Ottomans captured the city from the Knights of Malta, was due, in large measure, to the efforts of Rabbi Shim'on Lavi, a Spanish exile who lived in Fez in Morocco and arrived in Tripoli after first intending to settle in Palestine. In the seventeenth century there are echoes of a reaction to Sabbatean propaganda, from which Hirschberg (1981:163ff.) infers that the Jewish community was significant enough in size and organization to respond to the issue.[1] The research of Hazan (1982) on the poet Musa Bujnah has also shown that one must assume the existence of an active Jewish community at the time. It is only from the latter part of the eighteenth century that a consistent picture of Jewish life in Tripoli emerges, both in terms of internal communal structure and the place of the Jews in the wider society (cf. Slouschz 1908; Hirschberg 1981; Goldberg 1987b).

Qaramanli Tripoli

The Qaramanli era has been the subject of a number of studies,[2] so I mention only some main points relevant to our interest. There are no reliable figures on the population of the town, but one of the letters of Miss Tully (1957), whose correspondence is the basis of much of the detailed knowledge of the period, estimates the population of Tripoli at fourteen thousand. Her writings give an intimate picture of the

18

plague that ravaged the city from the end of 1784 to mid-1786. The population undoubtedly began to grow at the end of the eighteenth century and is placed at less than thirty thousand by Noah (1819:356) in the second decade of the nineteenth.

A sketch of the various "ethnic" elements constituting the population of the regency of Tripoli is given by Dearden (1976:8–11). The ruling family was supported militarily by the janissaries, and by the Kuloghlis—the offspring of Turkish men and local women. The indigenous inhabitants were made up of city dwellers (Moors), some of whom were descended from Spanish Muslims (Moriscos), and of rural (including nomadic) Arabs. Heterogeneity was increased by Berber-speaking tribesmen from the interior and blacks from the Sudan, often reaching Tripoli as slaves, who became part of Muslim society. There were some Christian merchants from Malta and Italy, and it was common for the European consuls to engage in commerce.[3] The Catholic fathers, from France, dealt with the ransom of Christian captives. A small number of Europeans reaching Tripoli, fleeing from the obligations of debt, or of prison, became renegades from Christian society and converted to Islam, bringing technical or military skills sought by the Qaramanli rulers. The skills of the Jews, too, were frequently crucial to the Qaramanlis.

The situation in Tripoli was broadly similar to that of other North African cities which were seats of patrimonial domination (cf. Hermassi 1975:22ff.). There was a "fundamental antagonism" (Streicker 1970) between the centralized government of the city and a series of fragmented tribal structures which were the basis of social and political life in the countryside. The form of rule called "sultanism" by Weber (Hermassi 1975:23) held sway, as the rule of the town was modeled after the Ottoman polity from which the Qaramanli rulers had severed themselves. Tripoli may also be viewed as an "administrative city" (cf. Fox 1977), whose organization was mainly an expression of state power. The commercial wealth of the city was to a great extent an adjunct of that power, based on the control of the caravan trade with the Sudan, which included traffic in slaves, and the state support of piracy.

One student of the period (Folayan 1979:43, quoted by Pennell 1982:113), in attempting to describe the essence of the system, states: "the words 'country' and 'state' are used generally as terms of convenience to describe the area that corresponds to present-day Libya, but which was, in the period under study, a loose polity held together mainly by the authority of the Pasha." The court, as the town and the society as a whole, was the scene of intrigues in which people tried to manipulate relationships to further their own ends. The Jews were part of this shifting scene of overlapping ties and networks.

The perspective of North African social structure as based on dyadic ties and networks of ties has been emphasized in recent anthropological work.[4] This view argues that it would be mistaken to interpret social structure solely in terms of given "ethnic" or "kinship" categories. However, it is precisely the given or "ascribed" features of social personages which often enabled them to individualize[5] their ties to maximize the advantages of given situations. The fact that certain non-Muslims, or Muslim slaves, reached positions of influence did not mean that "individuals" in the contemporary Western sense of the term had formally free access to all social positions. As Gellner quips (in reference to neighboring Tunisia), "it seems that in pre-modern conditions, only eunuchs, priests, slaves or politically-emasculated minorities can behave in a proper bureaucratic manner. There is pariah bureaucracy as well as pariah capitalism" (1983:174). The Jews thus had a defined place in Tripolitan society, stemming, in the first instance, from their status as dhimmis in Islamic theology and law. At the same time, this special place accorded the Jews created a complementarity between them and other sectors of Tripolitan society, which, when combined with a practical flexibility, led to their involvement in many different aspects of the life of the city.

The Jews in Tripoli

As already stated, the Jews were a long-standing part of Tripoli's population. Their contemporary Arabic speech probably represents an old urban dialect, compared to that of the Muslims, which is more similar to the speech of migrants from the countryside (Goldberg 1983). A tradition recorded by Ha-Cohen (1978:81) claims that the Jews originally resided in the eastern part of the town, near the center of economic activity, and in proximity to the government castle. He finds the tradition plausible when considering the residence patterns of the Jews in the small towns in his own day. In the period of Qaramanli rule, however, the Jews lived in a special quarter in the western segment of the town, up against the city wall, and several European consuls probably lived adjacent to it (Dearden 1976:106). The Jewish cemetery also lay to the west of the city walls. This arrangement may reflect the Muslim prohibition against placing the nonbelieving Jews between them and Mecca (Pascon and Schroeter 1982).

A reasonable estimation is that the Jews constituted about a quarter of the overall population. The writings of Miss Tully (1957) state that during the plague, half of the Jewish population died, along with two-fifths of the "Moors." Regarding the growth at the end of the eighteenth century, Ha-Cohen reports that early in the reign of Yusef Pasha, Jews were attracted to Tripoli both from the countryside and from other Maghrib countries (1978:117–18). He also states that Jews from Italy, seeking to take a second wife, settled in Tripoli, for rabbinic law there (and elsewhere in North Africa) had not adopted the ban on polygamy which had become institutionalized among European Jews. Such a move was, in most instances, probably motivated by barrenness of the first wife.

From an organizational point of view, the Jewish community was headed by an official known as the qaid. The existence of such a position enabled the government to place its tax-collecting burden on the shoulders of one man, who then had to concern himself with how this burden would be distributed within the community. Much of Jewish communal life revolved around raising funds, both for the external demands of the government and for internal needs (charity to the poor, the payment of ritual functionaries, and the like).

From the sources available (cf. Goldberg 1987b), the ad hoc nature of meeting these problems, rather than through established institutions, was striking. As has been discussed for Morocco (Bar-Asher 1981; Deshen 1983, 1984), the contingencies of collective life were met by an intricate meshing of individual leadership and communal initiatives, in which rabbinic authority was one factor, but wealth and closeness to the authorities (which went hand in hand— bribery was also part of the system) were of commensurate importance. The qaid, for the time of his appointment, was probably the most preeminent of individuals within the Jewish community (or more precisely, within the community of successful merchants) who had access to the court. His duties were carried out, most likely, in a somewhat irregular manner. Tully (1957:135), for example, mentions that the qaid of the Jews left the town in order to avoid the plague. Occupancy of the position seems to have changed with relative frequency, for it could mean a financial drain on its holder and even bring great danger, as well as great benefit. We thus find that in addition to this official link between the community and the government, individualized ties between Jews and the wielders of power were fashioned in many different ways. A well-connected Jew might even use his ties to weaken the hold of the Jewish community on him, and one document may indicate that a wealthy Jew fought the communal assessment of taxes by intimating that he had the option of converting to Islam (Goldberg 1987b:182, n. 14). While such a step was indubitably rare, it underlines the nature of the dynamic social field in which Jewish life played itself out.

Jews in Tripoli, as elsewhere, specialized in commerce and crafts, and came into daily contact with many Muslim customers and clients. They were frequently the only craftsmen available to provide services to the palace. Their ubiquitousness meant that they were often at the scene, participating informally in political life, while not sharing in the capability to exercise formal power. A sense of their involvement in the life of the town may immediately be gained by referring to the trade for which Tripoli of that period was infamous in European eyes, that of piracy.

The Jews themselves were victims of piracy. Among the captives taken by the Tripolitan corsairs[6] it was not unusual to find Jews. It was in this manner that the De la Penha family reached Tripoli in the seventeenth century (Khalfon 1986:42), and that the grandfather of Mordechai Ha-Cohen first reached Tripoli at the time of the Napoleonic Wars (Ha-Cohen 1978:118n.). It was incumbent on the leaders of the community to raise money for the *mitzva,* or religious commandment of *pidyon shevuyim,* the ransom of captive Jews, whatever their provenance.

The Jews were also involved in the benefit side of piracy (De Felice 1985:7). Ha-Cohen briefly relates the following incident from the first third of the nineteenth century (1978:270). Yitzhaq Guweta was a wealthy merchant and scholar who was born in Tripolitania. As a merchant, he was involved in the commerce linked to piracy based in Tripoli. At an unspecified date (before 1832), he held a ship full of wine which had been commandeered by Tripolitan corsairs. Much of the income from such merchandise was destined for the coffers of the pasha of Tripoli (i.e., the treasury of the regency), but Guweta sold the ship and its cargo and never returned to Tripoli. He took up residence in Trieste, where he continued to be a successful merchant.[7]

Jewish skills were called on in the trade in captured persons. Well-to-do or aristocratic passengers would travel the seas wearing simple clothing so that they would not be identified if taken prisoner. Jews familiar with European languages and dialects interviewed these passengers to ascertain their origin. An examination of the hands of the captives might also reveal the extent of their exposure to manual labor (Dearden 1976:20).

The involvement of Jews in piracy constituted one of the more dramatic examples of Jewish presence in the affairs of the society. In the following sections I present other examples and discuss the complex position of the Jews in relation to the rulers, the court, and the general populace. The final sections of this chapter interpret some "folkloristic" material from the same period which suggests complex symbolic links between the internal structure of the Jewish community and the wider Muslim society. The practices analyzed appear to condense the intricate pattern in which the Jews were "officially" set off from the rest of society but simultaneously were enmeshed with the life of the town at almost all social levels.

The Qaramanli Rulers

The latter decades of Qaramanli rule were characterized by episodes of political turbulence, exacerbated by natural calamities such as drought and the plague. European powers made considerable efforts to limit the activities of pirates operating out of North African ports. Their continued success in doing so, especially in Tripoli, meant a significant decrease in the state's revenues. The pashas were thus forced to exact heavier taxes (including special taxes on the Jews), bringing about discontent in both the town and countryside under their control. This discontent was utilized by rival contenders for the throne, from within the ruling family.

In 1790 Ali Pasha Qaramanli, who had ruled since 1754, was growing old and could do little to limit the growing animosity among his three sons. In a dramatic series of moves the youngest son, Yusef, murdered his eldest brother (who had the position of bey, i.e., commander of the troops) in front of their mother in her room in the castle. This act established a state of civil war in which Yusef took up position outside the city, supported by various groups of villagers and tribesmen, while Ali was aided by the middle son, who was less endowed with leadership abilities.

The fighting between these two factions took its toll on the local populace, and some of the Tripolitan notables appealed to the sultan in Istanbul to reestablish direct rule over the city. The sultan's response was to grant a *firman* to one Ali el Jezairli (commonly known as Ali Burghul), a corsair-adventurer, granting him rule over the regency based on forces that he raised through his own means. Burghul's forces arrived in Tripoli in 1793, and he easily was able to take up the position of pasha because of the divisions within the local leadership.

As was almost predictable from the outset, Burghul's installation in Tripoli was the beginning of a "reign of terror" (Slouschz 1927:25). He taxed the population heavily, particularly the Jews. Local notables suspected of loyalty to the Qaramanlis were executed. During his rule, several Jews were implicated in a plot to bring about his downfall. Among those to suffer was a son of Rabbi Avraham Khalfon.[8]

Avraham had held the position of qaid for a period of time, and his son, David, also a prominent figure in the community, was condemned by Burghul and burned alive.

According to Ha-Cohen's account (1978:103), a Jew by the name of Rahamim Barda (see below) was instrumental in negotiating an agreement between the competing segments of the Qaramanli family, who, with the aid of the bey of Tunisia, were able to drive Burghul out in January of 1795. The salvation of the city also brought redemption to the Jews, and a special hymn was composed by Khalfon retelling the events of Burghul's downfall and the Jews' delivery (Hirschberg 1965:180ff.). A local Purim festival, known as *purim burghul*, was established to commemorate the happy day. It was the second local Purim to take root among the Jews of Tripoli, just as similar special Purims had been accepted in other Jewish communities to mark parallel events in their own histories (cf. *Encyclopaedia Judaica* 1971, 13:1396).

Within half a year of the Qaramanlis' return to power, Yusef acceded to the throne as the result of his father's abdication and his own success in driving his brother Ahmed into exile. Resourceful and energetic, Yusef attempted to set the regency on a course of economic and political recovery. While, with the aid of a firm (if arbitrary) hand, he met with initial success, wider historical developments were to put this goal beyond his reach. He at first attempted to reactivate and buttress state-supported piracy, but confrontations with the European powers, and the famous encounter with the United States marines (Dearden 1976:155–210), eventually put an end to this source of revenue. He also worked to revive the caravan trade with the Sudan, including the lucrative trade in slaves, but this too waned as a result of growing European pressure. Indeed, by 1832 he was close to being a puppet in the rival hands of the British and French consuls, both of whom held over his head the double threat of indebtedness and military intervention.

The end of his reign bore clear parallels to his own seizure of power. In the 1830s he was threatened by both rebellious tribes, who cut off the caravan routes to the south, and a nephew-bey claiming to be the legitimate heir to the throne. As he had done to his father, he was besieged by troops in the Menshia, the garden-laced countryside just outside the walls of the city. Again, notables secretly appealed to Istanbul to rescue the city and establish direct rule over the town and province. At this period, the recent takeover of Algeria and the strong French presence in Tripoli convinced the Porte that this was the appropriate step to be taken, and Ottoman rule was directly reestablished in June of 1835. Yusef Pasha died three years later. If we follow the condition of the Jews during his long reign, we see how their situation varied not only under different rulers with their various whims, but under the rule of a single individual reacting to changing fortunes and circumstances.

The Rulers and the Jews

I have already discussed the position of the qaid, indicating that his link to the ruler should not be seen in formal bureaucratic terms, but as the principal tie among a variety of individualized relationships between Jews and powerful personages. One of the qaid's main functions was collecting taxes, as the Jews were seen as a potential source of revenue to the treasury. Upon coming to power, Ali Burghul immediately imposed a heavy impost on the Jews. When Yusef Qaramanli ascended to the throne several years later, he understood that for the Jews to contribute to the weal of his realm, their freedom of action should be encouraged. He also rescinded the rule requiring them to wear black clothes, demanding only that they wear black head coverings and shoes (Dearden 1976:142n.). Ha-Cohen describes an episode in which the Jews of Zawia, to the west of Tripoli, were supported by the pasha in their desire to build a synagogue, against the opposition of a local notable (cf. Goldberg 1980:51–53, 145–46).

As an adjunct to their commercial skills, Jews were able to assist the pasha in carrying out executive and administrative functions. During the conflict with the United States, a Jew was sent by the pasha to an American squadron to carry out negotiations (Noah 1819: 343). In 1810, Yusef's secretary was a Jew (Rossi 1968:269), and Jews were in charge of the minting of coins for the realm (Ha-Cohen 1978:124). Lyon (1821:32–33) found Jews serving as tithe collectors in the Gharian region. It should be remembered, of course, that granting high official positions to non-Muslims could be advantageous to a ruler, as they were not serious contenders for power. Toward the end of his career, however, when he was in desperate need of funds, Yusef returned to the former tactics of arbitrarily imposing heavy taxes on the Jewish community.

Ha-Cohen indicates (1978:125) that in this latter episode, the Jews attempted to utilize their links with the pasha's harem in order to abolish the heavy taxation. This, too, was a time-honored practice, as Jewish women apparently cultivated ties to the harem in seeking to influence the court, for both individual and communal ends. Several writers stress the importance of a certain Jewish woman, in the time of Ali Qaramanli, who was a close confidante of the pasha and was popularly known as "Queen Esther" because of her ability to intervene with the sovereign on her people's behalf.[9] Dearden, with a dose of "orientalism," gives his view of the importance of Jewish women in the life of the court in those days:

> Indeed, to Lilla Halluma, the Bashaw's lonely wife, to Lilla Ayesha, the Bey's wife, and to the separated *harims* of the Princes Ahmed and Yusef, where the painted, bejewelled women, in their stiff silks and brocades, sat out the long days and nights in isolated splendour, the appearance of these freely-moving Jewesses, whose creed and sex released them from the Islamic restrictions controlling Moslem women, were often the only means of communication with each other and with the world outside. (1976:114–15)

It was not only women who were able to gain access to the intimate workings of palace life, but some Jewish men attained this vantage point by virtue of their abilities as singers. This is documented by Féraud (1927:284), citing Vallière, and is mentioned several times by Ha-Cohen (1978:110,116). The Jews apparently were seen as specialists in music, as they were summoned by Yusef as part of his celebrations in the Menshia, before taking over as pasha (Tully 1957:252).

In general, aside from being merchants, the Jews, and other "foreigners," were almost the only ones known for specialized abilities in crafts. This too could be quite critical to the ruling house, as skills in metalworking were necessary to maintain weapons acquired from elsewhere. One example is a Tunisian Jew who supplied lead bullets to Ali Burghul, but who nevertheless was executed by Burghul, a ruler who was easily roused to suspicion (Ha-Cohen 1978:104). The narrative of Ha-Cohen also describes how, in 1832, a certain Mordechai Mizrahi, who was an English subject, utilized a new method to train the cannons of the pasha's forces on the rebels camped at the outskirts of the city (1978:129). This may be contrasted with Dearden's account of the rebellion a generation before, when cannon fire, "directed by an elderly Russian," kept back Yusef's men, even though the cannon had no trunnions with which to achieve accuracy (1976:121–22).

The interdigitation of the Jews in the life of Tripoli, at all levels, was problematic when it came to public recognition of this fact. At the time of Ali Burghul's official entrance to the city, Dearden's narrative depicts "black-clothed figures of a horde of terrified Jews driven with violence down the streets" (1976:131), as if they had no place in town life. Their very status as formally outside Muslim (but not Tripolitan) society, however, could be used to official advantage. Under Yusef Pasha, Jews were employed as hangmen, which provided an extra grain of fear to deter would-be dissidents. Not only would their end be bitter, but they would suffer the ignomy of having their lives taken by infidels.

The support and protection of Jews by a sovereign, with the aim of encouraging their commercial activities, was a well-known stratagem in the region, as in the medieval world generally. This policy, however, always had to take into account the possibility of opposition to the Jews' success, or to the blatant display of their success, on the part of those who spoke on behalf of Islam. Such spokesmen might represent the learned 'ulema, who, basing themselves on Muslim law, were expected to let their opinions be known to the ruler. Such was the case of Ibn Ghalbun, who in the mid-eighteenth century opposed the building of a synagogue in the town of Misurata (Rossi 1936: 170ff.). But a stand against the exaggerated well-being of the Jews could also take on a more populist and demagogic nature.

Popular Anti-Jewish Sentiment

While many Muslims came into frequent contact with Jews, and related to this contact as part of normal daily life, it was not unusual for popular sentiment to be stirred up against them. One case is described by Ha-Cohen for the period of Yusef Pasha.

> In 1800 a marabout came from Wadai. The Muslims honored him as was their wont; every mad marabout was holy in their eyes. When he saw that he was honored by them and commanded their attention as a seer, he exhorted them to despise and reject the Jews because they deny Muhammad the true prophet; he spoiled things for the Jews in the eyes of the Muslims.
>
> He became jealous of the success and the fine clothes of the Jews, and he presented his case before Yusef Pasha saying: "Do you not fear for your soul on the Day of Judgment, to give an accounting before Muhammad the Prophet, that you have given freedom to the Jews who despise his religion, so that they dare wear fine clothing to the extent that one cannot distinguish between a faithful Muslim and an infidel Jew?"[10]
>
> Yusef Pasha at first did not accede to his demands and said to him: "They all are creatures of the handiwork of the Blessed; why should their lot be less for they work diligently at all manner of occupation and have earned the wearing of fine clothes! Not so the Muslims who embrace pleasure and waste their money in food, drink, and evil pursuits."
>
> "I have saved my soul," said the marabout; he did not, however, desist from misleading talk or from spreading bitterness and enmity, until finally Yusef Pasha agreed with him. The pasha issued an order to the head of the Jews [qaid] that an announcement be made in all the synagogues that the Jews no longer be allowed to wear finery. This decree

weighed heavily on the Jews, for they would not be able to sell their fine clothes; Muslims would not bear the disgrace of wrapping their bodies with clothes that had been worn by the Jews.

The marabout did not live long after that, and the decree was revoked. However, the hatred that his preachings spread among the Muslims remains to this day, and they are still hostile toward the Jews. (1978:117)

Popular religious fervor could take extreme forms during the celebration of the *mulid* (birthday) of Muhammad by the 'Isawiyya brotherhood. During these days Christians and Jews had to remain indoors at the risk of their lives, while the ecstatic procession of the 'Isawiyya devotees dominated the street. The following paragraph, written by Ha-Cohen for his own days (the Ottoman period; see chap. 3) gives a sense of the general atmosphere during this celebration.

On that day the great passion of religious hatred is multiplied sevenfold. No member of another religion dare approach the camp of the Muslims, as he will be treated as a defiling object. Commerce and crafts cease on that day. No one dares risk his life and oppose the wild madness, for there is no guarantee against religious hatred. If an 'Isawi senses a stranger's presence, the stranger's fate is sealed, for he will pounce on him like a wild animal, with no one to defend him. Onlookers, however, may stand at a distance, at the windows and on the roof tops, to gaze on this wondrous scene. (1978:164)

This characterization is confirmed by Lyon (1821:11), who, while visiting Tripoli, witnessed the attack on a Jewish boy who ventured out during the mulid and was beaten to death.

The Jews, then, were a basic part of the local social scene and were also an integral element of the Muslim's cultural and religious world, even if in a negative way. Reference to Islam could place the Jews in varying perspectives. They could be viewed primarily as nonbelievers who should be distinguished from and humbled before the Muslims, or they could be viewed as part of "mankind" (cf. Goitein 1971a), who are thereby entitled to the same treatment as other "creatures of the handiwork of the Blessed." When the latter aspect became prominent, a reaction calling for a return of the Jews to their "proper place" in Muslim society often followed. These swings, which could be swift and dramatic, represented different values and interests within Muslim society. The Jews themselves, despite the social position achieved by certain individuals, were relatively powerless as a group in influencing which conception would take the upper hand.

Jews and Muslims in Jewish Lore

The participation of the Jews in the everyday life of the society, coupled with the attempt to "deny" this reality, represented a basic contradiction of cultural assumptions and their expression in daily behavior. Often such contradictions receive expression in ritual behavior or in play. This perspective may help us interpret a folklorelike account, from the period, preserved in the writings of Mordechai Ha-Cohen.

Following his statement that in the days of Yusef Pasha numbers of Jews came to settle in Tripoli after having been ransomed from corsairs, Ha-Cohen (1978:118) indicates that the Jews all resided in two adjacent quarters of Tripoli, the *hara kebira* (large [Jewish] quarter) and the *hara zeghira* (small quarter), and describes a Sabbath afternoon pastime which gave saliency to the residential division:

> In former days, each Sabbath after the morning meal, the Jewish toughs [*biryonim*] would gather on the western wall of the town, adjacent to the Jewish quarter. The members of the *hara kebira* with their special red flag would stand to the north, while the members of the *hara zeghira* would stand to the south with their white flag. They would exercise and then organize themselves as two armies, fighting without any weapons. Some would wrestle with their opponents, attempting to throw them to the ground, and others would box, skillfully hitting both head and foot. However, he who overcame his rival would be careful not to hurt him excessively. They would *take captives from one another and redeem captives* [italics added] with bravery and cunning.
>
> The women and children would stand crowded, watching the two teams play on the wall, praising that which emerged as the winner. For the most part the members of the *hara zeghira* were victorious as they were both courageous and clever. But the *hara kebira* team had two heroes, light of foot, who easily jumped great distances. When the fighting became difficult they swiftly ran to release the captured members of their side.
>
> Even though they liked and married one another, it was not possible for a member of one quarter to visit his friend in the other quarter during the fighting. But when the period set aside for fighting was over, a white flag was raised signifying peace, and one was able to visit the other.

These roughnecks constituted a "gang" which served, in an informal but definite manner, to defend the honor of the Jews. According to the narrative, "the fear of the *biryonim* was upon all the high handed ones," and it was a terrible shame to the family of a Muslim if he were to be bested by one of the Jewish toughs. The account emphasizes that the members of the Jewish gang would not bow their heads to accept any authority.

The portrayal of the biryonim and the Sabbath games is followed, in Ha-Cohen's book, by several stories of confrontation between members of the gang and Muslim officials who unjustly opposed them. One of the stories relates that an official tried to arrest members of the Jewish gang, motivated by jealousy of their skill and feats, but that they escaped by a seemingly impossible jump from the wall of the Jewish quarter. When this official complained to the pasha, he supported the Jews saying, "if only all my soldiers were as brave as the Jews." The second story, following the same general theme, is more elaborate.

Another official called el-Kehya[11] forced a Jewish woman to have sexual relations with him and continued to visit her regularly. Her husband, because of the position of this official, was fearful of voicing a complaint. The head of the biryonim heard of the episode and, on his own initiative, slipped into the house of the woman to lay in wait for el-Kehya. His action came to the attention of the rabbinic court which summoned him before it for entering the house of a married woman while he and she were alone. Despite his protest that his action was to defend the woman and the honor of the Jews, the court administered him the punishment of receiving stripes, indicating that such action, at his own initiative, was not acceptable.[12] The council of judges then turned to the head of the community,[13] who revised the tough's plan by giving it communal backing.

The qaid decided to invite el-Kehya to his house, where the Jewish gang lay in waiting. After el-Kehya entered, they pounced on him and tied him up. The qaid threatened to bring him to the pasha, which would be both an accusation of his misdeeds and shameful exposure of his fall at the hands of the Jews. El-Kehya then promised to stop molesting the Jewish woman, and the Jewish gang returned him quietly to his home, keeping their end of the bargain to save his honor.

A sequel to this story tells of a third official who, offended by the Jewish toughs,[14] warns one of them that he will take his revenge on them. In preparation, the toughs get together and rent a room in the "central quarter" (a street linking the two *hara*s) as part of a plan to trap this official. The latter attempts to work in cahoots with el-Kehya, who at first cautions him not to meddle with the Jews, "for it is only by their slyness, which they imbibe with their mother's milk, that they survive their exile among the nations" (Ha-Cohen 1978: 122–23).[15] Despite this warning the official proceeds, the Jewish gang again gains the upper hand, and both officials are disgraced before the pasha.

All three stories stress the theme that the Jews are able, through strategies of cleverness and strength, but also by virtue of the rectitude of their case, to attain a fair response from a just ruler and circumvent the jealous courtiers who are close to the pasha (cf. Jason 1975:147ff.). The individualized relationships reflected in the stories do not mitigate the importance of the categories "Muslim" and "Jew" as establishing a basis for loyalty and action. Rather, they suggest that these valued notions did not have a simple and unidimensional translation into institutional forms or in the realm of social interaction. It was often precisely because the Jews were a priori ruled out from certain social niches that they could manipulate their special status to the fullest and maximize their economic and other sorts of personal advantage. Even the Jews' despised status itself, their lowliness, as we see in the story of el-Kehya, could be used as a threat to Muslim officials for furthering Jewish interests, just as the Jews' status could be used to the advantage of the local ruler.

Ha-Cohen's narrative, obviously folkloristic in many of its features, clearly fills the compensatory function of raising an ethnic group, in verbal performance, above those who seek to oppress it or keep it down. Correct as this interpretation may be, it is also too general to be sufficient. More specifically, the story reflects the intricate place of the Jews in Tripolitan society in relation to the pasha who was often their main protector. The court, as the town and the society as a whole, was the scene of ever-evolving intrigues following the lines of dyadic ties and networks. Ha-Cohen's rendering may be based on actual incidents,[16] and certainly gives a sense of the setting within which Jewish life, in its intertwined communal and individual aspects, played itself out.

The Sabbath Games and the Place of Jews in Tripolitan Society

The stories following Ha-Cohen's account of the Sabbath games, which recount the successes of the Jewish toughs, clearly indicate that among the meanings of the games was their "compensatory" significance to the Jews. (The games may also have had the concrete function of allowing the young men to enhance their skills in self-defense against Muslims.) In addition, the description of the games also must be linked, textually, to the section that precedes it, that is, the author's statement that some Jews reached Tripoli as a result of having been captured by pirates. This connection is reinforced by the use of the terminology of taking captives and redeeming captives in the course of the account. These textual links suggest that the game may be symbolic of central aspects of life in the society in general, both Jewish and Muslim, and may reflect the delicate balance of contradictions of which Jewish life in Muslim Tripoli was composed.

Although Ha-Cohen does not state so directly, the continuation of his story, in which the pasha compliments the Jews for their feats, implies that in addition to the crowd of Jewish onlookers ("women and children"), at least some Muslims were among the spectators of the Jewish competition.[17] If "games," as Geertz has asserted about Balinese cockfights (1973:448), may be a story people "tell themselves about themselves," it is helpful to add Turner's perspective that "to look at itself a society must cut out a piece of itself for inspection" (1979:96). Handelman (1989) gives an example of this process of "cutting out a piece of itself" in his study of the Palio race in Siena, where each year different *contrade* take part in the competition which grips the attention of the whole city. I suggest that the mock fights in the Jewish quarter constituted such an event of interest to all of Tripolitan society.

In contrast to the situation in Siena, where each *contrada* can be considered a conceptually equal segment to all others, and each year different contrade may be selected to represent the whole commune, the Jewish quarter in Tripoli is an already-packaged sector, with properties that make it conducive to this special symbolic role. As nonbelievers, the Jews are a category apart which has been encapsulated by Tripolitan society. With the symbolic "cutting out" they are flipped over, so to speak, and their partition into two barrios comes to stand both for Tripolitan society and for the nonbelievers (Europeans) who threaten to encapsulate it. The Jews are an old local population, but their quarter of the city is also the spot in or near which foreign consuls reside. The location of the mock battles, on the western wall of the town which faces the sea (a border zone par excellence), may also encourage this perception. Ha-Cohen's phrasing hints that the competition entails a temporary suspension of intermarriage between the two quarters, as befits the division between the faithful and the infidels. At the same time the sides remain in contact, each with its own heroes, who make forays into enemy "territory." There are no permanent victories but individual successes and periods of truce, with the struggle destined to renew itself on a periodic basis.

The Jews thus come to stand momentarily for the whole society from which they are "officially" barred. Their mock war, in which the taking of captives is central, condenses the drama that pervades, or pervaded, the political-economic base of the town. It is possible that precisely at the time when this base was being threatened, when the ability to maintain the corsair enterprise was nearly balanced against the forces attempting to suppress it, that the Jewish games, remote, yet very close to home, became particularly compelling to Tripolitan Muslims. The metaphorical connection is expressed in the words placed in the mouth of Yusef Pasha: "If only all my soldiers were as brave as the Jews, I would be pleased" (Ha-Cohen 1978:119,123). Just as the Jews are set apart socially, but linked to Muslim society through a myriad of individual ties, so they are circumscribed conceptually, but this conceptual boundary can be situationally transcended in the cultural interests of the wider society and the Jewish sport can be made to represent a tension-ridden theme running throughout the body politic.

Conclusion

We have presented a many-faceted picture of Jewish life in the context of Muslim Tripoli at the end of the Qaramanli period, stressing the pervasive but problematic presence of Jews in the life of the town. One might even go so far as to argue that it would have been surprising, in Tripoli of those days, to find Muslims appointed to some of the positions that Jews held, rather than the other way around. Noah, the American consul in Tunis who was himself Jewish, remarks that in Tripoli the Jews "enjoy rather more influence than in other parts of Barbary" (1819:356). Other English and American observers also note the prominence of Jews in government affairs, but describe it less kindly (Dearden 1976:93,189). It is possible that a "liberal" stance with regard to the Jews parallels the less severe treatment of European consuls in Tripoli in comparison to other North African ports (Dearden 1976:24). Whatever our assessment of the *social* situation, it should be appreciated that an institutional or interactional analysis does not exhaust our understanding of the complex nature of Jewish life in that situation.

In the last section it was claimed that there is a precise correspondence between the social and political issues highlighted, particularly the (declining) place of piracy and the Sabbath competition of the Jews which, we have argued, attracted the attention of Muslims as well. The presence of Muslim onlookers on the occasion of Jewish "sport" has been documented elsewhere, both in Tripolitania and in other parts of North Africa. In the Jebel Nefusa in Tripolitania (Goldberg 1980:111), Berber villagers gathered around to watch the water fights among the Jews that traditionally took place on the festival of Shavu'ot. Parallel ethnographic data have been collected by the author from informants originating in southern Morocco. In Illigh (cf. Pascon and Schroeter 1982) the Jews were invited by the local qaid to carry out these fights on the day after the festival of Shavu'ot. In the area to the west of Agouim in the Atlas, the Jews from the small settlements would spend the festivals together in the central *mellah*. During the "intermediate days" (Herr 1971) of the festival they would engage in a kind of "football" competition. Berber villagers would gather around and watch, each cheering for "their own" Jews.

In the Mzab region of Algeria, the Jews of the region of Ghardaia, split into two divisions perhaps called *sofs*, also had water fights on Shavu'ot (Briggs and Guède 1964:44). No clear function or meaning is attributed to this social division (pp. 20, 59–60). The fact that the Jewish "sides" are given names normally characterizing Muslim factions suggests their symbolic importance for the local society as a whole.

If such games do in fact interrelate with social processes and structure in a fine-grained manner, it is not accidental that the games in Tripoli changed their form soon after the end of the Qaramanli period. Ha-Cohen (1978:119) indicates that because of bad accidents the games were curtailed by the Turkish authorities in 1845 (the competition could take place on the ground, but not on the walls) and were completely eliminated in 1850. This may be symptomatic of more systematic and aggressive intervention on the part of the government in the internal life of the Jews, in contrast to the classic medieval policy of letting the Jews deal with their internal problems as much as possible. Such a policy became more in evidence later in the century, when the reforms (*tanzimat*) being put into effect in various places in the empire began to make their mark in Tripoli as well[18] and created a new context for Muslim-Jewish interaction.

The secretary of the Community Board of Benghazi (left) and the members of the rabbinic court, about 1920. Next to the secretary is Mordechai Ha-Cohen, author of Higgid Mordecai. *(Bet Hatefutsoth and the Cultural Center of the Jews of Libya.)*

A Jewish money-changer and onlooker, with a Muslim client. (Israel Museum, Department of Jewish Ethnography.)

Itinerant Jewish tinsmiths in a rural marketplace. (Israel Museum, Department of Jewish Ethnography.)

A Jewish man from Misurata in traditional garb, including a "Turkish" hat. (Yosef and Moshe Ji'an [Zarqina].)

A bride being accompanied from her house, in Tripoli, during a prenuptial henna celebration. (Cultural Center of the Jews of Libya.)

An "I.O.U." signed by a Muslim in Misurata for money lent by a local Jew, in January 1946. (Yosef and Moshe Ji'an [Zarqina].)

A tailor in Misurata. Young Jews dressed in traditional garb are learning to sew Italian-style clothing. (Yosef and Moshe Ji'an [Zarqina].)

A Jewish blacksmith in the 1960s, with a young Muslim looking on. (Cultural Center of the Jews of Libya.)

A Jewish-owned tuna-packing factory, with Jewish, Italian, and Muslim workers. (Cultural Center of the Jews of Libya.)

Jewish youths gathering near Fum el-bab, where regular stone-throwing games took place between them and Muslim youths. (Cultural Center of the Jews of Libya.)

The synagogue at Zawia after the 1945 pogrom. (Bet Hatefutsoth and the Cultural Center of the Jews of Libya.)

A meeting of the Libyan Liberation Committee in the late 1940s to which representatives of the Jewish community were invited. (Cultural Center of the Jews of Libya.)

Aerial view of the Old City of Tripoli. The Jewish quarter runs against the sea in the center of the background. (Cultural Center of the Jews of Libya.)

3 The Ottoman Period: Political Change and Traditional Rhetoric

The history of Libya's relations with the European colonial powers was different from that of the other North African countries. In 1835 the city of Tripoli came under direct control of the Ottoman Empire, ending the rule of the Qaramanli dynasty. This move by the Ottomans was prompted, among other factors, by the French takeover of Algeria in 1830 and Muhammad Ali's rise to power in Egypt.[1] Ottoman rule was established firmly in Tripoli, but it took about two decades to bring the tribal groups in the interior completely under control. From the middle of the nineteenth century, processes of westernization and modernization were initiated by the government. These included the gradual improvement of the condition of the Jews in the province. While in other North African countries the betterment of the Jews' position was unequivocally associated with European expansion and domination, in Libya the situation was more complex as the Muslim Turks often supported the Jews, whom they saw as partners in the process of developing the region. At the same time, basic conceptions of the place of Jews in Muslim society showed great tenacity in the local populace, and the Turkish governors of Libya clearly took these conceptions into account in carrying out their policies. This chapter traces the evolution of the condition of the Jews under direct Ottoman rule, with special attention to the complex interplay of competing notions of the place of the Jews in society during that period.

The renewed Ottoman rule in Libya coincided with the era of reforms (tanzimat) within the empire (see Shaw and Shaw 1977), which involved the buildup of military strength, the establishment of new laws based on European models, and the attempt to bring about administrative reorganization favoring economic growth. These reforms, first applied in the more central parts of the empire, also had their effect on Libya. Tripoli, for example, was selected as one of five provinces in which a new provincial administration law, promul-

35

gated in 1864, was to be put in effect (Anderson 1984:330). While Italian historians, after the Italian conquest of Libya in 1911, tried to downplay their importance, these internal reforms were an important factor in the beginning of modernization in Libyan society.

Many writers indicate that Tripoli was peripheral to the major concerns of the empire (Shaw and Shaw 1977:289), but this view can be exaggerated. It appears that a number of the governors were sent to Tripoli as a form of "honorable exile" during the Hamidian period (1876–1908).[2] These were men who were in disfavor with the Porte, but who, with a shift in political fortunes, might be recalled to more central posts. While events in Tripoli might have little direct effect on developments at home, it is nevertheless the case that some of the governors appointed there were well in tune with the social and political changes characterizing the rest of the Ottoman Empire at the time. Some of them were associated with the Young Turks and espoused liberal ideas concerning religion and the position of minorities (Simon 1979:19). The narrative of Mordechai Ha-Cohen (1978:168,170) also intimates that some of the *walis* (governors) were energetic in carrying out new policies precisely to impress their superiors and thereby gain a more desirable appointment.

The extent of Ottoman efforts toward reform in the province has been demonstrated and discussed by Anderson (1984). Her analysis considers such areas as the policy encouraging urbanization and land settlement, administrative reorganization, land reform, the development of commerce, and the furtherance of education. Many of these programs had an effect, directly or indirectly, on the Jewish population.

For example, the tendency toward urbanization (mentioned also by Ha-Cohen 1978:160) is clearly reflected in the demographic material available on the Jewish community. The data, while not extensive, are consistent and show steady growth and a movement toward the city of Tripoli (and other coastal towns) from the communities of the interior, beginning with the middle of the nineteenth century (Goldberg 1971). The opening of a new gate in the western wall of the town, in 1865, was carried out in order to facilitate traffic between the countryside and the city (Anderson 1984:330). It also had special significance to the Jews, who contributed to the costs of the project, as it enabled them to carry their dead directly from the Jewish quarter to the Jewish cemetery. Previously, their funeral processions had been forced into a long route through Muslim quarters of the city where they were subject to verbal abuse and physical harassment (Ha-Cohen 1978:154). This is only one instance of how the story of the development of Libyan society in the nineteenth century would be incomplete without reference to the role played by Jews during that era.

Part of the tanzimat program, in the Ottoman Empire as a whole, was to accord a more equal position to religious minorities—Christians and Jews. It must be kept in mind, of course, that the implementation of the tanzimat program took place under the growing importance of European power in North Africa. Often the treatment of minorities was of special significance to Europeans in their judgment of the "enlightenment" of Muslim rulers.[3] As we shall see, it was also perfectly comprehensible to Muslims that symbolic value be placed on the well-being of minorities. During most of the period in question, however, the Jews of Tripoli did not see the improvement of their situation *solely* in terms of the intervention of European power, although this factor certainly was not absent from the forces at work. To a large extent the Jews in Tripoli were viewed as part of the local society, and even those who were subjects or protégés of European states were considered loyal to the Ottoman Empire (Simon 1982).

The situation of the Jews under Ottoman rule has been studied in detail by Simon (1979), who points to the betterment of their situation in a number of areas. She has documented the good relations that developed between the Jewish elite and some of the Ottoman rulers in the latter part of the nineteenth century. The desire of the walis to guarantee law and order in the province certainly was welcomed by the Jews, and Jewish commercial activity was seen as necessary to the development of the region, even though it contributed to a growth in Italian influence. A clear stand was taken by a number of the governors in insisting that the rights of Jews were equal to those of other subjects of the realm, although the same attitude was not shared by some of the petty officials who had been recruited from among the local populace.

Simon's documentation (1979, 1982, 1984) is based on a wide variety of sources, both Libyan and "foreign," and both Jewish and non-Jewish. One of the important sources are the writings of Mordechai Ha-Cohen, both in his book (1978) and in many reports he sent to the Hebrew press abroad.[4] Ha-Cohen was both an observer of the events he discusses and a participant in them (Goldberg 1980). Given the volume of his writing and the fullness of the picture he presented, Ha-Cohen appears as one of the major historical "spokesmen" for the Jews of Tripoli during that period. In the discussion that follows I rely heavily on his work, not only for facts, which often are supported by other documents, but for a view of the overall significance of this period to the Jewish community.

Ha-Cohen begins his description of the Ottoman period in the

following manner: "From the time that Tripoli came under the protection of Turkey, the Jews began to shake off the dust of their
lowliness, for the ruling Turks did not have strong hatred of the Jews
as did the Arabs" (1978:146). With the aid of his narrative, I examine
the situation of the Jews in a number of areas, such as their basic security in the countryside and in the town, and the administration of
justice in the courts. In these realms, the ancient logic of the protection of a weak minority was confronted by ideas of equality of all
Ottoman citizens. Ha-Cohen's position as a modernizer, of both Jewish tradition and Tripolitanian society as a whole, is revealed in his
reaction to, and description of, the attempts to impose new inheritance laws and to conscript Jews into military service. The various
cases presented depict the intricate interplay of the traditional view
of the Jews and the new notions concerning religious freedom in the
context of Tripolitanian society.

Basic Security

In Tripolitania, as elsewhere in North Africa, a common expression of
the power and strength of a ruler was his ability to protect the most
vulnerable categories of people. An often-quoted description of the
reign of Mulay Ismail in Morocco (seventeenth–eighteenth centuries) states that even a woman or dhimmi (Jew) could walk from
Oujda to Wad Nul unmolested.[5] Referring to that statement, Stillman
(1975) cites Lewis's analysis (1971:19ff.) of blacks in Islamic society.
Lewis claims that the rhetorical device (which he calls *trajectio ad
absurdum*)—reflected in a statement that a Muslim must submit to
authority, *even* to a black—may be taken as evidence of the place of
blacks in the society in question. In a parallel manner the rhetoric
invoking Jews may be seen as based on a fortiori logic: if protection is
extended even to the most vulnerable, how much more so to the rest
of the population!

In this chapter, which traces the position of the Jews in Tripolitania during the period of direct Ottoman rule, we see that, in
spite of institutional changes that brought Jews into fuller participation in the civic life of the society, the Jews maintained symbolic
importance as a special social segment in current cultural rhetoric.
Not only did Jews continue to stand for a ruler's resolve to maintain
law and order, but based on the same logic they were placed in the
forefront of a governor's plan to reform. To follow these developments, I first consider the situation of the Jews in a context where the
twin issues of power and protection were most salient, that is, tribal
life in the countryside.

Outside the city of Tripoli, the Jews were often dependent for their basic security on local tribal leaders or strong men, rather than on government control from the city. This was particularly true in the mountainous regions to the south of Tripoli, such as the Jebel Gharian or the Jebel Nefusa. This situation has been described by Ha-Cohen (1978:283–84) and discussed in some detail, along with consideration of comparable material from Morocco (Goldberg 1980:40–61). The general Islamic notion of dhimma—a contract in which a religious minority agrees to live under the rule of Islam, and accept the signs of demeaned status in exchange for the protection of their life and property—held sway in the countryside, even without the buttressing of specialists in Islamic law and theology. In the tribal setting, the notion of dhimma was reinforced by the values of honor, which demanded that a tribal chief demonstrate his ability to protect the weak and vulnerable under his patronage. This situation is succinctly summarized in Ha-Cohen's description of the Jebel Nefusa:

> The Berbers, the owners of the land, do not show great hatred toward the Jews; instead, the Jews belittle themselves before them. The Berbers are constantly demanding homage, even though the Jews are the pillars of the society, the craftsmen and merchants. Nevertheless, even before the conquest of the land by the Turks, when the region was governed by neither ruler nor judge, the Jews lived in security, for every Jew had a Berber lord who championed his cause in any quarrel. When a Jew was wronged and his lord let it pass in silence, it was considered a disgrace to the lord who had not protected his servant,[6] the Jew. There were even times when the tribes went to battle in matters concerning a Jew.
>
> A Berber lord passed his Hebrew servant down to his children as an inheritance. If the Berber lord had many sons, each inherited a share in the servant. . . . [However], if the Hebrew servant met his obligation in giving homage to his lord and was able to accumulate money, he could redeem himself by paying a sum agreeable to both parties. With his money he could acquire a deed of manumission for that portion of the rights held by the seller. (1978:283–84)

It is within this context that the imposition of Turkish rule in the Tripolitanian countryside had particular significance to the Jews of the tribal areas. Brief mention of these developments is found in the writing of Adadi (1865:47b), who served as the head of the rabbinic court in Tripoli in the middle of the nineteenth century:

> and to this very day, in that mountain, there is not an Israelite family without an Ishmaelite master to whom the Israelite must make a token

payment each year. The Ishmaelite may sell him to another, and this arrangement persisted until only six or seven years ago, when the Turkish rulers took the area from the Arabs.

Ha-Cohen adds more information about the "liberation" of the mountain Jews under the Turks, stressing that the situation did not change completely; ties of patronage between Berber "lords" and Jewish families still remained:

> When the land was conquered by the Turks, a law was enacted that all Jewish servants were to be freed. Not only the masters, but also the Jews were allowed to wear the red hat of the Muslims without anyone objecting. Today, even those families who could not buy their freedom have all been released from servitude. But in such cases the lord calls upon them by name[7] to treat them with respect, and in return assists them to overcome any injury inflicted by other Berbers. (Goldberg 1980:74)

As mentioned, after taking Tripoli in 1835, the Ottoman authorities were faced with the task of gaining control of the whole province. This was not accomplished easily, and peace was established after a generation of intermittent battles. Ha-Cohen provides a detailed description (1978:133–45; see also Slouschz 1927:192–94) of the revolts of the tribal chief Ghoma against Ottoman authority. After escaping prison in Istanbul, Ghoma returned to the Jebel Nefusa and took the fort in Yefren in 1855. According to the narrative, Ghoma proclaimed:

> Guard the Jews—do not plunder them! Take not even a shoestring! Whoever harms the Jews—his blood will be upon his own head!" Some Berbers spoke evil of the Jews, saying: "Forbid them to wear a red hat [like the Muslims]; allow them to wear only black, as a sign of lowliness, as was customary before the coming of the Turks." Ghoma did not heed these evil-tongued people and replied: "If in the days of Turkish rule the Jews were allowed to dress as they please—how much more so under my rule?" (Ha-Cohen 1978:140)

In the interior, where, because of their basic weakness, the well-being of the Jews was a salient issue, the cultural logic associated with the notion of protection/patronage is thrown into bold relief and made explicit. If justice and freedom are applied to the Jews, it is a clear sign that this is based on justice and freedom given to the rest of the population. Ha-Cohen gathered much of his information concerning Ghoma's revolt from one of the chief's main lieutenants (Goldberg 1980:40), but the a fortiori logic growing out of the situation of protection is applied by him with regard to other incidents. An example is his account of Muhammad[8] Bey's revolt against Yusef Pasha, at the end of the latter's reign, as he attempts to establish his leadership in the countryside (Ha-Cohen 1978:129–30). In his description of the rebel leader 'Abd a-Jalil Sif a-Nasr, who fought in the area to the east of Tripoli, Ha-Cohen shows the other side of the logic, that the Jews, being the most vulnerable, are most likely to be attacked first as a sign of a challenge to the established authority. Resisting Ottoman rule in 1839, "'Abd a-Jalil's men accompanied by a mob stormed the villages of Zliten, al-Khoms and Mesallata, pouncing upon the booty. First the wealth of the Jews was plundered because they are well-suited to be the scapegoat who receives the first injury" (Goldberg 1980:57–58).

The historical evidence available from the nineteenth century seems to indicate a rise in the number of incidents in which Jews in the countryside were plundered and even murdered (De Felice 1985: 20ff.; Goldberg 1980:56). If this is a real change and stems not only from more extensive documentation, it may reflect an unstable situation in which the tribal system of protection was no longer effective and the rule of the Turks still not fully established. In this setting, and given the logic of protection, the Jews "naturally" served as an index of strength in the struggle between rulers and those who opposed such rule. Below, we see how this logic continued to operate during the period of Ottoman reform, even when the exercise of naked force was not as free as in the tribal context.

The Urban Setting: Justice in the Courts

Within the city of Tripoli, changes in the administration of justice were evident a decade after the Ottoman takeover. Under Mehmed Emin Pasha (1842–47), Rabbi Ya'aqov Mimun was appointed head of the Jewish community and was also assigned a seat in the local court. This clearly indicated a change in the tradition in which Jewish communal life was totally separate from that of the Muslims. At first, according to Ha-Cohen's narrative (1978:151),[9] Mimun's chair in the court was placed to the side of the other magistrates and was not decorated as were the chairs of the Muslim judges. In 1846, apparently as a result of his contribution to the court, a request was sent to Istanbul to enable R. Mimun to participate in judicial deliberations on an equal footing with the other justices. An affirmative reply was received in 1847, by which time Mimun had passed away. Nevertheless, the precedent was established.

Under the rule of Mahmud Nedim Pasha (1860–67),[10] the local court was reorganized in accordance with the Ottoman Provincial Reform Law and separate courts—criminal, penal, and commercial—were established. Jewish magistrates were appointed to each, and they were salaried by the government. Ha-Cohen's description (1978:158), on which these details are based, also implies that the pasha was no longer sitting in the court, as had been established practice during the Qaramanli period, or even during the time of R. Mimun. This put into practice the principle of separating executive from judicial powers. As we shall see, the administration of justice was not only a matter of adopting new principles, but was also encouraged by European pressure.

The Alliance Israélite Universelle, established in Paris in 1860, was as significant in Libya as in many Jewish communities in the Middle East.[11] We hear of the Jewish community in Tripoli turning to the Alliance in the case of Ali Kerkeni, a mayor (*shaykh el beled*) in the late 1860s who tyrannized the population of the city (Nachtigal 1971), Jew and non-Jew alike. According to Ha-Cohen's narrative (1978:155–56), Kerkeni was responsible for the murder of a Jew named Saul Raccah.

Raccah had been an employee of Kerkeni and, for some unspecified reason, fell in disfavor with this influential notable. The Jews believed that Kerkeni had Raccah murdered. As shaykh el beled it was Kerkeni's task to investigate the murder, but he made no effort in this direction, even to collect evidence. The Jews discovered drops of blood leading from the murdered man's house to the home of one of Kerkeni's employees. They also found other evidence, but not enough to prove guilt in court. At this point they turned to the Alliance Israélite Universelle in Paris and its branch in Istanbul (the local committee of the Alliance had been set up in Tripoli in 1861; see De Felice 1985:12). Through the pressure of the Alliance, Kerkeni was summoned to Istanbul (Alliance 1870–73). Apparently Kerkeni could not be convicted in court, but an order was eventually issued prohibiting him from returning to Tripoli. According to Ha-Cohen, all Kerkeni's efforts at bribery were to no avail. He died "in exile" after a few years.

Noteworthy in Ha-Cohen's narrative, in this instance as in others, is that he portrays the growing well-being of the Jews as going hand in hand with improved conditions of the populace as a whole. The pressure of the Alliance removed the scourge of Ali Kerkeni's rule from the city in general. The narrative states that the action of the Jews had the approval of the local Muslims, who "congratulated the Alliance and Sir Abraham Camondo (a leader of the Alliance)[12] of

Istanbul, for their word had prevailed over that of Ali Effendi Kerkeni"
(1978:156).

The Jewish Community and the Agents of Change

The changes under way in Tripoli of the nineteenth century
compelled the Jews to take into account a variety of factors: the inno-
vating Ottoman governors, the local Tripolitan Muslims, and the
growing Italian influence. Ultimately, the vortex of orientations in
this milieu raised basic questions of an internal nature: what was to
be the basis of Jewish identity and solidarity? Through the writings of
Mordechai Ha-Cohen we glimpse different stands on these issues, but
the differences that arose were not significant enough to deeply split
the Jewish community or to give rise to different ideological movements. The voice we hear most clearly is that of Mordechai Ha-
Cohen himself, who, in documenting the various events and developments, stated his position on the possibility of accepting the new
ideas that were part of the Ottoman reform, while remaining loyal to
his native Tripoli and to Jewish tradition.

As discussed, attempts at Ottoman reform were not carried out
in a political vacuum, but reflected, in part, growing European (in particular Italian) influence in Tripoli. This is exemplified by Ha-
Cohen's description of the celebration of the mulid (birthday) of
Muhammad by the ʿIsawiyya sufis, and this celebration's gradual
"toning down" as a result of increasing Italian influence in the
province:

> Italy enlarged the sphere of freedom in connection with the Muslim
> holiday called mulid [birthday]. It is an ancient and hallowed custom,
> celebrated annually, on the twelfth day of the third month of their lunar
> calendar. The month is called Rabiʿ Uwal. The holiday is holy to their
> Lord, and celebrated joyfully. For according to their reckoning it is the
> birthday of Muhammad their lawgiver. (1978:163)

Ha-Cohen then goes on to describe the celebration, featuring the
ecstatic *dhikr* (mystical exercise) of the ʿIsawiyya dervishes. The sufis
are followed through the streets and supported by onlookers who do
not themselves participate in the dhikr. As quoted in chapter 2, the
enthusiasm generated among the sufis and the crowd can turn into
"the great passion of religious hatred." Consequently, "Commerce
and crafts cease on that day. No one dares risk his life and oppose the
wild madness. . . . For if an ʿIsawi senses a stranger's presence, the
stranger's fate is sealed."[13] The account continues and tells of the resentment of the non-Muslims toward the restrictions that were

placed on them during the Muslim celebration. Ha-Cohen relates two
incidents, one concerning a Christian in 1883, and the second a Jew in
1904. In both cases a nonbeliever violated the traditional restrictions
but, with the support of the Italian consul, succeeded in affirming the
principle of "freedom of religion." In 1905 the Italian consul attempted to force Rajab Pasha to forbid the 'Isawiyya to perform the
dhikr, but this was opposed by the Muslim community. The celebration took place that year in a very subdued manner. Ha-Cohen's
account concludes with the following two paragraphs:

> All the peoples gathered round and cheered the Italians for stand-
> ing on principle and raising the flag of freedom, so that every man may
> go to his work and his toil, even on the holiday.
> In 5662—1912—when the city was captured by the Italians, the
> 'Isawiyya did not go outside at all, but performed the dhikr in a special
> place in the house of prayer. (1978:165–66)

The account depicts, in almost quantitative style, an inverse relation between the strength of Italian political presence and the
elaboration of the celebration of the mulid.

While the Jews obviously appreciated the opportunities provided
them by the intervention of the Alliance, or by growing European influence, they did not feel alienated from their native Tripoli. Many
saw themselves as the natural partners of the reforming governors
sent to Tripoli from Istanbul. For example, the steamship company
established in 1860, which began to provide regular mail service between Tripoli and Europe, was crucial to the Jewish merchants. Ha-
Cohen (1978:168ff.) reports that Ahmed Razzam Pasha, who gov-
erned the city in 1881–96 (see Martin 1985), utilized the advice of the
then chief rabbi, Eliyahu Bekhor Hazzan. Ha-Cohen describes
Hazzan's relationship with Ahmed Razzam Pasha in the following
terms:

> He selected the head of the Jews, the Hakham Rabbi Eliyahu Hazzan, to
> be his trusted adviser. He would speak to him in French, or with ges-
> tures, so that his [other] assistants would not understand what was
> being said. In the case of difficult matters, he would meet at night with
> Rabbi Eliyahu to take counsel. He did not go in the path of religious
> hatred, for all humankind among the Ottoman subjects was equal in his
> eyes. Even though he directed his efforts against the Jews who sought
> foreign citizenship, or the protection of foreign consuls, and forced
> them to be considered Ottoman subjects, he did not do this out of
> hatred toward the Jews but out of his love of Othmania and his hatred of
> foreign governments. (1978:168–69)

Thus fair and just treatment of the Jews was not seen as a monopoly of the Christian European powers, but there were expectations within the Jewish community that these norms could be established under Ottoman rule, even if this required bringing to bear outside pressure. We know from other countries that support for Jewish rights by European powers often helped drive a wedge between the Jewish and Muslim communities (cf. Bowie 1976; Shaw and Shaw 1977:128). This, however, does not appear to have been a major factor shaping the relations between the two communities in Tripoli, except during the final years of Turkish rule (i.e., on the eve of the Italian invasion). Ha-Cohen (himself an Italian national), who was well aware of the importance of foreign citizenship to those who held it, nowhere indicates that this issue fanned Muslim resentment against Jews (cf. Simon 1979:31ff.).

The adulation accorded (above) to Italy for its contribution to "freedom of religion" does not mean that Ha-Cohen (or the other Jews) had developed an unthinking loyalty to European civilization. His book also quotes at length the description of an incident in Benghazi of 1862, in which the French and British vice-consuls ignored appeals on behalf of several Jewish nationals who had been unjustly imprisoned (Goldberg 1980:173–77). In letters to the Hebrew press in England (Goldberg 1980:13), Ha-Cohen reports and praises several instances of fair administration. His text tells how Jewish soldiers, under the Young Turk regime, were not forced to eat nonkosher food and were given leave on Jewish Holy Days (Ha-Cohen 1978:185). Conversely, he does not hesitate to describe events in which the Italians discriminated against the Jews. In one instance the Jews of Tripoli called a boycott against the Bank of Rome (established 1907), after an order was issued that all employees had to work on the Sabbath (Ha-Cohen 1978:167–68). Similarly, and with characteristic detachment, he records the dismay of the Jews in 1911 when they found that the conquering Italians began to favor the subdued Muslim population at their expense (Goldberg 1980:191). He thus does not present improvement of the position of the Jews as an automatic concomitant of European intervention.

Change and Jewish Tradition

To understand how the Jews could at one time praise Italy, at another support the Ottoman governors, and on still another occasion side with the local Muslims against the Young Turks (see below), it is important to understand that the Jewish community in Tripoli at the end of the nineteenth century was characterized by a basic sense of

Jewish loyalty and religious-cultural identity which encompassed any non-Jewish influences it may have absorbed. While some Jews were wary of European influence on traditional belief and practice, others, including Ha-Cohen, were insistent that Jewish culture need not flee from contemporary ideas. Supporting Ha-Cohen in this position was the man appointed as hakham bashi, or chief rabbi of Tripoli from 1874 to 1888, Eliyahu Bekhor Hazzan.

Hazzan later served as the chief rabbi of Alexandria until his death in 1906. He was noted for his appreciation of some aspects of contemporary European culture. This was reflected in several of his *halakhic* (rabbinic-legal) decisions, which indicated an acceptance of changes in technology and society rather than an attempt to defend against them (Zohar 1983). In Tripoli, Rabbi Hazzan had been active in trying to reform Jewish education to include, among other subjects, the teaching of modern European languages.[14] While this was opposed by some members of the community as "planting the seeds of disbelief" (Ha-Cohen 1978:236), the majority supported the effort. Eventually the growing Italian presence (and capture of the city) brought about the acceptance of European-style education (Kahalon 1972; Goldberg 1983). While Hazzan was still in Tripoli, Mordechai Ha-Cohen was his ally in working toward educational reform.

While Ha-Cohen does not expound his religious philosophy in relation to the new cultural currents and social developments, several of his remarks indicate his basic orientation. At one time he contrasts modern times with the "religious hatred" common in the "Middle Ages" (1978:166). For him, however, "religious freedom" is not synonymous with "the freedom of religious conscience" of the individual, but rather refers to the unhindered opportunity for Jews as a community to follow their religious tradition, including the exertion of pressure on individual Jews to follow the dictates of the rabbinic law and community.[15] It is thus possible for him, while welcoming changes initiated by the Italians or Ottoman governors, to oppose the latter, together with the local Muslims, in the name of a sacred and time-honored tradition. The following is an example of such an incident under the rule of the Young Turks (Ha-Cohen 1978:184–85; Goldberg 1980:179).

The Turkish reformers tried to institute a law in which the state became trustee of a man's estate upon his death if his children were still below the age of twenty years. The local Muslims saw this as an abolition of the traditional rules of inheritance. It seemed that the government was trying to expropriate the land of any person who died without children and keep it from devolving upon his brothers or other heirs. Government officials began registering the estates of the local inhabitants, upon their death, despite popular opposition.

In May 1910 a wealthy Jew by the name of Saʿadan ʿAtiya passed away, leaving no children. The government officials approached his house to register the estate. The Jews organized and (apparently physically) prevented the officials from entering the house. The Jewish artisans and merchants then closed their shops and demonstrated in the streets. Upon seeing this, the Muslims struck as well and joined the demonstration. The crowd approached the governor's palace, and he (Ibrahim Pasha) agreed to admit a few of the leaders of the demonstration, both Muslims and Jews. When asked what the protest was about, the leaders claimed that there was united opposition to the new laws of inheritance. The pasha attempted to rebuff them, saying: "Is there not a clear commandment in the Holy Qur'an that one must establish a guardian for orphans?" (Sura IV, 6). Ha-Cohen, who was present then, was quick but respectful in his retort. The law of the Qur'an applies to orphaned minors, not to people of legal majority. The Jew Saʿadan ʿAtiya was of legal age, why should the law apply to him? The pasha asked the leaders to give him two weeks' time, after which he would announce a decision. He contacted Istanbul about the matter and received the answer that the issue should be referred to the local council of notables.[16] The council voted to do away with the new laws.

This incident plainly shows that the Jews were not permanently aligned with any one sector of the society, but took stands based on what they felt were Jewish interests. Ha-Cohen's participation in the demonstration and his taking the role of spokesman before the wali indicated a common purpose shared by the Jews and the Muslims in preserving their own (partially overlapping) traditions. Protection or improvement of the situation of the Jews could thus go hand in hand with the interests of the local populace.

Conscription of the Jews: A New Setting for the A Fortiori Logic

The period of Ottoman rule in the nineteenth century thus brought about greater protection of the Jews and their wider involvement in the civic life of Tripoli. It appears, however, that the dominant view among local Tripolitans continued to define the Jews in their traditional position of *ahl adh-dhimma* (the people of the dhimma) who had accepted the protection of the ruling Islamic power, with the acknowledgment of inferiority implied by that acceptance. Despite the weakening of some of the medieval social and political restrictions, the Jews continued to be perceived as a separate religious community characterized by a peculiar status. Freedom of religion, insofar as it was granted, was a condition gradually extended to a group and was not understood as the inviolable right of an individual. Features of the traditional cultural conceptions and aspects of the newly arrived ideas comingled in the social contexts emerging in nineteenth-century Libya.

The changing status of the Jews, therefore, was often grasped by the local Muslims in a manner different from that intended by the reforming governors. For some, an improvement in the Jews' status was interpreted as a decline in their own position and easily became a symbol and rallying point for those who wished to oppose the Ottoman innovations in general. A corollary of this understanding is that a sure test of the resolve of the Turkish pashas was the firmness with which they ensured the newly granted rights of the Jewish community. We see this in the case of Hafez Pasha (1900–1902), a governor who was vigorous in suppressing banditry in the region and who also attempted to impose a new land tax in the province (Ha-Cohen 1978:170–74; Goldberg 1980:59).

The peasants opposed this innovation and tested the pasha's strength by rioting in the Friday market of Amrus, on the outskirts of Tripoli, and robbing the Jewish merchants of thirty-three thousand francs. The pasha reacted forcefully, imprisoning the leaders of the peasants and demanding compensation for the Jews. The message of the pasha's actions follows the traditional a fortiori logic, here with regard to the property of the Jews, and not in the dramatic matter of their lives, as was characteristic of the incidents in the early part of the century cited above. If the governor is decisive in protecting the property of the Jews, then how much more so in other matters!

As I have argued above, a fortiori logic may also be applied in reverse, in the case of obligations. If there are certain duties that the Jews fulfill, it goes without saying that Muslims can be expected to meet those obligations. This view becomes clear in the struggle over conscription to the army and involves Ha-Cohen's own experience with Hafez Pasha and his successor, Husni Pasha (1978:175–78).

In accordance with an ancient tradition in the empire, the residents of Tripoli (along with other towns) had been exempt from serving in the army. If Hafez Pasha could not get the Tripolitan Muslims to serve in the army, he could at least compel them to pay the military exemption tax[17] and thereby acknowledge their obligations as Ottoman subjects. To this end he first pressured the Jewish community, members of whom, after the reforms of 1856 (cf. Shaw and Shaw 1977:100), were in theory if not in practice expected to serve in the military. A census was taken by Hafez Pasha in which the number of eligible Jewish males, subjects of the Ottoman Empire, was estimated at forty-five hundred. The pasha then demanded that the Jewish community pay a tax of 40,500 francs, or 9 francs per individual (combining, thereby, the traditional method of communal taxation with an obligation based on the modern conception of an individual's obligation to the state). Earlier, the tax owed by the community as a whole was 6,600 francs, and this new, high assessment might even result in the conscription of some Jewish men.

The pasha tried to enlist the cooperation of the leaders of the Jews in this effort, but was not successful. The treasurer of the Jewish community said to him: "There are 200 merchants who will willingly pay 9 francs in order to get the exemption, but the rest will simply not pay. They would rather be imprisoned, in which case the government treasury would have to support them" (Ha-Cohen 1978:176). In the midst of these events, Hafez Pasha received notice that he was being recalled to Istanbul.

His successor, Ahsan Husni Pasha, continued to pressure the Jews on the same issue. Arriving in Tripoli in late February 1903, he renewed the demand for payment of 40,500 francs in early June. The notables of the Jewish community were called before him, but claimed that the amount was excessive. The pasha then imprisoned these notables, an act reminiscent of the tactics of Hafez Pasha in his struggle with the peasants.

The Jewish community was alarmed at this move. On the following morning, Mordechai Ha-Cohen, sensing the mood of the people, went to all the synagogues with the following proclamation: "Brother Israelites! You all know that we are in great distress, and can rely on no one but our Father in heaven. For this reason, it is incumbent on every Jew to assemble this morning in the Great Synagogue and supplicate the Creator as one man" (1978:177).

This proclamation was, in effect, a call for a strike. It was heeded by all Jews (according to the narrative), including those who were citizens or subjects of foreign countries. Assembling in the Great Synagogue, the Jews "brought commerce to a standstill, and many of the crafts as well." The police were stymied, being unable to arrest everyone. The Muslims were very pleased at these events. The Jews "did not so much as give a finger to the Pasha," thereby preventing him from drafting them and from drafting the Muslims. They applauded the Jews, saying: "They number about 15,000 souls, and in no time at all they were able to organize and achieve unity. If only the Muslims were unified thus, no ruler could introduce new laws against their will."

This struggle between the Jewish community and the government over payment of the military exemption tax went on for the next several years, continuing into the reign of Rajab Pasha (1904–8). Again, Ha-Cohen (1978:181) notes that "religious hatred is foreign" to Rajab Pasha, even while this governor continued to press for payment of the tax. Over the course of time, compromises were offered to the Jewish population in which the original amount demanded was greatly reduced. The Jews remained united in refusing to make any payment until the Muslims were taxed first. Ha-Cohen clearly states that the Jews were mainly concerned with the resentment and hatred of the Muslims, the amount of money involved being a secondary consideration. They even resisted a suggestion of Chief Rabbi Hizqiya Shabbetai (he served in 1904–8),[18] who was recruited by the wali to propose that the payment of the tax be linked to an increase in the charity fund for indigent Jews. The matter was not settled during the period of Ottoman rule but in 1911, under the Young Turk regime. Jews were conscripted along with Muslims and were amply represented in the army. Of the 142 recruits from the city of Tripoli and its immediate environs, 59 or 41.5 percent were Jews (Ha-Cohen 1978:185; Simon 1979:18).

Conclusion

The struggle over the draft brings together several themes. From one point of view, imposition of military conscription may be seen as an aspect of the improvement of the Jews' status and their fuller participation in the evolving wider society. The new law was to be applied to them just as it was to other citizens of the realm. If the Jews enjoyed rights that they did not previously possess, then their new obligations were simply the other side of the same coin. Moreover, new demands were being made on all Tripolitans, and not only on the Jewish community.

Up to a point, melioration in the situation of the Jews goes hand in hand with the betterment of the whole population. If justice is done in the courts, if corrupt administration is eliminated, if security is established in the countryside, and if unfair taxes are avoided, both Jews and Muslims stand to gain and no one has to lose. The Jews are not only carried along in the general developments, but they sometimes appear in the limelight of new advances. In taking these positive steps they may win the approval of their fellow citizens of the

Muslim faith or may work in coordination with the ruling (Muslim) governors.

These developments took place, however, within the context of traditional understandings of the place of the Jews in Muslim society, which were still widespread in Tripolitania. The case of conscription highlights the limits this understanding placed on the innovations of the pashas. In spite of the improvement in the concrete situation of the Jews, there is little basic cultural revaluation of their social existence. The Jews are not viewed by the population at large as Tripolitan citizens "of the Mosaic persuasion," to borrow a phrase from the rhetoric of the European emancipation, that is, autonomous individuals who choose to follow a given private religious life. Rather, the communal definition of the Jews continues to be primary in public discourse, and this definition takes for granted the conditional place of nonbelievers in Muslim society. Thus, the actual social position of the Jews in relation to the Muslims of the town does not appear to have altered the ancient conceptualization of two separate and nonequal communities.

That this conceptualization continues to reign is made evident by frequent recourse to the a fortiori logic linking the Jewish and Muslim communities. If the two communities were perceived as equivalent segments in a wider society, such logic would make no sense. The very use of this rhetoric reveals that traditional presuppositions concerning Jewish existence in Muslim lands were not revised. As I have indicated, the a fortiori logic can work in two directions. It was used most commonly by leaders who demonstrated their power by extending justice and protection "even" to the Jews. The inverse of this logic is that challengers can test a ruler's strength and intent by probing his reaction to a violation against the Jews who are his concern. The Tripolitanian material also indicates another implication of the same logic—that a ruler can pressure all his subjects to meet their obligations by placing the Jews in the forefront of those who fulfill his demands. In each case, the location of the Jewish community in the social schema exposes them, on both sides, to the trial forays of ruler against ruled.

Hafez Pasha and Husni Pasha, in the early twentieth century, could no longer dramatically execute dissidents for violating the Jews as did the rebel Muhammad Bey (Ha-Cohen 1978:130; see above and n. 8), or as was threatened by Ghoma, in the nineteenth century, but they still appreciated the contingent existence of the Jewish community in the eyes of the local Muslims. Moreover, they utilized this traditional perception in manipulating the Jewish community in the service of their own progressive political goals.

4 Jewish Weddings in Tripolitania: A Study in Cultural Sources

As the previous chapter has indicated, the lives of Jews and Muslims were intertwined in both the city of Tripoli and the smaller communities of the countryside. Interviews conducted with Jews who formerly resided in the villages, as well as Ha-Cohen's text, show that Muslims traded, worked, chatted, and dined with Jews (see Goldberg 1980 and the next chapter). This regular contact undoubtedly resulted in cultural borrowing, transferring patterns of behavior and thought, common in one group, to the other. In the case of North African society, however, it cannot be ignored that a basic religious line divided Muslims from Jews, and that the distinction defined by this line framed, in a taken-for-granted manner, much of daily interaction. Moreover, this framing often restricted or modified the processes of cultural borrowing.

For example, in his analysis of Jews in Iranian society, Loeb (1976) has suggested that the devalued conceptual slot in which Jews were placed limited their influence on the Muslims with whom they came into contact. The encapsulation of Jews in North Africa was not as thorough as it was in Shiite Iran, but a similar mechanism may have been at work. Jews, representing urban life to Muslim villagers and nomads, and being on the average more involved with literacy, were an understandable source of cultural influence on Muslims, but this influence may have been mitigated because of its association with a non-Muslim source.

Looking at the other direction, Muslims, constituting the majority, were obviously targets of imitation by Jews. Jews, however, in seeking to maintain their distinctiveness, also had reason to hide or disguise such influence, so that despite the proximity of the two groups, we would expect there to be regular differences in their customs and culture. There were few spheres of life not affected by the play of contradictory forces of influence. In the present chapter, aspects of the dynamics of this cultural give-and-take are explored by focusing on a single topic—the wedding ceremony.

The challenge of understanding the culture of North African Jewry in the context of wider Muslim culture is presented succinctly in Chouraqui's (1952:261) chapter on Judaism in the Maghrib in the following words: "By the successive study of Oriental, Spanish, mystical, Arabo-Berber and French influences we succumb to the facile systematization suggested by history; it should be understood that these different currents converge and fashion the present reality while shaping developments yet to emerge." Despite this warning, students of the subject sometimes see the question from one perspective only, neglecting the complex interplay and emergent patterning of the various historical factors mentioned.

There have appeared a number of simplified views, held explicitly or implicitly, which detract from the richness and vitality of the subject. In one such viewpoint, the problem is not even recognized because the significance of Jewish culture is all but ignored. The unstated assumption here is that Jewish culture is only an accidental variation in the region, bearing no implications for an understanding of the Maghrib in general, the latter being "naturally" Muslim. In reply to this position one may quote Wansbrough's view that "the role of Judaism in Islam is structural, and impinges upon most aspects of Muslim society" (1977:41). I contend that this holds true for the recent past as well as in the historical periods to which Wansbrough refers.

According to another viewpoint, Jewish life was so influenced by the dominant Muslim culture that Jewish culture is basically a direct reflection of the former. This perspective appears in the following quote concerning the Jews of North Africa:

> Their roots were sunk deeply into the soil of the Maghrib. Their language was the local Arabic vernacular (with certain idiomatic differences); their ethos and values were those of the Maghribi Muslims; their personality traits and other characteristics were largely similar to those of their Muslim neighbors; even the Jewish and Muslim attitudes to the supernatural—with the all-pervading belief in magic, the evil eye, saints, amulets, apotropaic utterances and gestures—were practically identical, as was the personality of the God whom the Muslims called Allah and the Jews by one of his several Hebrew names.[1] (Patai 1971:206–7)

This view (reiterated in Patai 1986, chap. 6), which has much to recommend it, also is oversimplified, for a detailed examination of the life of Muslims and Jews in the region shows differences as well as similarities. In addition, it is not likely to be accepted by many North African Jews, and the very resistance to the notion is, in itself, a social force working to highlight and create differences. These points are illustrated in the material and analysis which follow.

From a third perspective, which focuses on parallels found in rabbinic writings and in the practices of Jewish communities elsewhere, the culture of the Maghrib Jews is seen primarily as a variant of general Jewish culture. This is undoubtedly a correct perspective, as I shall show, but very misleading if taken alone. Each of the viewpoints cited, separately, yields a one-sided picture. This chapter illustrates the complexity of the problem by focusing on cultural life in a defined region in which Muslims and Jews interacted, and thereby contributes to a balanced understanding of the topic generally.

In this chapter I analyze data, taken from three main sources, concerning various aspects of the marriage ceremony in rural Tripolitania. The first source is Mordechai Ha-Cohen's description of the wedding ceremony in the Jebel Nefusa (Goldberg 1980:122–26). This description was written in the first decade of the present century, but the author had been familiar with Jews of the Jebel Nefusa since 1886.

As a supplement to Ha-Cohen's account, I consider data from the Jews of the neighboring Gharian region who are now living in Israel. Some of these data have been presented elsewhere (Goldberg 1972, 1973). In addition, a partial description of a Muslim wedding is available from the villages of Bin'abbas (al-Ahmar 1976), one of the two localities in the Gharian region that had a Jewish community until 1949. While these three sources are not identical in time or space, they are close enough to allow productive comparisons.[2]

The exercise in comparison demands that we attend to a number of the levels of historical explanation briefly mentioned above. First is the overall similarity between Jewish and Muslim weddings, a similarity that is not surprising given the intertwined economy in which Jews and Muslims interacted on a daily basis. Close examination, however, shows significant differences in law, custom, terminology, and interpretation between Jews and Muslims (as well as between local communities within each religious category). This variation must be related to the difference in religious law, which influenced both the formal and the customary sides of the wedding ceremony. In spite of overall similarities in values and concepts, the diverse great traditions created subtle contrasts in practice among the two religious groups. The weight of traditional texts and symbols was ever present in the ceremonies of the Tripolitanian Jews and provided a basis for ongoing interpretation and reinterpretation.

These points are illustrated in the course of our presentation of ethnographic data. We begin with the wedding ceremony in the Jebel Nefusa (translated from section 99 of Ha-Cohen's book). As Ha-Cohen's description is discussed, new material is introduced allowing a detailed appreciation of similarity and difference in custom among Muslims and Jews in rural Tripolitania.

The Jewish Wedding in the Jebel Nefusa

The obligation to marry is incumbent on a male at twenty years and upon a female from the age of thirteen years.[3] Generally a youth picks a maid at the well. Each evening, at the time for drawing water, the daughters of the town go out to draw water from a well called Ba-isi, with their pitchers or leather water pouches on their shoulders. The women and girls drink from the well and draw sufficient water for all their needs.

When a young man finds a girl to his liking, she may no longer be seen with him face to face. For, from the moment she is spoken for, she shies away from him; she covers her face from him with the veil of shame.

The bridegroom counts out a sum of money according to the bride-price of virgins and gives the father of the maiden the bride-price and a gift. The bride-price is the price of a virgin, the value being six hundred francs, or at minimum, one hundred francs. It is a great disgrace for a girl if her father does not receive a higher price. The bridegroom contributes wheat, olive oil, and the like to help the bride's father with the expense of the wedding feast, in addition to the gifts of betrothal that are customary on the festivals. If the father of the bride is generous and good-hearted, he will give a dowry to his daughter equivalent to the bride-price and sometimes he will add extra money from his own pocket.

He who has only daughters profits from the bride-price; nonetheless, the father of girls mainly is concerned that they not fall to a man of evil deeds.

The items in the dowry are appraised by assessors in the presence of the bridegroom at twice or three times their value and price, and are so written into the marriage contract (see Tractate *Ketubbot*,[4] p. 66).

As soon as the wedding festivities begin, the bride must demonstrate her bashfulness. She runs from her parents' home to the home of one of her relatives, wrapped in a veil of modesty. Her face remains covered, and she is not to be seen with any man until the time of the wedding ceremony.

The groom, too, must depart from his father's house. He is accompanied by a youth, one of his friends, who is called the *shushbin*[5] and whose task it is to guard him through the days of the wedding festival.

Before the wedding festival the groom sends a species of an herb called henna to the bride's home, so that the hands and feet of the bride can be painted red by her and her female relatives.

The wedding celebration precedes the festival of Tabernacles [the fifteenth day of the Hebrew month of Tishri, in the autumn]. On the eve of the eighth of Tishri the bride is brought from her house of exile to her father's house. On the eve of the ninth of Tishri the bridegroom brings a basket of cosmetics wrapped in a silk sheet, together with the *bsisa,* to the house of the bride's father.

After the Day of Atonement [the tenth of Tishri] they take a hand mill and a plough, spread kerchiefs over them, and seat the bride on the kerchiefs (as a sign of her mastery of ploughing and milling). After that they paint her hands and feet cosmetically. They also expose her hair, letting it flow down before the crowd, while the kerchief covers her face. They sprinkle myrtle bud powder on her, and other perfumes sent by the groom.

The evening on which the bride is led from her father's house to her husband's is called *lilet a-raḥla* (the night of the journey).[6] Prior to her departure from her father's house, she must swallow seven twisted cotton wicks dipped in olive oil.[7] The bride walks slowly the entire way; her face covered by a veil. Two women support her, one on her right hand and one on her left. The other women clap hands and sing love songs composed for the bride. Wax candles and a torch are carried before her, while the men chant hymns. When she arrives at the groom's room she takes a chicken's egg out of her bosom and throws it against the wall of the house, soiling the wall. This is a reminder of the destruction of the Temple.

The seven blessings are recited on the night preceding the eve of the Festival of Tabernacles. The rabbi reads aloud the marriage contract, in front of the assembled, to make public the sums written therein, because, sometimes, the witnesses do not sign the marriage contract. The public reading by the rabbi is sufficient. For the most part there is no marriage contract that is not the subject of disagreement between the relatives of the bride and groom. Sometimes the seven blessings are not read until midnight.

During the day of the eve of the Festival of Tabernacles the bridegroom may not leave the portals of his house, for this is his wedding day, the day that gladdens his heart. Instead, he remains dressed in fine clothes and makes glad the woman whom he has chosen. He is given to her entirely for one day.

On the morning of the Festival of Tabernacles his companions gather to parade him to the synagogue. He is wrapped in a fringed prayer shawl and walks with very small steps, accompanied by hymns. If he should take a large step, one of his companions whispers in his ear,

"Keep your steps slow, have you another day of joy like this?" He rises and blesses the Torah scroll, and is accompanied by hymns. Afterward, the prayer leader passes a small glass of brandy to all those present in the synagogue. This takes place after he finishes reading the portion of the Torah beginning: "And Abraham was old . . ." [Genesis 24] in a special Torah scroll prepared for that reading. He pledges money to the Land of Israel funds, and the additional portion from the Prophets is read, beginning with the words: "I will rejoice in the Lord . . ." [Isaiah 61:10].

Every bridegroom must serve as a prayer leader at least once during the festival, reading the Additional Prayer[8] of the festival. If he is not familiar with it, another person may prompt him, in a whisper. All the grooms in one synagogue pull straws to see who will read on the first day, who on the second, and so forth.

When the groom returns from the synagogue, dressed as when he came, his friends and comrades come to his house, eating and drinking and making merry at his table. For one month he does not enter a room in which his parents are found together with his bride, for he is embarrassed to face them. (Ha-Cohen 1978, sec. 99)

Contexts of the Tripolitanian Jewish Wedding

Some aspects of the wedding ceremony may be understood in the context of the local ecology and economy. For example, the established time for weddings was at the end of the summer, before the Festival of Tabernacles. Many of the Jews in the Jebel Nefusa were itinerant peddlers and craftsmen who, as described in the next chapter, spent weeks and sometimes months away from home. Only at festival seasons was everyone present to partake in celebrations. Moreover, it was at this time of the year that Jewish artisans (blacksmiths, coopers, shoemakers, etc.) were well supplied with food, payments in kind having been given by Muslim clients after the harvest. Thus, while the Jews were not primarily farmers, their celebrations must be understood in terms of the local agricultural cycle and their place in the economy, which was complementary to that of the Muslims.

For this reason it is not at all surprising that parallels occur between Muslim weddings and the Jewish celebrations, as has been amply demonstrated by Ben-Ami (1974) while discussing Jewish weddings in Morocco. I show that in Tripolitania, similarities exist at the level of both general values and specific practices. It would be too simple, however, to see the customs of the minority as replicating the culture of the majority. While influenced by the immediate cultural environment, Jewish conventions took on distinctive meanings in terms of their links to a wider Jewish social system and religious tradition. This is exemplified by a discussion of bride-price in Jewish and Muslim local practice.

Bride-price: Concept and Terminology

The notion of bride-price illustrates the intricacies of cultural similarity and difference. In his description, Ha-Cohen uses the Hebrew word *mohar*, a biblical term (cf. Exodus 22:16), which is an obvious cognate of the Arabic *mahr*. The *mohar* described by Ha-Cohen, however, does not affect a marriage as the mahr does in Islam (Spies 1936), that is, the woman is not transferred in a full legal sense by this payment. Jewish law normally requires a monetary transfer,[9] accepted by the woman, in order to bring about a marriage. This, however, takes place during the wedding ceremony itself, along with the signing and the reading of the wedding contract.[10] The payment described by Ha-Cohen, however, represents an initial agreement between families to give their children in marriage. As such, it is both an indicator and a test of the prestige of these families within the community. Its payment finalizes the discussion over the conditions which later will be entered into the marriage agreement itself. The families may even stipulate that a fine should be paid if one side breaches this initial promise. Should this happen, however, it only affects the tie between the families, but there is no change in the marital status of the young man or woman. Their personal status is not affected by the payment of the mohar, and no bill of divorce is required if the agreement is abrogated. The payment mentioned, then, is an agreement on *conditions* and is directly parallel to the *tenaim* (Hebrew: conditions) agreement known elsewhere in the Jewish world.[11] The term for Ha-Cohen's mohar in local speech reflects this directly. In most Tripolitanian communities it was called *shart*, Arabic for "condition."

The term *shart* is also used by the local Muslims, but here the meaning appears to be more directly tied to the formal marriage transaction. Al-Ahmar gives the following account:

> The people of Bin'abbas distinguish between the *mahr* (bridewealth) and the *ash-shart* (marriage condition). *Ash-shart* is paid in cash as part of the *mahr*, which also includes animals, dresses, silver or gold articles, grain and other consumable items. . . . *Ash-shart* is handed over to a girl's father when the marriage contract is concluded. But not all the amount is paid at once. The main part of the bridewealth is paid over soon after the writing of the marriage contract and is called *muqaddam*. The remaining small part, called *mu'akhkhar*, is left over as a debt between two sides as long as the marriage survives. (1976:110,120)

Jewish practice in Tripolitania does not recognize the *muqaddam* and *mu'akhkhar*,[12] but again a focus on terminology alone can be misleading. The Jewish ketubbah stipulates the amount to be paid to the wife in case of widowhood or divorce. It thus may be functionally equivalent to the mu'akhkhar of the Muslim mahr but is not derivative of it. The payment written into the ketubbah is based on the ancient Mishnaic law.

In both Jewish and Muslim marriage in Tripolitania, then, a payment is made to the father of the bride at the outset, and a stipulated payment is made in the event the marriage is dissolved. There is a similarity in the terminology employed in both communities, but not an identity. Even though the influence of the Muslim environment is evident, each form of marriage must be understood in terms of its own tradition of religious law.

Premarriage Festivities: Judaic Influences and Muslim Borrowings

In both Jewish and Muslim practice the formalities required by religious law take up a small part of the overall ceremony, but are surrounded with elaborate festivities giving prominence to the wedding in communal life. The same sort of complex interaction of traditions is also evident in those aspects of the Jewish wedding which are not directly dictated by rabbinic law. One way of showing such Jewish influence is to point to a precedent for local practice in an ancient text, as Ha-Cohen does when citing the custom of writing a large sum into the marriage contract (above), or in the section of his work in which he describes the woman's role in nineteenth-century Tripolitania in terms of the Mishnaic code (Goldberg 1980:126).

Early rabbinic law itself took into account regional variations in the festive customs surrounding rabbinically required actions and sometimes saw these customs as firm indications of the strictly legal part of the ritual. Thus, in certain places, the "gifts of betrothal that are customary on the festivals" (Hebrew: *shiblonot*), mentioned in Ha-Cohen's description above, were given only after a marriage tie had been made and their existence could be taken as evidence of the marriage relationship having been established. In another example, the practice of a bride participating in a wedding procession with her hair uncovered was taken as evidence of her having been married as a virgin (below). The enshrining of these local customs in rabbinic discussion provided a basis for their repetition in different times and places over the generations.

In discussing the data available from Tripolitania, I put forth a further claim—that within the Jewish community, customs and attendant values common to Muslims and Jews were *structured* in such a way as to reflect normative Jewish concepts, even though there may have been no explicit reference to these concepts. This claim is pursued with regard to the ceremonies that took place during the nights preceding the legal marriage, which were commonly known among the Jews as *lilet el-ḥenna* (henna night). In the Muslim Binʿabbas community, the night before the formal wedding was known as *aṭ-ṭubail el-kbir* (the great drumming). The following analysis describes the prewedding celebration as it took place among the Jews of the Gharian, a region adjacent to the Jebel Nefusa which included the community of Binʿabbas.

In the evening before the wedding, many girls and women gather at the home of the bride. Here the bride undergoes beautification, which began the day before, involving dressing, cosmetic preparation, and combing of her hair. Later in the evening the bride is brought outside and sits on a low stool. Her head and body are completely covered by a large cloth, except that her bare feet, which have been covered with henna, extend outward. She is surrounded by women and girls, who sing songs appropriate to the occasion. Elsewhere, others are standing or milling about in same-sex and age-homogeneous groups. Prominent here are the young men, of approximately marriageable age, including some who recently have married. The groom is among these young men and, at this point, is not distinguished from the others by dress or behavior.

After the bride comes outside and sits down, the practice of "giving money" takes place in the following way. One of the young men takes some coins out of his pocket and begins making his way toward the bride. In doing so he has to thread his way through a circle of girls and women who are surrounding her. Upon reaching the bride, he touches her henna-covered feet with the coins and then drops them in a basket on her head. At this point the women ululate (*zgharit*). The boy retreats, and the coins are taken out of the basket by an old woman who is the "mistress of ceremonies" over much of the female side of the proceedings. She is usually a widow and keeps the money as a gesture of charity. This is not the only money involved, however. A handful of shiny new coins are dropped into the basket at the same time, making the total sound like a large sum of money. These coins are not kept by the old woman, but continually are returned to the "outside," that is, to the circle of boys, by the "best man" (*shushbin*), who is usually a recently married friend of the groom. The shushbin brings out the new coins and gives them to the next young man, who goes into the circle, touches the bride's feet, and drops the money in the basket. He, as do all the other boys, adds money of his own. Throughout this process, there is no outward indication that the groom is distinguished from his fellows.

Some of the features of this description, and that of Ha-Cohen, closely correspond to aspects of the Muslim celebration. For example, in both cases an emphasis on charity is deemed appropriate in the context of the wedding joy. As described, in the Gharian Jewish community an old woman is, in a discreet fashion, given charity. In the Bin'abbas wedding, a specialized singer who praises various public values also stresses the importance of helping relatives and needy people. Again it would be an oversimplification to view these similarities only in terms of direct cultural borrowing. In the nineteenth century it was customary for a wealthy Jew celebrating a wedding in the city of Tripoli to prepare a table for the poor of the community (Adadi 1865). Parallel customs are known from European Jewry as well (e.g., Pollack 1971:36), so the local custom in the Gharian appears as one expression of a widespread cultural value in Judaism.

In other instances, direct Jewish borrowing from Muslim surroundings seems more likely. The singer at the Bin'abbas wedding also recounts how a man can become well off if he works hard at planting and at harvest time. Ha-Cohen's account describes the Jewish bride sitting on a kerchief spread on a hand mill and plough "as a sign of her mastery of ploughing and milling." This custom was probably borrowed from celebrations in the Muslim community where there was a fuller involvement in agricultural production. Note, however, that the Jewish bride sits on a mill, associated with the work of women, and a plough, which, in a Middle Eastern context, is eminently a sign of maleness (the Qur'an 2:223 explicitly likens women to fields which men plow). In the Muslim ceremony, the singer refers to male activities which are clearly set apart from female ones (cf. Bourdieu 1977:132–39). In the Jewish ceremony, the task of ploughing is less clearly marked by gender. Thus while common values were shared by Jews and Muslims, the expression of sexuality among the Jews appears to have been relatively muted, greater emphasis on the male/female dichotomy being found among the Muslims. These differences in emphasis were realized in practice in other ways, as I now discuss in greater detail.

Sexuality and Social Values: Jewish Tradition and the Structuration of Local Practice

In both celebrations, Jewish and Muslim, there is a ritual exposure of hair.[13] The association of hair and sexuality is very old in the region and very widespread. In the Mishnaic code, as mentioned above, the testimony that a bride's head was uncovered at the time of her wedding was accepted as evidence that she was a virgin (i.e., it was not a second marriage, and her ketubbah was accordingly valued higher).[14] The ceremony differs, however, in the Muslim and Jewish communities of the Gharian region.

In the Muslim wedding, the exposure of hair occurs as a group of males stands opposite a group of females. The young men stand in a semicircle, with the groom in the middle, and opposite them is a line of nubile girls who kneel down and let their hair flow in front of their faces. They dance in this fashion, moving their hair, waists, and arms. The public appearance of femininity is more restricted in the Jewish wedding. Only the bride is involved. Her hair is let down, and the only other parts of her body exposed are her fingers and toes. There is no dancing in front of men, although some Jewish women danced among themselves in the fashion described.[15] A greater expression of sexual contrast and opposition, however, is reported from a Muslim community in eastern Libya, making the Jewish/Muslim contrast clearer.

Mason (1975) reports that in this Muslim community, the young men, in a separate room, line up against the wall and dance, making pelvic movements obviously reminiscent of the sex act. The groom does not participate in this dance but sits solemnly on the side. After the dance has begun, a young girl, usually related to the groom, is sent to the men's room as a representative of the women. This girl dances in front of the men and signals to individual male dancers to sing love songs. These songs are supposedly to refer to women generally. If the song seems to become overtly intimate and relate to the specific girl dancer, she may strike the male in question on his head with a baton in her hand. Mason's description and analysis cannot be fully presented here, but there is obviously the presentation of sexuality and an emphasis on the distinctiveness of the sexes. At the same time, the ceremony indicates the constraints that define the socially valued form of sexual expression. Briefly, in Mason's words, "female virtue and male honor are very clearly represented in the confluence of symbol and act" (1975:657). Thus this local custom seems to state, through ritual acts, values that are widespread in Muslim culture. Similarly, I believe that aspects of the Jewish celebration just described are related to sexuality and also to standard, normative notions established in Jewish tradition. To show this, let me supplement the description with more detail.

With reference to the coin-placing custom in the Gharian, I was told that in Libya some boys would file the coins, thereby creating very sharp edges. When approaching the bride and placing the coins on her henna-covered feet, they would dig the sharp edges of the coins into her flesh. The bride was not allowed to cry out or show any feeling. Afterward the coins would be placed in the basket, as described, and the young men returned to their fellows' company. It was not expected that the groom would do this to the bride, however. Most people could not explain this practice, but one man, who usually was more expressive than the other villagers said: "After you had done this to the bride you felt as if you had 'screwed her.' "[16] Aided by this interpretation, I think it is possible to place the ceremony in the context of standard Jewish tradition.

In Jewish law, the initial act of the formal marriage process, an act that changes the personal status of the couple, is known as *qiddushin.* The term comes from the same stem that signifies "sanctification." It is unclear why the term is applied to this act, but the Talmud offers the reason that through this action the man prohibits the "whole world" from sexual access to the woman as if she were a sanctified object (i.e., set apart for a special purpose).[17]

The young woman, who, before the marriage, is potentially available for sexual union with all the males in the community, now becomes forbidden to them, save for one—her husband. It seems that it is exactly this legal notion that is ceremoniously acted out in the celebration described. As emphasized before, all the young men of the community, including the groom, participate in the henna ceremony of placing coins on the bride's feet and then in the basket on her head. My informant's interpretations of the sexual connotation of this act are paralleled by the fact that each male appears to give the bride some money, one of the standard ways of acquiring a wife according to Mishnaic law.[18] Thus, during the henna night, a few days before the wedding, the groom participates as do all the other young males. It is only several days later, during the formal marriage including the qiddushin, that she becomes his wife and he takes on his new status singling him out from among his fellows. The whole ceremony exhibits, in folk practice, themes of sexuality, gender distinctiveness, and rivalry which are shared with Muslim culture, but it also takes on a specific form that is intelligible in terms of the Jewish "great tradition."

In attempting to unravel this thicket of distinctiveness on the background of commonality, it may be useful to refer to a lead provided by S. D. Goitein. In *Jews and Arabs*, Goitein (1955:147) notes that family life among the Jews and Arabs historically has been "extremely different." Among the Jews, he states, the warm intimate family featuring the husband and the wife has been highlighted, while among the Arabs the clan—with brothers, uncles, and cousins—has been central.[19] Following up this notion, and working with my ethnographic data, I suggest that one way of stating the differences between related traditions, such as the Jewish and the Muslim, may be the relative emphasis placed on different structural contrasts. Thus the contrast of the world of males versus the world of females seems to have central importance in Muslim rituals (particularly the one described by Mason), while the contrast (and complementarity) of the nascent individual family to the community is given prominence in the Jewish celebration.[20] Both themes, defined by contrasts, are present in the Jewish and the Muslim cases, but the stress is different. This is illustrated, in the Jewish instance, by aspects of mate selection which appear in the wedding ceremonies.

Mate Selection and Community: "Official" Explanations of Local Practices

The importance of community as providing the context for mate selection and marriage is stressed in both the Jewish and Muslim cases. On the day before the wedding in Bin'abbas, Muslim women from the whole community are invited to the home of the bride to help grind flour for the feasting. This is a major occasion for the exchange of information concerning possible matches. It is also a rare opportunity for young male relatives of the bride to closely view some of the village girls who have been secluded from them since puberty.

Matchmaking takes place at the Jewish wedding as well and has a ceremonial side to it. I refer again to the description of the coin-placing ceremony. When putting the money in the basket on the bride's head, a young man may quietly mention the name of a girl in the community. The mature women who surround him at this time understand that this is a "trial balloon" in the attempt to obtain a wife. The young man's gesture activates a network of inquiries concerning a possible match. If the girl and her family are interested, the matter will be pursued. If not, the matter is dropped and no one loses face.

While the dynamics of these maneuvers are easily understood in terms of a small Mediterranean community in which interaction is intense and the sense of family honor well developed (cf. Bourdieu 1977:34–35), it is instructive to consider this part of the ritual as well in light of Jewish lore and the explanations of informants. When responding to my queries as to the significance of different aspects of the henna ceremony, some persons explicitly claimed that the reason the new coins are added, in addition to those actually given by each young man, is that in this way everyone seems to be contributing the same amount, and no distinction will be made among those who give more or less. Thus, although there were clear wealth and status differences in the community, and these must have influenced the process of mate selection (cf. Goldberg 1972:101), part of the wedding ceremony stressed an egalitarian ethic in which each young man was recognized for his personal merits. In presenting this explanation, the villagers to whom I spoke acted as if there were some "correct" interpretation which they had once been taught. Although they did not quote a specific source, their account is reminiscent of a well-known Mishnaic passage which states that on the festive days of "the Day of Atonement and the Fifteenth of Ab the daughters of Jerusalem would go out in white clothes, borrowed from others, so as not to embarrass whoever did not have any. . . . The daughters of Jerusalem would dance in the vineyards saying, 'Young man, lift up your eyes and behold. Whom do you choose?' "[21] It would be hasty or even frivolous to claim that the Tripolitanian custom is directly derived from the passage, but the similarity in values underlying both should be noted.

In interpreting the customs of the Jewish wedding, as presented in Ha-Cohen's account and in the retrospective reports of Tripolitanian Jews, informants often provide a crucial element. The informant who made explicit the sexual connotations of placing coins on the bride's toes allowed us to link this custom to a standard Jewish source, although he himself made no such expressed linkage. The second interpretation (of the circulation of new coins), which I have just cited, intimated that there is an official, "correct" version of understanding the custom. It should be appreciated that the continuity of such a practice stimulates various explanations attaching praxis to classic text, and that this in turn reinforces perpetuation of the custom in question. Explanations like these, oriented toward the great tradition, have the implicit purpose of strengthening loyalty to tradition and highlighting group boundaries. This is particularly clear when a custom that is shared with the Muslims, and intelligible in a local context, is expressly placed within a set of concepts peculiar to Jewish tradition. This may be seen in the custom of breaking an egg which takes place toward the end of the wedding festivities.

Breaking the Egg: The Judaization of a Custom

In Ha-Cohen's description of the Jebel Nefusa wedding he mentions the custom of breaking an egg against the wall and explains the act as a reminder of the destruction of the ancient Temple in Jerusalem. This explanation immediately resonates with the widespread practice among other Jewish communities (including Tripoli) of breaking a glass at the termination of a wedding ceremony, and the accompanying comment that even in the hour of their greatest joy, Jews remember the destruction of the Temple. When looked at comparatively, this interpretation is obviously partial, for in Libyan Muslim weddings the practice of breaking an egg before entering the house is found as well. Ha-Cohen himself puzzles over this interpretation, when citing a parallel rite forming part of Jewish weddings in the city of Tripoli:

> When she [the bride] reaches the groom's house, the people refrain from entering until the groom ascends the roof and, with all his might, throws a jug full of water crashing to the ground—in memory of the destruction of the Holy Temple. The women cry out [zgharit] with joy, but it would be proper to sing a lament, because the crash recalls the mourning over the Holy Temple. (1978:277)

The bride in Tripoli has to step through these broken pieces to enter the house and then throws an egg against a wall of her new home. In the Tripolitan case, the Temple-mourning explanation is linked to the jug smashing and egg breaking, and, with respect to the former, Ha-Cohen questions the appropriateness of the women's response, rather than the interpretation itself. It is therefore clear from the Tripolitanian material (as well as from a comparative point of view) that supplemental levels of explanation are required.

Looked at as a widespread symbol, it is not difficult to formulate the hypothesis that the breaking of a glass, jug, or egg involves mimesis of the end of virginity, a rupture that is irreversible. With regard to the Libyan Muslims, al-Ahmar's informants claim that the breaking gesture helps bring harmony to the new house, while Mason (1975: 660) suggests that it may symbolize the loosening of ties between the bride and her family. These, in fact, may be two sides of a single process. It is quite possible that all these significations are relevant to the Jewish community as well and that tradition has seized the opportunity of attaching itself to a multivalent and powerful symbolic act. Moreover, the Temple-mourning gloss may serve to hide the source of a custom that appears to have been adopted from the non-Jewish surroundings.

Conclusion

This study of the Jewish wedding in rural Tripolitania has stressed the complexity of cultural influences shaping practice at any given point in time and has attempted to point to some ways of sorting out that complexity. As suggested at the outset, it is futile to try to neatly separate the different layers of historical influence, particularly those of remoter periods. Whatever the historical source of practices, their incorporation into a new community often involves reinterpretation—the adding of some meanings, the revision of others, and the dropping or denying of significations that previously were important. A more detailed study of these matters would also attend to the social settings in which traditional texts and notions are transmitted, such as synagogue study sessions and "sermons," in order to understand which concepts, terms, or values were familiar to which segments of the population.

The overall approach, built upon variation within a given region, has been stimulated by the work of the Language and Cultural Atlas of Ashkenazic Jewry (Herzog 1965). This research, focusing on "bilingual dialectology," has systematically compared linguistic features of a Jewish language (Yiddish) and the non-Jewish languages (e.g., Polish, Russian) that coexist with Yiddish in the same area. A mapping of parallel linguistic features within the same region shows clear and expected influence of the general languages on Yiddish dialectology, but also demonstrates that the Jewish language is not simply a "sponge" that mechanically absorbs influences from the environment. The distribution of linguistic features in space also reflects lines of communication internal to Jewish society.

The same type of analysis is obviously relevant to the distribution of cultural traits and should be applicable to North Africa as well as to eastern Europe. A preliminary analysis of this nature has been carried out for Tripolitania (Goldberg 1974, 1983). In the present chapter we have looked at some of the factors that account for variation within a single region. This included a special emphasis on the influence of the "great tradition" on local practice, in terms of both specific laws and a cultural format within which local customs are given Jewish meanings. In addition, there may be some customs which should be seen primarily in contrast to the neighboring Muslim traditions. This perspective is explored in greater detail in chapter 6.

5 Itinerant Jewish Peddlers in Tripolitania at the End of the Ottoman Period and under Italian Rule

hapter 2 discussed the situation of the Jews in Tripoli during the early nineteenth century, while chapter 3 considered the situation of the Jews in the small villages of the hinterland during the course of that century. These chapters brought into view diverse aspects of Muslim-Jewish relationships. One aspect was the official position of the Jews in respect to the formal institutions of society. A second view emphasized the actual forms of contact and social interchange obtaining between Jews and Muslims in the life of the region. This chapter focuses on the countryside and analyzes a specific focus of Jewish-Muslim interaction by examining the activities of Jewish peddlers. It then highlights some symbolic features which pervade that interaction, in particular the equating of Jews with women.

In the middle of the nineteenth century about 40 percent of the Jews of Tripolitania lived in small communities in the hinterland (Goldberg 1971), and many of them engaged in itinerant peddling. By the mid-twentieth century, this figure had dropped to about 25 percent, but the image of the Jewish peddler was still a significant one, even to the Jews of the city who had relatively little contact with rural regions. Jewish children in Tripoli heard stories about the adventures of these peddlers who spent much of their time "alone," wandering from one Muslim settlement to the next. From a methodological perspective, it is precisely this position of structural "weakness" that provides the background to cultural concepts and images which come into clear focus when examining the activities of Jewish peddlers in detail.

This discussion is divided into three parts. The first outlines the importance of itinerant peddling within the context of the long-distance caravan trade in which Tripoli was a major terminus in the nineteenth century. The second part describes the role of the *tawwaf*, the itinerant peddler. It describes his sources of credit, merchandise, routes, methods of transportation, interaction with Muslim villagers both male and female, and his consumption or resale of the goods acquired through barter. The third part examines the role of the peddlers as shaped by a combination of economic factors, on the one hand, and by traditional values in Tripolitanian society concerning Jews and Muslims and men and women, on the other.

The work of Mordechai Ha-Cohen, who himself worked as a merchant linking these small communities to Tripoli, serves as a source for documenting the life of the peddlers in the nineteenth century (Goldberg 1980). In addition, I utilize data taken from interviews with former peddlers active in the present century. While aware of the pitfalls of treating life in the countryside as "timeless," a comparison of Ha-Cohen's work with the interview data strongly suggests that there were many continuities in the economic and social situations, and I surmise that my symbolic analysis holds for the nineteenth century as well as for the recent past. Some attention has been paid to the effect of the Italian takeover, but this, I argue, only partially modified the traditional social and cultural forms.

The peddlers interviewed came from the towns of Amrus, Tajura, Mesallata, and Yefren, and were familiar, through their travels, with a variety of localities throughout Tripolitania.[1] Discussions with other former village dwellers, particularly from the Gharian region (Goldberg 1972), provided supplementary information. There was wide agreement in the description of itinerant peddling drawn by the different informants, along with variation in the extent and depth of the interpretations offered.

Itinerant Trade and Its Ties to the City of Tripoli

In both this century and the preceding one, Jews formed a significant proportion of the population of the city of Tripoli. At the same time, many also resided in the rural market towns lying along the major routes in the Tripolitanian countryside. Here and there one finds historical information on the economic links between Tripoli and its hinterland, but the information is too sparse to yield a detailed and clear pattern.

Early images of Tripoli have sometimes pictured it as an island, serving as a node of trade between both eastern and western directions and the north (Europe) and south (the Sudan), with much less important connections to its own rural hinterland.[2] In an analysis of the town of Sefrou in Morocco (including a discussion of the place of the Jews in the economy), C. Geertz (Geertz, Geertz, and Rosen 1979) has emphasized the shift in Sefrou's importance from forming a link in trans-Saharan trade to being the center of a regional market network. Under the two hundred years of Qaramanli and Ottoman rule (1711–1911) in Libya, more regular contact was established between Tripoli and the Fezzan in the south, and between the former city and its hinterland. The Jews definitely played a role in this trans-Saharan commerce (Goldberg 1980:8), as well as in the more localized trade.

Mordechai Ha-Cohen,[3] who traveled as a merchant to the interior of the country (in particular the Jebel Nefusa), gives the following account of the itinerant peddlers of that region and their ties to the city of Tripoli:

> They bring merchandise from Tripoli on the humps of camels: pepper, cumin, coriander, ginger, spice-stems and all kinds of spices; honey, sugar, tea, coffee, tobacco; rose and myrtle, spikenard and saffron, cassia and cinnamon and all sorts of spices; powders and pure frankincense and incense and the ointments of women; antimony powder for women to darken their eyes; walnut shells for them to paint their lips as a scarlet thread; henna plants to color their hands and feet red; mirrors, hair combs, glass beads and corals, matches, thread, needles and other merchandise too numerous to mention.
>
> All the Jews peddle, scattering throughout the district with a bundle on their back, or on a donkey, to barter with the Berber and Arab women for grain, olives, olive oil, figs, butter, lamb's wool, goat hair . . . chicken eggs and so forth. (Goldberg 1980:81)

Based on this description, Goldberg (1971) has interpreted the role of the Jews as occupying an intermediate position in the flow of goods and services between Tripoli and the most rural of villages and nomadic encampments. While it is clear that the Jews found a niche in the rural Tripolitanian economy, it is difficult to estimate how central a role they played in the total functioning of the economic system. Ha-Cohen describes recent changes in the situation, wherein Muslim Berbers from the Jebel Nefusa began to compete successfully with Jewish traders. He states:

> Originally, all the trade was in the hands of the Jews and no one could compete with them, for commerce requires planning and talent for which the Jews are well-adapted. Recently the Berbers have begun to undertake trading and many have been successful.
>
> With regard to peddling and bartering with the women, however, no one can enter the Jews' preserve; it is a Muslim rule that Arab or Berber males may not look upon their own women, for it may lead to evil thoughts, but Jewish men can look upon them freely. (Goldberg 1980:82)

Ha-Cohen wrote at the turn of the century, toward the end of the Ottoman period. Based on interviews with itinerant peddlers who worked in the Tripolitanian countryside during the Italian period, my impression is that the process described above may have developed even further. With the general development of commerce and the growing competition attendant upon direct Ottoman rule in the province,[4] the Jewish peddlers specialized mainly, or even only, in goods sold to women. The symbolic significance of this specialization is discussed after a detailed consideration of the economic and social activities of the Tripolitanian Jewish peddler or tawwaf.

Peddling in the Tripolitanian Countryside: Economic Aspects

This section gives an account of the activities of the peddlers from an economic point of view, while the next considers the same process from the perspective of the social interactions and meanings that were part and parcel of the economic exchange. The economic description is divided into the following topics: (*a*) learning the trade of the tawwaf, (*b*) obtaining the goods to be sold, (*c*) getting information on the routes to be followed and deciding on the length of the journey, (*d*) the items bartered and the goods received in exchange, (*e*) the problems of transport, and (*f*) disposal of the goods received in barter.

Learning the Trade

There were peddlers who learned the trade at a young age (at around the age of *bar-mitzvah*)[5] and those who began it later in life, even at the age of forty. For both young and old this work provided a good income. One person stated that after a month of peddling he had enough food in his house for a year; others described how they were later able to purchase land or build a store as a result of the income derived from peddling. At the same time, peddling was described as very hard work, requiring exposure to the sun and time away from home, so not everyone was attracted to it. Young men learning the trade often began to work with a relative, typically not a father, while the older men entered a partnership by investing capital and working with an established tawwaf.

Obtaining the Goods to Be Sold

Peddlers could obtain merchandise in a variety of ways. Goods could be purchased in Tripoli or in one of the major market towns of the hinterland. A man from Mesallata might purchase his goods there, but if he had the wherewithal to purchase them in Tripoli and trans-

port them to his area, he could save money. Often goods were purchased on credit, so there had to be a relationship of trust between the
supplier and the peddler. The supplier might be a Muslim or a Jew,
although some informants mentioned purchasing only from Jews.
Others said that generally the Muslims sold more cheaply, with one
informant stressing that it was less embarrassing to ask a Muslim for
credit. In some instances, certain goods might be sold only by Jews or
Muslims, reflecting an economic specialization along ethnic lines.

Information on Routes and the Length of the Journey

While the Jewish peddlers were the middle men par excellence of the
region, their activities were closely linked to the agricultural/pas-
toral economy and they had to be knowledgeable about the peasants'
situation. (There were also Jews who owned land and worked on the
land, although usually in partnership with Muslims.)[6] In eastern Tripolitania, near Garabulli or Mesallata, the peddlers typically traveled
among nomads' encampments, while in the west (Jebel Nefusa) they
more often visited settled villages. In their hometowns they would
receive information from Bedouins and villagers who came to market
as to which regions had had more rain and where the nomads were
located. Peddlers might be away from home for as short a period as a
week or as long as several months. Two weeks seems to have been a
modal length of time. During the harvest season (the fall), their jour-
neys were the longest. Their movements were also regulated, of
course, by the annual cycle of Jewish festivals.

Severe drought could drastically disrupt the economic rhythm of
the region. Nomads from eastern Tripolitania might move as far as
the Benghazi area in search of pasture. In the Nefusa Mountains,
whole villages might be temporarily abandoned, the population turning to seminomadism in years of drought. Events such as these
directly affected commerce. Well-to-do merchants could make profits in times such as these. Household items and clothing sold by the
nomads and villagers at very low prices during drought years would
be hoarded by merchants in Tripoli and resold when the prices were
high. Needless to say, the peddlers, who were directly dependent on
the produce and purchasing power of the rural population, were hard
pressed in times of drought as well.

Items Sold and Items Received in Barter

The essential trade of the Jewish peddler was in spices, cosmetics and
cosmetic equipment (combs, mirrors), and trinkets. I found a striking
similarity between the information gathered from contemporary in-

formants and Ha-Cohen's description from the beginning of the century. Below is a list of some of the main items sold.

Arabic Terms	English Translation
khal	*antimony*
henna	*henna*
židra	*myrtle leaves for the hair*
swāk	*walnut bark for reddening lips*
lubān	*a kind of chewing gum*
harž	*beads*
mašt	*comb*
mraya	*mirror*
kašik	*spoon*
ugīd	*matches*
yibrausilk	*needle and thread*
zhar	*flower water from orange peels*
bzar	*tumeric*
qranfel	*cloves*

In addition, tawwafs might sell other items, according to the demand in the countryside. Some sold sugar and tea, while others said that these items would be sold by Muslim peddlers or small shopkeepers in the villages. Sometimes these goods were sold by Jewish peddlers in small quantities, in between the villagers' main purchases in the market. Some peddlers sold baraccans or caps woven by their wives. Still others might sell copper pots or agricultural instruments purchased in Tripoli. A tawwaf might also be a tinsmith, mending household items and retinning the inside of worn copper pots. In one instance a tawwaf and tinsmith (*yekazdir*) traveled together, forming a partnership.

The items received in barter also show variety. Most commonly mentioned were barley, wheat, olive oil, and goat hair. Peddlers also acquired lamb's wool and camel hair, and tattered clothes and rags. Other goods included dates and eggs. They also accepted payment of pieces of copper from broken vessels or small bits of silver from broken jewelry. Most of this barter was carried out with women, as discussed later in the chapter.

Transportation

The tawwaf typically traveled with a donkey. Peddlers from Tajura described how they would travel from their home to Garabulli (a market town) with a horse-drawn cart, store their goods there, and continue through the countryside with a donkey. A sack, cut in half and slung over the donkey's back, was the typical mode of carrying merchandise. A man who had acquired too many goods to carry, but did not yet want to return home, might leave these goods with a Muslim acquaintance (see below), asking the latter to bring them to his home, by camel, on the nomad's next trip to the market. This was most common in the east, where the clients of Jews were mainly Bedouin. Alternately, the Jew would pay a Muslim for this service. Other peddlers simply returned to their base whenever their donkey was fully loaded or rented a room to store goods, bringing them home by hired camel themselves.

Disposal of the Goods

There was variation, too, in what might be done with the goods obtained. Some were consumed at home, others sold directly in a market, and still others sold to Tripolitan merchants. A man would attempt to ensure that he had a good supply of barley or wheat in his house before selling the grain. The same is true for olive oil, and eggs too would be consumed at home. Lamb's wool was spun by Jewish women to make baraccans and carpets. If a surplus of produce, eggs, or lamb's wool remained, these might be sold as well. Rags were primarily for resale, as was goat's hair, used for Bedouin tents. The broken copper would be resold, while broken pieces of silver might be accumulated until there was enough to bring to a silversmith (a specialty of Jews in Tripoli), to be refashioned into new jewelry. Thus some peddlers seem to have acquired enough to make their home life comfortable, without too much resale, while others appeared to play a significant role in moving goods from the countryside to more central markets. Fuller information is required to warrant generalizations about the role of the Jews in the local economy, but their importance probably varied with the season and the overall state of the region's economy.

Social and Symbolic Aspects of Peddling

The discussion thus far has focused on economic aspects of itinerant trading. It became apparent to me while analyzing the data collected that economic analysis in itself was insufficient to grasp and explain the particular place of the itinerant Jewish merchant in the local economy. An examination of the items cited by Ha-Cohen and those listed above shows that the peddlers dealt first and foremost in goods used by women. This specialization may be understood as resulting from a conjunction of two major cultural values. On the one hand, traditional Middle Eastern life was based on a clear separation of the world of women and the world of men, where the women were concerned with the interior of the house and the activities carried on therein. It was seen as a basic violation of social convention for a "strange" male to intrude into this realm. On the other hand, the Jew occupied a special status, because of his religion, which enabled him to be viewed as lower than Muslims in nonreligious spheres as well. The Jewish peddler, weak and dependent, was in some ways analogous to women and was allowed, therefore, to have face-to-face contact with them in the intimacy of homes, while Muslim males could not have this access. The sale of cosmetics and spices, therefore, became a Jewish preserve, bringing Muslim and Jew together, each dependent on the special goods and services the other had to offer. At the same time, the Jew, for his part, was also bound by traditional religious rules which regulated the nature of his contact with Gentiles. The following discussion analyzes the forms and meanings of social interaction between Muslims and Jews which arose on the basis of these factors in the various phases of itinerant peddling described above, showing how the economic and symbolic domains were linked in a closely knit fashion.

Peddlers on the Road

In considering the routes of the peddlers and the peddlers' relationships with the surrounding population, the question of physical security immediately comes to mind. The social situation of the Jews, during the Italian period, was one of relative well-being and stability. The Jew was "like a king," our informants told us. The Muslims dared not attack him. Incidents of adult Muslims robbing or attacking Jewish peddlers were extremely rare, compared to the Turkish period (Goldberg 1980:56–57,84). On the other hand, there were incidents where Muslim youths seeking to amuse themselves accosted peddlers in the desert. The peddlers would get rid of these youths by giving them small items such as mirrors or needle and thread. It should also be noted that the peddlers very often traveled in pairs, although they explained this as "preventing boredom," rather than as a means of protection.

Our informants expressed diverse opinions on the relations between adult Muslims and Jews. Some attributed the rarity of attacks to the fear of reprisal by the Italians. Others emphasized cultural values, underlining the notion that to attack a Jew was considered shameful. Although one man told of a case in which, threatened by a

Muslim at a crossroads, he dismounted from his donkey and hit the Muslim, this type of incident was considered unusual.

To interpret these accounts we must understand the conceptual place of the Jew in Muslim culture; his special status was marginal,[7] yet central in certain niches or social contexts, and possessing more than a negligible ritual importance. Ample evidence from Morocco, for example, shows the ritual importance of the Jews, and the social ambivalence of their status, in the context of a cultural symbiosis of the two communities.[8] In addition, the element of shame, which plays an important role in the cultural life of the entire Mediterranean region, infused the realm of Muslim-Jewish relationships in Tripolitania.[9]

The following example illustrates one aspect of the importance of shame. Certain Muslim clients of the itinerant peddlers could allow themselves to request lodging and food from their Jewish associates during a visit to the market towns where the Jews resided. Made to another Muslim, such a request for hospitality would have been shameful. On the other hand as mentioned earlier, Jews sometimes turned to Muslim suppliers to provide them with goods to peddle, on credit—this request being less shameful than if it were made to another Jew. We are thus confronted with a rigid system of interaction, based on established cultural values, in which the existence of an "other" cultural group introduces an element of flexibility, and the Jews thereby play an important functional role. The point is developed as the discussion continues.

Peddlers among Bedouins and Villagers

The peddlers' sojourn among the villages and encampments where their clients resided involved various practical arrangements. These arrangements are discussed under the rubrics of (1) lodging, (2) food, and (3) the "friendship" tie.

Lodging. The majority of our informants recognized that the itinerant Jew, for the most part, was well received by the surrounding population. He could ask, and would receive, lodging from families with whom he had no previous contact. He would be invited to pass the night under, or nearby, the tent, or in a room within the household. In some cases, in the mountainous Nefusa region, the Jew would sleep in a dugout section of the house complex. Typically, there was an expectation that the Jew would entertain his guests with storytelling, and most peddlers seem to have had the ability to provide this kind of diversion. In the villages, although less in the Bedouin encampments, the itinerant peddler was also a person who brought news of events in the outside world.

The hospitality extended to the Jew may be seen as part of the general morality of extending protection to the traveling and often defenseless "stranger." As described by Mordechai Ha-Cohen, the Muslims of the villages in Tripolitania

> desire to honor their guests by preparing them an elegant meal and gladly bring them everything they need in a generous manner. If something is lacking in the house, they will borrow from another in order to properly honor their guests. In particular, if a mounted warrior comes to their house, or even an ordinary Jew, they earn a good name by honoring him greatly. (Goldberg 1980:50)

In addition, there sometimes seemed to be an interest in the special religious needs of the Jew. One peddler reported that villagers familiar with the Jews would wake them in the morning, saying, "get up Jew—put on the straps" (i.e., phylacteries), knowing that the Jew had to say morning prayers before eating and continuing on his way.

One of our younger informants, however, expounded the situation in a completely different manner. From his point of view, the Jew was tolerated rather than welcomed. According to him, the peddler had to sleep some fifty meters from the tent because he was suspected of casting evil spells on the Muslims. This behavior toward the Jew was derived from a belief that a Jew, by sleeping under the tent, had the power to kill his host's livestock and family members. This story shows the ambivalent nature of the relationship between the two communities, even while it contradicts the bulk of our information. As in other instances, the variation in our data is of interest not only because of the "average" portrait that it yields, but because of the competing underlying meanings at which it hints.

Food. The rules of *kashrut* (foods permitted and prohibited by Jewish law) dictated that the Jewish peddler should dine with his own utensils while on the road, but would accept the bread and milk of the Muslims. In the region of Jebel Nefusa, the Talmudic-based practice[10] in which a Jew would throw a splinter of wood into an oven, thereby making the bread partially "his own" rather than "Gentile bread," was recognized and even encouraged by the local Muslim population. Several informants said that when among Bedouin, they would seek to lodge with a family that could provide an ample portion of milk, that is, those who had substantial flocks.

The following anecdote highlights the double-edged relationship between the two cultural groups. A peddler arrived in an encampment of seminomads, and the wife of the family prepared for him a number of flatbreads which he rapidly gulped down. The husband arrived later and asked the Jew if he had been fed. The Jew answered: "Oh, just a few small things." The Muslim then ordered his wife to bake some more bread which the peddler again gobbled up. During the night, the wife told her husband her version of the story. In the early hours of the morning the Muslim asked the Jew to help him lift some very heavy sacks of wheat. The Jew lifted them by himself. The Muslim then told the Jew that had he not lifted the sacks, he would have been killed, because it would have been as if the Muslim's food and hospitality were worthless.

Is this anecdote real or myth? It does not matter for our analysis, as the essence of the story lies in the ambivalence of its message. On the one hand, the Jew is seen as worthy of Muslim hospitality. On the other the transgression of norms befitting a guest threatens to bring on a punishment far beyond that which a Muslim transgressing the same norms might expect. The threat of death hovering over the Jew shows that the peddler is something "other," neither entirely rejected nor entirely accepted.

The "Friendship" Relationship. Sometimes Jews would lodge with an established acquaintance, referred to as *ma'aruf* or *ṣaḥbi*. The former term may be translated as "known" and the latter as "my friend." As a designation of client relationship, the terms may vary geographically, *ma'aruf* being more common in the Jebel Nefusa and *ṣaḥbi* more common in the east. A full analysis would depict the range of usages in different situations. At the moment I confine the discussion to some brief remarks.

One meaning given to the term *ma'aruf* was a person who renders a service, and another meaning was a person "known" among strangers. The term could be applied to a long-standing Muslim associate of a Jew who shares the income from herds or cultivated land owned by the Jew, or to a Muslim doing a service for a Jew such as transporting merchandise from an encampment to the Jew's house in town. Mordechai Ha-Cohen gives the term in reference to the established clients of Jewish artisans (Goldberg 1980:83), who paid in kind at the end of the agricultural season rather than paying in cash. Our informants similarly indicated that a ma'aruf is someone who might be given goods by the peddler without receiving immediate payment. The term thus may refer to relationships that are superficial, a stranger known among unknowns, or to a more long-standing tie, even to the extent of the establishment of intimacy (cf. Rosen 1984:160).

The concept of friendship in the Muslim culture of Morocco, according to Geertz (A. Cohen 1979), is understood differently from the notion of "friend" in contemporary European culture. For the Muslim, the term involves the components of trustworthiness and fidelity, not personal warmth or nonerotic love. One informant noted that the term *ṣaḥbi* would be used by a Jew to refer to his established Muslim client, but that the Muslim would refer to his Jewish associate as his *yahudi* (Jew). Here again we have contradictory notions of equality and inequality thickly intertwined with one another.

The Barter Situation

The main actor opposite the Jew in the barter situation itself was the Muslim woman. The marked separation between the feminine and masculine worlds[11] in Muslim North Africa shaped the economic role of the itinerant peddler. A "strange" man should not engage in a frequent and sustained relationship with a woman. At the same time, women had exclusive charge over certain household wares and items of personal use. Men could keep women protected from strangers by going to the market to buy meat and vegetables, or by purchasing tea, coffee, and sugar from Muslim peddlers specializing in these goods. These latter products were used by men as much as by women in the entertainment of male guests. Women's special competence concerned personal items such as trinkets, cosmetics, and kitchen spices, and it was shameful for men to be closely involved in these matters. The Jew, by virtue of his marginal identity, could enter into relationships with Muslim women and trade in these items (cf. Geertz, Geertz, and Rosen 1979:171).

The itinerant peddler not only sold these goods, but often specialized in yekazdir, the retinning of copper kitchen utensils. In Muslim culture, according to our informants, one does not take kitchen utensils out in the sun, in front of strangers. The objects symbolize the female world, the secrets of the house, and reproduction. As Bourdieu explains (in an Algerian, Berber, context), the house, the refuge of the secrets of nature, is a feminine domain (1973:102–5). Our informants agree that Muslim men would not want to engage in yekazdir; that would have been shameful (i.e., both "feminine" and "Jewish"). The Jew could permit himself to touch these utensils, to enter into the female world, suffused with symbols of reproduction. Thus, a symbolic analysis rounds out our understanding of the special economic place of the itinerant Jewish peddlers.

As stated, Bourdieu separates the Muslim world into two symbolic zones; the masculine domain which is the world of the "outside," and the feminine domain, confined to the home: "Woman has only two dwellings, the home and the tomb" (1973:104). Bourdieu and other researchers indicate that a self-respecting man must not be seen too much around the house, in the company of women. The Jewish peddler, however, spent much of his time in direct contact with women, bartering with them in goods of a feminine "nature." Our informants indicated that Muslim women did not observe the standard forms of female modesty in front of the Jewish peddlers, being unveiled and not even covering their hair. One explicitly claimed that the Jew was seen to be "like a woman"—*lihudi kif limra*.[12] Viewing the Jew in this way meant that it was not shameful for the intimate feminine secrets of the house to be exposed to him.

This suggests an interpretation in which the two domains, masculine versus feminine, and Muslim versus Jew, are closely linked. A man must protect his honor, and the sexuality of the women in his home is one of the main symbols and embodiments of that honor. Any laxity in the behavior intended to protect that honor brings shame. Thus a woman may be beaten, or even put to death, for bringing dishonor upon the males who protect her.[13] Let us recall the anecdote of the Jew who, overstepping the bounds of propriety expected of guests, might be put to death. On the one hand, the host has the obligation to provide hospitality and protect his guest. On the other hand, if his weak and dependent guest dishonors him, he may punish the guest with death. Just as females must provide certain services for males, and abide by the code of honor and shame, with the power of judgment in the hands of males, so the Jewish peddler must provide services for his Muslim host and not dishonor his protector upon whose will he is ultimately dependent.

In Tripolitania, as in Morocco (Rosen 1984:159–60), Jews may be likened to women.[14] In both instances there is an insistence on the separation of social categories, a demand for submission, and, at the same time, the necessity of maintaining relationships. Men cannot do without women, and Muslims cannot do without Jews. The peddling Jew is transformed into a woman both metaphorically and metonymically. First, his political weakness and submission are likened to the submission of women to men. Second, his peculiar economic activities bring him into the private female domain of the Muslim rural family. As such, the Jew fills a special economic role which he alone can assume.

Conclusion

Many studies have explored the importance of the concepts of honor and shame in Mediterranean society in general, and in North African society in particular. The link between honor/shame and gender differences is well known. It has been pointed out that elsewhere in the Middle East, ethnic groups may be ranked in terms of honor (Zenner 1972), or that certain occupations, such as that of peddler, may be perceived as "feminine" (Atkinson 1832). The present analysis shows how these various associations adhere together in a single bundle.

Surprisingly, little attention has been paid at either the cultural or interactional levels to the values of honor and shame in Muslim-Jewish relations. Notions of honor and shame spontaneously arose in the interviews conducted with Jewish peddlers. It would be shameful for a Muslim to harm a peddler or not to receive a Jew in his home. It would be shameful for one Muslim to request hospitality of another. According to Mordechai Ha-Cohen (quoted above), the first source of shame was even stronger than the second: a Muslim villager was prepared to borrow food from another Muslim in order to properly provide for a guest.

Our data thus show the linkage and overlapping of three sets of cultural contrasts: honor and shame, male versus female, and Muslim as opposed to Jew. We have explored various ways in which the conceptual opposition of *Jew/Muslim* may be symbolically linked to that of *woman/man*, with the values attached to norms of shame and honor providing a set of standards relevant to both of these symbolically merged domains. In the case of the itinerant peddler, alone among Bedouin camps and Berber villages, his marginality and social weakness allowed the full play of symbolic forces which turned particular males into actors enveloped in female symbolism. If our analysis of this focus of interaction is correct, it is likely that the same set of symbols also was at work, in a less bold fashion, wherever Jews and Muslims came into contact.

6 Jewish-Muslim Religious Rivalry in Tripolitania

The analysis in the previous chapter focused on the countryside, where Jews, in small communities, lived much of their lives in close proximity to Muslims. There, where interpersonal relations were very salient in communal structure, honor was a central value animating social life, and notions of honor and shame easily intertwined with the concepts and sentiments separating and linking Muslims and Jews. Even though the distinction of Muslim from dhimmi is, at the bottom, a religious one, explicit attention to matters of religion in this setting was relatively muted. Ha-Cohen contrasts the Muslims of Tripoli, who "are eager to argue about matters of religion," with the villagers who "do not have religious hatred toward the Jews, but are still very proud" (Goldberg 1980:49–50).

This clearly suggests that an explicit concern with religion informed Muslim-Jewish relations in the urban setting more so than in the villages. It was in the larger towns, of course, that the religious leaders and intelligentsia of both communities were to be found, so town residents were more likely to have been exposed to views emanating from classic Muslim or Jewish sources.[1] Our argument is not concerned with elite religious ideologies, however, but with elements of popular culture in which religious themes received expression. This is not to assert that the average townsman, who had little formal education (and the townswoman usually had none), was well versed in the sophisticated formulations of classic texts. What is claimed is that an analysis of popular culture as experienced by Muslims and Jews, while composed of many features characterizing the folklore of competing groups everywhere, often reveals elements of specific concern with religious and even theological topics. This component of popular culture probably was nourished in the urban centers, but there is every reason to assume that it had the potential of spreading to the countryside as well.[2]

A clear element of religious rivalry may be found in the collection of texts about the city of Benghazi in eastern Libya,[3] presented by Panetta (1943). Among these tales are several whose main theme is opposition between the Jews and Islam. Characteristically, these narratives do not relate explicitly to the local setting, but portray a conflict between a Jew and Muhammad. For example, one story, which purports to explain why the orbits of the gazelle's eyes are black, recounts how this animal sought to save Muhammad from a Jew, and the Jew, wondering at this act, decided to accept Islam (pp. 183–85). A similar tale, which also culminates in the conversion of a Jew (pp. 181–83), explains the "enmity" between the Jew and the camel, and also provides a reason for the Jews' not eating camel flesh. This was a salient difference in the practice of Muslims and Jews, for while they both followed forms of slaughtering which separated them from the Christians, Jews were restricted from eating camel meat, while Muslims were not.[4] Such nonverbal ritual acts formed part of religious "debate," as much as did explicit verbal arguments (Goldberg 1980:50–51).

The genre of tales recorded by Panetta in Cyrenaica must have been known in Tripolitania as well. Slouschz (1927:50) records the notion that Jews are "descended from a camel," and one of Panetta's narratives (pp. 177–78), explaining the special smell of Jews because of another incident involving Muhammad, is also documented from Tunisia (Saint-Paul 1902). This story attributes the Jews' odor to the fact that they are descended from corpses, and is linked to the practice, cited from Tunisia of the last century (Hesse-Warteg 1882:113) and by Tripolitanian informants, of referring to them as *jīfa* (carrion). It was probably by exposure to a combination of influences, in which formal religious doctrine and practice intermingled with popular conceptions, that the attitudes toward Jews and Judaism by rank-and-file Muslims were shaped. As will be shown, the debate between the religions was not carried out solely at the verbal level, but was embedded in the everyday ritual life of the two communities.

This argument will be pursued, with regard to Tripolitania, by presenting and analyzing a section of Ha-Cohen's work that can be entitled "Abraham the Proselyte,"[5] which tells the story of a prominent Muslim who converted to Judaism. Ha-Cohen, in a footnote, indicates that the narrative (written in Hebrew) is based on a popular sacred song, probably a *qaṣṣa*,[6] which was sung (in Arabic) by the elderly Jewish women in his day. Ha-Cohen regards the incident, which begins in 1688, as historical, and states that the document attesting to the religious conversion is still extant.[7] While recent research has shown the importance of the poet Musa abu-Jinah, who appears in the story (Hazan 1982), there is little information concerning him or the other rabbi (Agib) mentioned, reflecting the general lack of data from that period. It is not my purpose, however, to evaluate the historicity of the account, but rather to utilize it as a way of learning something about the world of cultural meanings current in Ha-Cohen's time which were shared, and argued over, by Muslims and Jews. While, as we shall see, there are polished literary elements in the tale as they appear in Ha-Cohen's book, the fact that his narrative partially derives from a popular song known to old women means that the story reflects the most common and nonliterate layers of the local culture. We also shall see how reference to nonverbal culture, customs that both united and divided Jews and Muslims, helps realize the overall religious message of the story as a whole. We proceed by first presenting a translation of the story, which we have broken down into episodes, giving them thematic titles.

Abraham the Proselyte

The Sabbath Egg

In the year 5448-1688 there was a wealthy Muslim named Hmayid who lent money to a Jew named Yosef ben Hizqiyahu. On the Holy Sabbath he was seized by a spirit of zealousness to press the Jew Yosef to repay the money, and disturb his Sabbath rest. He came to Yosef's house just as Yosef and the members of his family began to partake of the second[8] Sabbath meal.

"Welcome *sidi* [sir] Hmayid," said Yosef, "do you care to dine with us from the tasty Sabbath *tfina?*" (saying this in order to flatter him).

"I will not eat," said Hmayid. But his words faded away. "I did not come to fill my desire for Jewish delicacies, but came . . ."

Yosef insisted that Hmayid eat until he finally agreed to dine (for he thought, "I will eat his food and then laugh at him,[9] because after the meal I will press him for the money and he will have no escape").

They set a place for him and brought first an egg from the *tfina*, as it was customary (in those days) to apportion an egg to every person in the household at the beginning of the Sabbath meal.

Hmayid sensed an exalted taste in the egg and also sampled the other delicacies, and all of them had a lofty odor. He was utterly amazed, saying, "I have tasted all the delicacies the world has to offer, but nothing has pleased my palate so much as this exalted taste." He asked: "Please tell me with what you season the food?"

"Pardon me, *sidi* Hmayid," said Yosef. "The lofty taste is not from the spices, but from the food warmed specially for the Sabbath."[10] (Ha-Cohen 1978:93–94)

Theological Debate about the Sabbath and the Torah

"What is the Sabbath, and what is its taste?" said Hmayid, "that it can make food so fragrant?"

"We are commanded in the Torah of Moses (may he rest in peace)," said Yosef, "to sanctify the Sabbath day to commemorate the creation."

"But the Muhammadans and Christians believe in the Torah of Moses and in the creation," said Hmayid, "if they warm food on the Sabbath will they merit such a taste?"

Yosef said, "They all believe in the creation of the universe and in the Torah of Moses, but the other religions were received from a human lawgiver, while the Children of Israel received the Torah directly from the Almighty, with thunder and lightning.

"Everyone gives honor and glory to the Torah of Moses," said Hmayid, "but we have it written that the Jews forged parts of the Torah of Moses."

"Excuse me *sidi*," said Yosef, "do not believe in vain words which are not reasonable. Long before Muhammad, prophet of the Ishmaelites, the Jews were scattered throughout the world, and each tribe had with it a copy of the Torah of Moses. Other nations and tongues, and the disciples of Jesus son of Miriam, also possessed copies. How can it be conceived that one tribe of Jews, in any one place, would arise and change so much as one letter? Would they not fear for their lives that challengers could disprove them on the basis of the other copies that they had?" (Ha-Cohen 1978:94)

Proselytization

Hmayid was silent for about one hour but then said, "Oh, how sweet are the words of truth. It is impossible to accept belief in the falsification of the Torah of Moses because we have never heard of one group that had possession of a variant version. Is it permissible for you to present to me the Torah of Moses, that I may hear it?"

Yosef then presented to him the Five Books of Moses but said it is impossible to learn it on one foot.[11]

From that day, Yosef's words began to take root in Hmayid's heart. He began to be suspicious of the Muhammadan religion and spent his time coming quietly to Yosef's house each Sabbath to learn the Torah from him and to understand its interpretations. He also learned the hymn *Yigdal Elohim Ḥai . . .* which summarizes the thirteen principles of faith.[12] Finally, he decided to enter the covenant of the Jewish religion. He also persuaded his mother and his sister to accept Judaism and divorced his wife who hated the Jews.

One Saturday night Hmayid went to the house of a Jewish sage named Musa abu-Jinah who was chanting hymns with great joy. Rabbi Musa abu-Jinah paused from his chanting in order to pay respect to the presence of Hmayid. But Hmayid said, "How pleasing to me are your utterances which gracefully exult the Creator! I did not come to interrupt your joyous pastime, but when you finish the chants I have to speak to you in secret." After the chanting was over, Hmayid disclosed his inner thoughts, that he desired to enter the covenant of the Jewish religion.

Rabbi Musa, who knew very well that the exile weighed heavily upon the Jews and feared that there would be trouble were Hmayid to be proselytized, did not agree to say yes, but also did not refuse. He said to him, "This is my counsel: Go to the wise Judge Rabbi Yosef Agib, who is well versed in the Talmud, and very perspicacious. He will tell you the path to follow."

Hmayid went with a broken heart and constant worry to Rabbi Yosef Agib because he had not been promised by Rabbi Musa that he would be accepted as a willing proselyte. He poured out his heart in front of Rabbi Yosef, saying, "Please, my lord, I do not wish to accept the Jewish religion for reason of profit, for God has been gracious to me and I have everything. Neither do I seek carnal pleasure, that I have become attracted to a Jewish girl,[13] for my carnal desire is dulled . . . . I know for certain that the Jewish religion is true, and that the other religions are as nought compared to it, and for this reason I have come to take refuge under its wing."

Rabbi Yosef, at first, did not want to accept the Muhammadan proselyte for he feared that evil would befall the Jews because of religious hatred. But Hmayid persisted in his pleas and said, "Trust in the Lord and do not be afraid, for the conversion will take place secretly and when the opportunity arises I will take my family to a place where no one knows me and will profess Judaism openly."

After that Rabbi Yosef presented him with some of the commandments, both simple and difficult ones.[14] He then informed him of the severity of the punishment should he backslide because of the strict commandments. But Hmayid said to him, "I knew all this before I came to you, and have accepted it with great love." Then Rabbi Yosef took secret counsel with the assembly of judges, and agreement was reached to accept a righteous proselyte. He was circumcised a second time,[15] and ritually immersed with the intention of proselytization and was given the name Abraham.[16]

His mother was called Rebecca and his sister Yaquta. His two sons were circumcised and immersed with him. (Ha-Cohen 1978:94–96)

"False" Accusation and Deliverance

Abraham the proselyte was filled with joy upon accepting the religion. He rejected all the delights of this world. He lavished a great deal of money on the purchase of a scroll of the Law, decorating it with silver ornaments and plush wraps. However, there lived in his neighborhood a certain Muslim named ibn-Shalluf who began to be suspicious that there had been a conversion. He injected the poison of suspicion into his neighbors in order to watch Abraham's steps and to search his every deed.

On the holiday of Passover, it was as if an invisible hand hinted that enemies were stalking his tracks. He prepared a meal of *kuskus* made out of *matzah* crumbs, so that it would appear to everyone that he was eating leavened food made from farina. He also ate meat with the juice of the fruit called *ḥab'aziz*, which looks like milk.

The neighbor ibn-Shalluf maligned Abraham the proselyte before Muhammad Pasha Sha'ib al-'Ain[17] and his lieutenants, saying, "The Muslim Hmayid is observing the Jewish religion, he is careful not to eat leaven." On the night of Passover, the pasha and his assistants went to investigate his food and found the remnants of his meal—leavened kuskus and meat in what looked like milk. They were then satisfied that he was falsely accused for he had eaten leaven, and meat with milk, in opposition to the Jewish religion (Ha-Cohen 1978:96)

Abraham's Observance of the Sabbath

In 1689 the new month of Tishri[18] fell on a Monday. As the Muslim months are set by witnessing the new moon, they began that month, which was called *dhu-l-ḥijja*, on Tuesday, because the new moon was not seen on time. On the twelfth of that month is the Festival of Sacrifice on which the Muslims slaughter sheep. The assembly of judges was worried that if Abraham refrained from slaughtering the sacrifice on the Sabbath, which was the twelfth day of the Muslim month, the omission would be felt, and zeal would be aroused against the Jews. They permitted him to slaughter on the principle that "the Torah releases in the case of compulsion." During the slaughter, his conscience struck him because of the desecration of the Sabbath; his hands slipped and he soiled his clothes with blood. An Ishmaelite woman, who was standing by silently, saw how brave Hmayid's hands slipped during the slaughter. Abraham was concerned that the incident would become known. He won her over by giving her the liver[19] and the lung and a good portion of meat.

Conclusion

Some time passed and Abraham fell sick. His appointed time had come. His last request to the assembly of judges and the Jewish notables was to spare no effort and try to steal his body from the Muslim cemetery and to bury him in a Jewish grave. The Jewish notables succeeded in honoring the request of the deceased through great effort and cunning. (Ha-Cohen 1978:96)

Structural Aspects of the Story

The central theme of the story is clear. A Muslim sets out to disturb a Jew in his Sabbath observance. Contrary to his original intention, the Muslim finds himself attracted to Judaism, first through a sensory experience and later by theological conviction. He wishes to convert to Judaism and eventually does so. This places both him and the Jewish community in danger, but they succeed in avoiding harm and in thwarting the designs of accusers.

The overall narrative is built up of smaller units, each of which reiterates the theme of Jewish-Muslim conflict. A great many tales on this topic have been collected from Middle Eastern Jews who have migrated to Israel; the tales are subjects of a study by Jason (1975: 125–71). One common topic is the special taste of Sabbath food which cannot be duplicated by non-Jews. Another well-known theme is that of religious dispute between Jew and Gentile.[20] A third motif is that of the false accusation of a Jew by a non-Jew (here, having the twist of being true). In the present study, these individual units have been incorporated into the vita of a righteous man, "Abraham the proselyte."

Hmayid/Abraham's career takes a full turn, and this is expressed in several literary devices. At first he wishes to disturb Yosef's Sabbath. Later he is cautious not to interfere with Rabbi Musa on the conclusion of the Sabbath. In the last episode he himself, like Yosef, tries to observe the Sabbath despite the pressures of the Muslim surroundings. At the beginning of the tale Hmayid confronts the Jewish religion in order to get his money back, while in the end he lavishly spends his money in decorating a Torah scroll. The movement of the story is also underlined by literary allusions to the biblical narrative. At the outset, Hmayid uses an expression attributed to Esau (see n. 9), but later, when claiming that God has been gracious to him and that he has everything, he mouths the words of Jacob (Genesis 33:11). The name Yosef, given to the Jewish protagonist, may hint that he, like his biblical namesake, resists the temptation of the Gentile environment.

Most of the sacred legends dealing with Jewish-Muslim confrontation do not explicitly concern themselves with theological matters,[21] but simply highlight Jewish-Gentile conflict and take it for granted that God, or a sainted rabbi, is on the side of the Jews. One explanation of the theological focus of the present narrative is that the author, Mordechai Ha-Cohen, was an educated individual who had a highly intellectualized approach to life in general (Goldberg 1980:10–14). While this undoubtedly is true, I do not believe the explanation is sufficient. As stated, Ha-Cohen took the details of the story from a popular song, sung by women, who had no formal theological training. In addition, I have heard of similar discussions of the classic question concerning the falsification of the Torah and refutation of the argument (Baron 1957:86–96; Perlmann 1974:110) from members of the "lay intelligentsia," religious specialists living in the small communities in the Tripolitanian hinterland. Theological dispute thus appears as an integral part of the story.

The strength of the theological argument to the reader of the tale, or to the listener of the song on which it is based, however, did not derive only from the superior logic of one point of view or from a more accurate mustering of historical facts. The implicit debate takes on force by linking official religious views with "nonverbal" elements of the narrative: the religious customs and practices mentioned which were universally observed by members of the society in question. Hmayid is in danger (as is the Jewish community) when the pasha sends his agents to conduct a religious investigation by examining the contents of his plate,[22] and manages a second narrow escape when a simple Bedouin woman observes an unusual movement in his style of slaughtering. An analysis of three of the customs referred to in the narrative shows yet another level on which the debate between Judaism and Islam was carried out in everyday life.

Customs in Debate

A number of customs appear in the narrative which are relevant to the normal religious life of Jews and Muslims. Among them are (*a*) the Jewish Sabbath and the eating of an egg on the Sabbath; (*b*) circumcision; and (*c*) the *'id al-adha* celebrated by the Muslims. The mention of these customs is not accidental, and their presence is crucial to the story. Each carries connotations of the Muslim-Jewish *religious* dispute and thus states, on a nonverbal level, theological contentions parallel to those made explicit by Ha-Cohen.

The Sabbath

The Sabbath is a Jewish institution that saliently separates Judaism from Islam and Jews from Muslims. It does not seem that the Muslim "day of assembly" was established in polemic opposition to the Jewish Sabbath (Goitein 1965:592–94), but it is easy to see how the difference in the day on which public worship is held could serve as a symbol marking the separation of the two communities. The "day of assembly" is not officially a day of rest, although in some places it seems to have taken on that characteristic to some extent. In any event, it stands in contrast to the Jewish Sabbath for which forbidden work is enumerated into a long list of categories and subcategories. The salience of the Jewish Sabbath to Muslims was strengthened by the attenuation of commerce on that day. A local proverb stated that "a market without Jews is like a document without witnesses" (Moreno n.d.:51).

The difference between the Sabbath and the day of assembly was of special interest to Mordechai Ha-Cohen, who mentions it several times in his book. It appears in a polemic context when Ha-Cohen has a long discussion with a prominent Muslim (Goldberg 1980:10–11). Ha-Cohen tries to best the Muslim in debate by claiming that if the Muslims accept the Ten Commandments (and do not view them as being included in that part of the Torah which had been tampered with), then they should also accept the Jewish Sabbath which is one of the Ten Commandments. This debate over the Sabbath, moreover, was of interest not only to a religious intellectual, but was of wider concern in the area, as is attested to in mundane practices associated with its celebration.

One of the categories of work explicitly prohibited on the Sabbath is that of kindling a fire (Exodus 35:3). At the same time, the Sabbath is a joyous day celebrated in a family setting, which involves the preparation and consumption of a festive meal. While food may not be cooked *on* the Sabbath, food which has been prepared prior to the Sabbath may be kept warm on a steady flame which is lit before the Sabbath (Friday evening), but burns slowly during the day. Throughout the traditional Jewish world there are special Sabbath foods which can be prepared and kept in this way.[23] In Tripoli and Tunis such a dish is called *tfina* (D. Cohen 1964:151–54). The egg referred to in the story is part of the tfina.

The tfina and particularly the egg are thus trademarks of the Jewish celebration of the Sabbath, and we find that special attention is paid to them in tales. In stories that I collected among the Jews of the Gharian in Tripolitania (Goldberg 1967:215–16), the tfina appears as a focus of Jewish-Muslim conflict. In these stories the Muslims attempt to harass the Jews by stealing meat from the pot of tfina and substituting frogs instead. Because the Jews cannot cook on the Sabbath, this means ruining their celebration of the day of rest, just as Hmayid intended to spoil Yosef's Sabbath in Ha-Cohen's narrative.

In the narrative, Ha-Cohen mentions that the custom of giving an egg to each member of the family before the Sabbath meal was once more widespread than it was in his own day. This practice, like many others that were once common in the city of Tripoli, was still in force in the villages of the interior up until 1949. In an ethnological survey of former residents of these villages (Goldberg 1974, 1983), information about the practice of serving an egg before the Sabbath meal was gathered simply to discover the geographical distribution of that trait. One informant, from Mesallata, volunteered information indicating that the egg carried connotations of Muslim-Jewish religious rivalry. He said that should a person consider converting to Islam, people would make him recall the fond memories of childhood by saying "remember the Sabbath egg." The same notion was found among informants from Tripoli, and in the village of Yefren people recall a story in which a Muslim woman converts to Judaism after tasting the Sabbath egg.

All these incidents are reminiscent of the story of Hmayid. The man from Mesallata, in an interview on the topic of the Sabbath, gave a bit of information which inverts one aspect of the text presented here. He said that sometimes a Muslim would come to repay a debt on the Sabbath, and the Jew was allowed to accept the money by simply telling the Muslim to put it on the table (so the Jew would not be forced into a monetary transaction on the Sabbath). This would avoid the possible "trouble" that could arise as a result of a direct refusal.

It thus appears that Ha-Cohen's account reflects a cultural milieu in which common practices reflected firmly held religious ideas and sentiments. Symbols such as the egg, whose basic meaning is found internal to a given tradition (the enjoyment of and delight in the Sabbath), carry additional meanings when placed in opposition to rival religious symbol systems. At the same time, the tfina, of which the Sabbath egg forms a part, could form the occasion of good neighborliness between Jews and Muslims. Thus, Jewish women in Tripoli in the middle of the last century would bring the tfina to be warmed in the ovens of Muslim homes in case their own fires went out on the Sabbath.[24] Which meaning became salient on what occasion depended on the context and situation.[25]

Circumcision

Circumcision is another practice common to Muslims and Jews, and simultaneously a point of difference between Judaism and Islam. In Judaism, a biblical verse (Genesis 17:12) explicitly commands that circumcision be carried out on the eighth day after birth. According to rabbinic law, this can be set aside only if the health of the child is in question. In Islam, by contrast, circumcision is only considered a "commended" act by several schools, as it is not mentioned in the Qur'an (Levy 1957:251; Wensinck 1986). Most Muslims, however, popularly regard circumcision as marking the entrance of a young boy into the Islamic religion and nation. This popular view of circumcision is also common in Judaism, although technically it is not the act of circumcision which "makes" a child Jewish. In several villages in the Tripolitanian interior, the men would shout "yehudi, yehudi" as soon as the circumcisor performed the operation (Ohel 1973).

The time of circumcision is another factor separating Jewish from Islamic practice. A linguistic text from Tripoli (Cesàro 1939: 207) indicates that some importance was attached to this difference: "The time of circumcision is variable. Some circumcise on the fortieth day, but this is rare, so as to be different from the Jews[26] who circumcise on the seventh and fortieth day.[27] Most of the residents of Tripoli circumcise from the second to the seventh year." Cesàro's informant clearly shows an instance of conscious dissimulation of Jewish practice on the part of Muslims.

The difference in the timing of circumcision has always symbolized the separation of the Jews from the "sons of Ishmael." This is seen in the biblical story in which Ishmael is circumcised at thirteen years, while Isaac is circumcised at eight days (Genesis 17:23 and 21:4). Moreover, the difference in circumcision practice is linked to another point of controversy between the two religions—who is the rightful spiritual heir of Abraham. The crowning story in Abraham's career of faithfulness to God is the episode of the sacrifice of his son. A *midrash*[28] links the circumcision to the episode of the sacrifice as follows:

> Isaac and Ishmael were engaged in a controversy: the latter argued, "I am more beloved than thou, because I was circumcised at the age of thirteen"; while the other retorted, "I am more beloved than thou because I was circumcised at eight days." Said Ishmael to him: "I am more beloved, because I could have protested, yet did not." At that moment Isaac exclaimed: "O that God would appear to me and bid me cut off one of my limbs! then I would not refuse." Said God: "Even if I bid thee sacrifice thyself, thou wilt not refuse."

The theme of this story, which probably predates Islam, was developed further when Islam claimed that Ishmael was the victim, and not Isaac, and therefore Abraham's rightful heir. There is a minority opinion, however, among Muslim theologians, that on this point Islamic tradition does not differ from the Torah (Eisenberg 1927:532; Paret 1971). What is noteworthy about the present argument is that this minority view is not only confined to scholarly tracts, but had some popular currency in Tripolitania. In Ha-Cohen's account of some of the Muslim celebrations in the town, he states: "On the twelfth day of the month of *dhu-l-ḥijja*, it is a great holiday for the Muhammedans. They slaughter sacrificial rams commemorating Ishmael's ram, but some say[29] it was Isaac's." (1978:42). Again we find that a religious tenet in which Islam and Judaism differ, and which has the potential of becoming a subject of theological debate, is given direct expression in popular usage. The same point of contention may be seen by further examination of the celebration of the Muslim Great Festival.

'Id al-adḥa

Most general accounts of Islam, focusing on the "five pillars," describe the pilgrimage to Mecca, while there are relatively fewer detailed ethnographic accounts of the celebration that accompanies that event in specific locales throughout the Muslim world—the Great Festival. The centrality of Mecca, it seems, carries with it connotations that set off Islam from Judaism, particularly the association with Ishmael. According to tradition, Muslims were first enjoined to face Jerusalem in prayer, but this was later changed to Mecca (Levy 1957:157). It was Abraham and Ishmael who built the Ka'ba, and the latter is believed to be buried nearby, together with his mother Hagar. When pilgrims sacrifice at the conclusion of the *hajj*, it is preferable to do so at a point where Abraham prepared the sacrifice of his son (Von Grunebaum 151:33). Again, my interpretation of religious rivalry does not rest on standard meanings attributed to these rituals, but focuses on specific practices involving the Jewish community in the Muslim Tripolitanian setting.

The Jews, who constituted a small minority in Tripolitania, were not unaffected by celebrations central to the Muslim majority. This was particularly true in small rural communities, where the Jewish population usually numbered several hundred souls. Jewish merchants sold new clothes to their Muslim customers in preparation for the Great Festival, and Jewish blacksmiths sharpened the knives to be used in slaughtering. Jews were even involved in aspects of the slaughter itself. It was customary in several of the villages for a few notable Jews to visit their Muslim counterparts and skin the carcasses of the slaughtered animals. It is significant that the leaders of the Jewish community were expected to perform this menial task. It seems that the act was viewed as a statement of the relationship between the two communities, in which the Jews acknowledge the supremacy of the Muslims and, by implication, Islam.

In recent times, under Italian rule, the Jews were less dependent on local goodwill for their protection and security, but customs such as these persisted in the rural areas. One informant claimed that the Jews performed this service "partially out of respect and partially out of fear." In one community in 1945, the Jews gave a sheep to the Sudanese troops who came to guard them during the disturbances in November of that year (Goldberg 1975 and chap. 7).

In Tripoli and several other villages, there was another Jewish custom associated with this Muslim festival, which appears to have been more widespread in the past. In these communities some Jewish household heads would arise early on 'id al-adha and slaughter an animal *before* the Muslims sacrificed.[30] In one case an informant was quite explicit that the Jews did this in order to be the first to receive the merit of the blessing. If one leans toward structural analogies, this custom might be seen in relation to circumcision,[31] mentioned above, where Jews circumcise at the age of eight days and Muslims later. The unspoken logic from the point of view of the Jews may be: just as we circumcise early, so we can slaughter early. One also is reminded of the biblical story of Jacob and Esau wherein the former usurps the blessing intended for the latter by reaching his father earlier. What is clear from this custom, which has absolutely no basis in Jewish halakhic tradition, is that there existed explicit rivalry between the two communities over the same spiritual rewards. Mention of the Great Festival and the slaughter in Ha-Cohen's story, therefore, as in the case of the other customs already discussed, restates and reinforces the message of the text as a whole.

The Social Context of Religious Rivalry

I have attempted, through the analysis of the text presented above, to illuminate cultural dimensions of Muslim-Jewish religious rivalry at the end of the previous century. Systems of cultural meaning and concrete patterns of interaction, though interrelated, are not replicas of one another. Thus, the narrative cited is not intended as a description of the concrete social relations obtaining between Jews and Muslims in Tripolitania. However, note should be taken of some sociological aspects of the topic discussed.

In his book on Jewish-Gentile relations, Katz (1962) discusses the attitudes of Jews toward Gentile religions in various periods. He contrasts the degree to which there was direct confrontation in the religious realm during the Ashkenazi Middle Ages with that of both earlier and later periods. During the Ashkenazi Middle Ages the Christian community constituted a significant audience in front of whom Jews acted out the devotion to their own faith. This may be seen in the drama of martyrdom, in which those who sacrificed their lives did so fully intending to rebuke the Gentile onlookers through their deaths. It may also be seen in the serious attention accorded to the question of proselytization by rabbinic scholars. In other periods, by contrast, Christianity was no closer to Judaism in terms of formal doctrine and practice, but Jewish religious life went on while largely ignoring the outside world.

If we consider the Tripolitanian case in terms of this rivalry/ignorance continuum, we find it closer to the medieval situation. I do not base this statement on consideration of incidents of extreme stress, proselytization, or martyrdom, but on the analysis I have presented of standard rituals forming part of normal life in both communities. Each of these rituals—the Sabbath, circumcision, and the Great Festival—has basic meanings relating to the central values, doctrines, and laws of the respective religions. At the same time, each carries significance deriving from its opposition to symbolic forms in the rival tradition. From this point of view the practice of these customs must be viewed in terms of the overall cultural milieu, which includes both the Islamic and Jewish traditions and in which matters of religion were taken seriously. At the very least we must assume a certain area of overlap in which there was a common ground of meaning on which rival religious claims were made, understood, and "answered" through the ritual acts of members of the opposite faith.

By likening the situation in Tripoli, at the turn of the twentieth century, to the Middle Ages, there is no intention to deny the significant developments wrought by the Ottomans in the nineteenth century (see chap. 3). Changes did take place in political and legal realms and may even have affected attitudes among part of the Muslim elite. It appears unlikely, however, that the new definition of the place of the dhimmi in Muslim society, introduced by the Ottomans and carried forward during the brief reign of the Young Turks in Tripoli, altered the basic cultural and religious orientations of the majority of Muslim society in this regard. The improved position of the Jews (or, at least, of the Jewish elite) during the last decades of the nineteenth century may even have been the cause of a certain backlash in attitudes toward the dhimmi. In any event, the social setting was such that the traditional concepts, reflected in Ha-Cohen's story, continued to have meaning and retained the potential of shaping action.

Some of these points are relevant in evaluating aspects of our methodology. As indicated at several points in the discussion, customs and practices that had disappeared or were disappearing from Tripoli still could be found in the villages of the interior. Implicit in a number of examples has been the assumption that data pertaining to life in the villages in the second quarter of the twentieth century can illuminate cultural features of life in Tripoli several generations before. This is linked to another assumption that the influence of the Ottoman regime in the region only slowly spread into the rural areas. Patterns of Jewish-Muslim interaction and cultural exchange which prevailed in Tripoli during the last century still found counterparts in the rural setting.

At the same time it should be appreciated that the Ottoman presence and Ottoman reform, along with growing European influence, did have an effect, particularly in the city and in the countryside as well. Principles of religious equality began to be translated into social reality, albeit slowly and unevenly. As we have already surmised, these political and legal developments may have aroused religious resentment in the local population, at the same time that they countered its direct expression. The reforms may thus have had the effect, in some segments of the population such as lower-level officialdom (Simon 179:19), of heightening the saliency of religious tensions, based on preexisting traditions that culturally defined the terms of religious rivalry. This may be the background of Chief Rabbi Hazzan's decree, in 1885, that Jewish children should no longer engage in the practice of joyfully celebrating the burning of Haman dolls in the street, on the holiday of Purim (Ha-Cohen 1978:198).[32] Whatever degree of intercommunal tension existed during Ottoman times as a result of growing Jewish participation in civil life, it is probable that notions of religious rivalry and tension continued to persist, and perhaps grew, during the Italian period, as is discussed in the following chapter.

Conclusion

This chapter has focused on religious rivalry between Jews and Muslims as expressed in popular culture. Utilizing a text based on a genre of oral literature common to Muslims and Jews, I have shown that the theme of the text—rivalry between Islam and Judaism—is also echoed in everyday practices which played a role in the religious life of all of Tripoli's inhabitants (the Christian Maltese of the town do not concern us at this juncture). These practices reinforced, in a multitude of ways and settings, systems of cultural meaning. Such meanings are not to be viewed as rigid models for daily behavior, just as complex cultural systems cannot be interpreted as simple mirrors of social interaction. Thus the same symbols might sometimes be used to declare religious rivalry and on other occasions to highlight common identities and harmonious relations. Jews and Muslims were both the Children of Abraham—a source of solidarity *and* a point of contention with regard to spiritual birthright (see chap. 7, "The Riots and Other Social Dramas"). Religious food taboos could set both groups off from Christians (many Muslims would eat meat slaughtered by Jews) or could place them in opposition to one another (Muslims ate camel flesh; Jews did not). Even while the formal political and legal frameworks within which daily life was carried out underwent significant changes, these quotidian practices, in which religion was interwoven with the basic threads of the fabric of social life, ensured the maintenance of distinctions in which Muslim and Jew, believer and dhimmi, while in continual interaction, were also constantly defined anew as belonging to rival social and spiritual categories.

7 The Anti-Jewish Riots of 1945: A Cultural Analysis

Italian rule brought with it a series of changes shaping Tripoli as a whole, including its Jewish community. The development of the Jewish community under the Italians is the major focus of a comprehensive historical study by De Felice (1985). During this period the city and its Jewish community were affected by many forces, including colonization and economic development on the one hand and Arab national reaction to the Italians on the other, both of which fed into the events of World War II and the growth of Zionism within the Jewish community. Within this vortex of political and social change, Jews and Muslims continued to interact on a daily basis, and the age-old ambivalences and complexities of that interaction persisted, both reflecting and helping define the new historical situations.

Italian colonial rule was the shortest in North Africa, and years of relative stability were punctuated by dramatic incidents, sometimes including physical hardship and violence. Less than three years after the Italians were driven from the city of Tripoli by the Allied forces, the Jewish community was rocked by a pogrom[1] (in November 1945) in which more than 130 Jews and one Muslim were killed in three days of rioting. Many observers see this event as the watershed determining that most Libyan Jews would leave their native country[2] and immigrate to Israel, when it became possible to do so. It is the thesis of this chapter that this episode must be placed in the perspective of the traditional Libyan Muslim notions concerning the Jews and the threat to these notions posed by Italian colonial rule. While the riots were clearly rooted in the specific political conditions that characterized Libya at the time, they also took the precise historic shape of older cultural outlooks and symbolic forms. In pursuing this argument, I first outline the political-legal situation of the Jewish community under Italian rule and then supplement this with a depiction of everyday life in a number of spheres. It will be seen that in spite of relative stability imposed by the Italians, tensions between

97

Muslims and Jews continued to be present, and at times the religious aspect of these tensions was apparent. A discussion of the events prior to, during, and after World War II, which were extremely trying for both Libyan Jews and Muslims, provides the background for an analysis of the riots. These are discussed in terms of the data at hand, but also considered in the context of theories concerned with "collective behavior." I argue that both historical understanding of the riots and social science theory relevant to such events can benefit by attending more fully to cultural perspectives.

The Jewish Community during the Italian Period

The Jews of Tripoli constituted, at the beginning of the Italian era, a well-defined religious and ethnic group with an important economic role, most of whose leaders had a modernizing outlook but this orientation was not the substance of a systematized ideology. De Felice (1985:82) portrays the Jewish community at the beginning of the Italian era in the following terms:

> a lively sense of tradition, reflected in both individual and community life, characterized Jewish life in Libya during the Italian period. Jewish life followed time honored forms, and was "entirely dominated in public and private by one law and one tradition." These were so tightly knit and interdependent that it was almost impossible to distinguish between the effects of Jewish law and tradition and outside influences resulting from centuries of contact with the surrounding Arab society. "Jewishness was intense and shared by all."[3]

After the experience of Turkish rule, this community, along with its clear sense of Jewish identity and commitment, also viewed itself as very much part of the local urban scene.[4]

De Felice's analysis traces both external causes and internal developments which led to "an irreparable splintering of the Libyan Jewish community into two camps, the traditionalists—mainly the poor and socially marginal—and the modernizers—mainly the rich and the enterprising members of society." The two groups, De Felice claims, "were linked on a religious and spiritual level in ways which grew more and more formal and perfunctory" (1985:81). The former group continued to become more "marginal to society" and eventually moved en masse to Israel.

These developments, however, did not unfold along a unidirectional path. At one level, the situation of the Jews was better at the beginning of the Italian era, when there was an expectation that they would quickly come to resemble emancipated Italian Jewry, than it was at the end of that period when the Jews of Libya became subject to the racial laws enacted in Italy. At the same time that Italian rule and contacts with the local Italian population encouraged many Jews to modify their traditional way of life, political developments led to the assertion of a renewed solidarity.

The internal structure of the Jewish community of Tripoli (Comunità Israelitica della Tripolitania) was legally formalized by the Italians in 1916. At first there was an attempt to introduce a form of leadership based on elections, but this led to severe conflicts within the community. Later (in 1929), during the period of fascist rule, when there was a growing need of the colonial administration to achieve a modus vivendi with Libyan Muslims, an Italian (non-Jewish) official was charged with the administration of the Jewish community (De Felice 1985:108ff.). While at the time of the conquest, many Italians thought that the Jews of Libya would quickly be transformed into the likeness of contemporary Italian Jewry, some colonial officials began to insist that they were, in fact, socially similar to (or even "below") the indigenous Libyan Arabs. Throughout the period of Italian rule, the receptive orientation toward European culture which had developed among the Jewish elite at the end of the nineteenth century continued to grow and formed part of what De Felice views as a process of the splintering of the community. The developments of the 1930s, however, including attempts to quicken the pace of "civilization" of the Jews by enforcing the opening of shops and school attendance on the Sabbath,[5] both highlighted and ensured that even the most "advanced" members of the community retained a clear sense of Jewish identity and attachment to tradition.

The colonial situation, as elsewhere in North Africa,[6] thus established a complex set of dynamics among Jews, Muslims, and Europeans. Some of the Jews, particularly the well-to-do,[7] felt themselves socially close to the Italians at the same time that many others continued to live and work in proximity to the native Arab/Muslim population. While for the latter, who constituted the large majority of Jews in Tripoli and in Libya, daily relations with the Muslims continued according to familiar forms, the fact of Italian domination was always in the background. The conventional gestures that signaled the special status of the Jews might continue, particularly in the countryside (e.g., not riding mounted on a donkey when a Muslim passed by on foot), but could also, in the new context, be viewed as demeaning abuses. Before considering this question, I sketch some of the trends of the Italian period regarding contacts (and separations) among Jews, Muslims, and Italians, which are summarized under the general categories of residence and work, technical change, schooling, and the synagogue and leisure activities.

Social Trends among Jews, Muslims, and Italians

Residence and Work

In Tripoli the Jews lived in both the traditional Jewish quarters of the old city and the new part of the town. The movement out of the Jewish quarters began during the Turkish period (Ha-Cohen 1978:118) and continued under Italian rule. There are no official figures about the percentage of Jews in the new city during the Italian period, and one observer estimates that the number reached from three thousand to four thousand people (Rubin 1988:39). Based on the estimates of informants, it is unlikely the figure ever reached as high as one-fourth of the Jewish population.

The Jewish population had been concentrated in two adjacent quarters (the *hara kebira* and *hara zeghira*), in the western quadrant of the city. To the northeast of those quarters was a concentration of the European/Christian residents, including many Maltese; this also was the location of several of the European consulates. To the southwest of the Jewish quarters were the predominantly Muslim residential areas. The "crossroads" of the old city was to be found at the meeting place of *suq el harrara*, running in a southwest to northeast direction, and the *arba arsaat* street running from southeast to northwest. Here the first-mentioned street (*suq el harrara*, which was a continuation of *sciara homet gharian*) divided the Jewish quarters from the Muslim area. The second street led northeast to the heart of the old European area, which included the Catholic church and branches of several banks. In the opposite direction this street paralleled *suq el turk*, a prestige market (first built by the Turks and developed as a tourist attraction by the Italians) in which Jewish, Muslim, and Italian shops were intermixed, and led out through *bab el hurria* to the new city. In the larger streets of the new city, European-style shops were built, many of which were owned or run by Jews.[8]

In each area of the city the diverse ethnic elements of the population mixed on a daily basis, although there were differences in the character of the interaction. The majority of the Jews continued to live in or adjacent to the Jewish quarters. I know of no instance in which a Jewish and non-Jewish family lived in the same dwelling unit in these neighborhoods. There were areas in the heart of the Jewish quarter where one rarely saw a Muslim; in the words of one informant: "it was just like Tel Aviv."[9] Similarly, there were areas in the old city in which it is said that Jews rarely walked, in particular at night. When Jews began to move out of the Jewish quarters in Turkish times, probably reflecting a situation of overcrowding, a few took up residence on a street where houses of prostitution were concentrated, as rooms rented there at a lesser cost. At the same time, this was a poorer area where Jews were more likely to meet abuse on the street.

The traditional Jewish quarters were mainly residential but also included many grocery stores, greengrocers, butchers, restaurants of various scale, and street vendors. In other words, individuals pursuing commerce could find much of their clientele within the limits of the Jewish quarter, as well as reside there. However, procuring supplies (meat, vegetables) always took them to other markets in and around the city. The craftsmen, for the most part, plied their trades outside of the Jewish quarter even while continuing to live in it. Shoemakers, carpenters, builders, and silversmiths usually had their shops in the southeastern quarter of the city, in the interlaced network of market streets, some of them named after craft specializations (e.g., *suq en najjara*—carpenters; *suq es siyyagha*—silversmiths).

A considerable number of Jews established residence in the new city built up during the colonial period. Jews living there mainly had other Jews and Italians as their neighbors. These Jewish families were often found near one another, but not in any exclusive concentration. Jews and Italians lived in the same European-style multistoried apartment buildings. It appears that even Muslims who could afford to move into these areas often preferred not to because the houses were not built in a way that secluded the interior of the house, as was Muslim custom (cf. Goitein 1971b:292 on this difference in Muslim and Jewish homes during the Middle Ages). A number of well-to-do Muslims invested in real estate in the new city, and often all the management of their affairs was carried out by Jews who were more familiar with the market and the details of managing these matters. This arrangement also allowed Muslims to minimize contacts with Europeans/Christians.

Technical Change

The period between the two world wars was characterized by the continual introduction of items of contemporary western technology, which can be illustrated by a widespread Jewish craft in Tripoli—tailoring. The importation of sewing machines was an important innovation, and the provision of electricity meant that these machines could be powered by motors. At the same time, the pressing irons continued to be heated by coals, since there were as yet no electric appliances satisfactory for this purpose. The presence of electricity also meant a change in the working hours of certain craftsmen, who previously ceased their labors when sunlight was no longer available. Another shift was from the practice of sitting on the floor while working on clothes (or shoes, or while coppersmithing) to working at a bench. Many craftsmen serving the traditional population of the city did not partake in these changes during this period, but whether slow or rapid, these changes also reflected the differential involvement of Jews with Muslims and Italians (Goldberg 1982).

Tailoring had always been a common Jewish occupation, and there is mention of the tailors' market (*suq el tuarzi*), in which Jews were active, from the middle of the last century. Jewish women also worked at tailoring, in their homes, for Muslim customers. A market in Tripoli, known as "the market of women," formerly was where Jewish women would receive materials from clients to be sewn at home into traditional Muslim garb. This pattern of organization appears to have changed in the early part of this century, perhaps influenced by the growing use of sewing machines. In the middle of the Italian period, Jewish tailors seemed to specialize in either Muslim or European clothing. Those specializing in the latter, who often first worked as apprentices to Italian tailors, gradually grew in prominence. A massive shift toward working within a European-style market, and away from the Muslim sector, became apparent only after World War II.

Schooling

In traditional Muslim society schooling was inextricably linked to religion, so it was taken for granted, in Libya as elsewhere, that different groups would organize basic education in separate frameworks. In the latter part of the nineteenth century, various steps were taken within the Jewish community to modernize education (Kahalon 1972), a trend that continued under Italian rule and tutelage. To the extent that this brought Jews into contact with non-Jews, it almost always involved greater contact with Italians rather than Muslims. It has been argued both that the Italians did little to promote indigenous Muslim education (Appleton 1979) and that Muslims were not quick to respond to initiatives in that direction (De Felice 1985:69). While in the third quarter of the nineteenth century some traditionalist elements in the Jewish community opposed plans to introduce the teaching of European languages on the grounds that it would plant the seeds of disbelief (see chap. 3, "Change and Jewish Tradition"), the overall trend toward study in the framework of Italian schools became clear during the colonial period (Goldberg 1984:84–86; De Felice 1985).

Almost all the Jewish males, during the Italian period, had some elementary schooling, while the situation is less clear with regard to the schooling of women.[10] Typically, education for the men involved a combination of traditional Jewish schooling and attendance at a school run by the Italian government. A large proportion of the Jewish students studied at the Pietro Verri school, located in the old city, adjacent to the Jewish quarter, near the Jam'a Mahmud mosque. Other Jewish students attended a school located just outside the city walls, to the west, which was set up for children suffering from trachoma. This school was attended by Italian and Muslim children as well, and included daily examinations and treatment in a clinic. Many Jewish students from families living in the new city attended the Scuola Roma, together with Italian children, and others were scattered in several schools in the new city. In these schools boys and girls studied in the same classes, while they were separated in the Pietro Verri school. A few men had studied only in the traditional synagogue schools, and a few had led the life of "street urchins" while officially enrolled in school, but barely attending in reality. In some instances, male children were sent to the traditional Jewish school at a very young age (four to five years old) with the notion that they should get a basic religious education before attending the Italian school at age seven or eight. More typically, as the Italian period grew in length, children attended the Italian school in the morning and received Hebrew and religious instruction in the afternoon.

For most of the colonial period there were no separate "high schools" for Jewish students, as there were elementary schools. Jewish children who attended these schools studied together with Italian students. Most of these students came from new city families. In the 1930s attendance of post-elementary schools became problematic for the Jews because the Italian authorities insisted that all students attend school on the Sabbath (De Felice 1985:132ff.). Later, the fascist racial laws barred full Jewish participation in the school. In 1938 a separate Jewish high school was set up, employing Jewish teachers from Italy who were no longer allowed to teach there. This attempt did not last long, and the educational system throughout the city was severely disrupted by the bombing and fighting during World War II.

Synagogue Life and Leisure Activities

Both within the traditional sector of the Jewish population and among those exposed to greater contact with and influence from Italians living in Tripoli, the Jewish community continued to be the main framework of social life. There were many synagogues in the old city,[11] and the synagogue was a focus of daily life. Most Jews, even those who had moved to the new city, continued to attend the synagogue, particularly on the Sabbath and most certainly on the festivals. Often synagogues were described as having one *minyan* (prayer quorum) after another, both for the daily morning and evening prayers. The synagogue was a place where people gathered in the evening, after work, not only for prayer but for participation in "associations" located in each synagogue. In such an association men would gather to study a certain sacred book. Many associations had a charitable purpose or might constitute a self-help burial society. Less than ten synagogues were operative[12] outside of the old city, and most of the families moving away continued to be traditional, if not always strict, in observance.

New forms of leisure, not tied to religious occasions, began to develop, such as attendance at the cinema (which the poor could not afford) or walks along the *lungomare* (boardwalk), where Jews mixed with Italians and (to a lesser extent) Muslims. Casual intercommunal contacts in themselves, however, were not a product of the colonial situation.[13] While a certain sector of middle-class Tripolitan Jewry began to assume the tastes and life-style of the local Italians, they were not necessarily accepted by the latter. The establishment of the Maccabee social and sports club, with a general Zionist but non-ideological orientation, may also be seen as a Jewish answer to exclusive clubs formed by Italians. De Felice (1985:177ff.), while emphasizing the cleavages within Jewish society during the Italian period (above), also acknowledges the reemergence of Jewish solidarity during the stressful years of racial legislation prior and during World War II.

Jews, Muslims, and Italians: Religious Aspects

There is no doubt that Libyan Jews as a whole look back at the Italian period favorably, despite specific hardships and repressions that developed under fascist rule from the mid-1930s until the British took the country at the end of 1942 and the beginning of 1943.[14] For the Muslim population, on the other hand, Italian rule meant colonial oppression (cf. Anderson 1986, and Roumani 1987 on this period). In addition to political opposition and military struggle, which continued in Tripolitania until 1924 and in Cyrenaica until 1932, Libyans resisted the challenges to a way of life tied up with religious loyalty and identity. From a cultural point of view, these reactions cannot be seen in isolation, because the position of Jews in Libyan

Muslim society was not just a matter of shifting political fortune but had meaning for the local Muslims and for the Jews. The well-being of the Jews was not only a question of successful economic competition or political upstartsmanship on the part of a minority, but, from the perspective of the Muslims, constituted a challenge to the basic conceptual foundations of society. To appreciate this we return to the latter part of the nineteenth century and, as in the other chapters, attempt to trace aspects of Muslim-Jewish interlaced worlds of meanings through some of the details of custom and everyday life.

In chapters 2 and 3, a brief account of the mulid was given—a holiday when a procession of 'Isawi[15] devotees took over the streets of Tripoli, during which, traditionally, Jews and Christians felt safe only if they stayed indoors. Ha-Cohen's account (1978:163–66) follows the celebration of the mulid over time, and it is clear that the celebration was subdued gradually with increasing Italian influence in the province. Eventually, as cited earlier, "when the city was captured by the Italians, the 'Isawiyya did not go outside at all, but performed the dhikr in a special place in the house of prayer." In brief, Ha-Cohen's narrative shows an inverse relation between the strengthening of Italian political presence and the elaboration of the celebration of the mulid. It is therefore not surprising that one of the more severe incidents of the colonial period, involving a serious attack by Muslims on Tripolitan Jews, took place, in 1927, on the eve of the mulid (De Felice 1985:76).

Religious occasions served to highlight the consciousness of the potential tension between Jew and Muslim, but these strains also existed on an everyday level, side by side with constant contact and frequent cooperation between members of the two communities. Here, too, the Italian presence gave prominence to factors already built into Tripolitan life. With the Italian capture of the city in October 1911, a need was created for translators who could serve as a bridge to the civilian population. The local Jews, even those who knew Italian imperfectly, were natural candidates for these jobs. A reporter on the scene at the time indicates that often Jewish translators would give misleading translations in order to prejudice the Italians against individual Muslims or Arabs in general. In his view the Jews were quick to "grab the chance of avenging themselves for numberless slights and injuries endured at Arab hands" (McClure 1913: 283; cf. De Felice 1985:34, 42, 312, n. 44).

There is no doubt that political developments had their effect on Muslim-Jewish ties, as highlighted throughout De Felice's study (1985). The perception of Jews as supporting the Italians undoubtedly exacerbated tense relations, particularly in the city, but these cannot be seen as the cause of social distance between Muslims and Jews. Similarly, the few cases of Jews accused of collaborating with Arab rebels in the early 1920s (De Felice 1985:73–74), or the tendency in the 1930s for colonial policy to maintain a reserved relationship with Libyan Jews, did not bring the two communities measurably closer. Most people continued to live within the cultural contours that defined Jews' and Muslims' perceptions of one another in previous periods, and contemporary events resonated with these traditional understandings.

In some areas of the countryside, such as Misurata, there were Jews who seemed sympathetic to the anti-Italian forces, probably reflecting a mixture of preference and lack of choice. One man from that town said that the red ("Turkish") hat many Jews wore was called *taqiʻa ḥurra*, the hat of freedom, because the Jews identified with the Arabs who sought to shake off the Italian yoke. It is possible that the term in fact derives from the previous century, when wearing red hats was a sign that the Jews were no longer under the heels of the local Muslims (chap. 3, "The Jews in the Countryside: The Logic of Protection"), but was reinterpreted to fit the twentieth-century political context.

It is therefore important to complement the kinds of information which normally constitute political history with ethnographic data from a variety of realms. For example, De Felice's assertion that the Jews were very sensitive to any show of favoritism on the part of the conquering Italians, and often overdramatized incidents that pointed in this direction (1985:34), is illustrated by reference to "a protest by 'many Jews of Tripoli' at the fact that on the occasion of the king's birthday [in the fall of 1913], Jewish leaders were not invited to the parade and reception offered by the governor" (p. 306, n. 21). To this may be added another incident, with an explicit religious component, from the preceding year (May 1912). On this occasion, some Jews believed they discovered the grave of Rabbi Shimʻon Lavi, the "patron saint" of the local Jewish community,[16] as the result of excavations by the Italians related to the water supply system. The celebration of the Jews, and their plans to erect an elaborate structure honoring R. Lavi, was of concern to Muslim leaders who feared that such acts would be perceived as a Jewish triumph and arouse the wrath of Muslims. They successfully brought an end to the plan by "proving" that the bones in the grave were those of a Muslim buried there in the last generation. This is but one example of the traditional forms of Muslim-Jewish rivalry which continued to exist throughout the colonial period, alongside the events and incidents more directly comprehensible to the colonial authorities.

We do not have a great deal of ethnographic information on Muslim life in Libya at the time, but it is useful to recall that the information in the linguistic works of Cesàro (1939) and Panetta (1943), which were cited in the context of our discussion of religious rivalry (chap. 6, introduction and "Customs in Debate"), was gathered during the Italian period. In the countryside, the Jews' traditional special status was still evident in usages of daily interaction. Thus, a Jew was expected to greet a Muslim first, rather than the other way around, and a Jew would address a Muslim as *sidi* (lord, sir), while the Jew would be addressed by his first name. Asymmetry in relationship was also expressed on religious occasions, as indicated in the previous chapter. Also, when the Muslims' festivals approached, it was more likely that they would insist that Jews conform strictly to the daily etiquette of subordination.

There were, of course, many expressions of interethnic jostling which had no direct reference to religion. One vignette from the city of Tripoli (Piccioli 1935:85) depicts how Muslims in a coffeehouse took delight at an episode in a Garagush shadow play in which the hero sodomizes "Yahudi," who is trying to rescue the qadi's daughter. Travelers from the nineteenth century and later cite a jibe, apparently institutionalized in daily life, in which drivers shouted at their beasts the words *ya yahudi* or *rumi* (Christian), or *isa* (Jesus) (cf. Richardson 1848:80, 1853; Slouschz 1927:118). A Jewish story from the Italian period (Khalfon 1986:153), about a jokester who took vengeance on one such driver by causing the animal to spill its wares, indicates that these practices were still part of public awareness.

Ethnic infighting is often a characteristic of lower-class culture,[17] but it should be appreciated that in twentieth-century Tripoli, matters of traditional culture were always close at hand. One informant, a poor inhabitant of the Jewish quarter who tried to minimize his contact with Muslims because he explicitly was afraid of them, explained the subtleties of his interaction with lower-class Muslims (e.g., a porter). When asked how he addressed these individuals, he said he would use the appellation *Hmid* whether or not this was the man's first name (a Muslim of higher status would typically be addressed as *sidi*). His explanation was that this would be perceived by his interlocutor as highly complimentary because the name was based on the same linguistic stem from which the name of the Prophet was formed. He then looked at me slyly, chuckled, and pointed out that *Hmid*, if written with Hebrew orthography, had the same numerical value[18] as the Hebrew word *kelev*, or dog. Not only "religion" but textual play could be threaded through the meanest of mundane interaction.

Most Jews, when asked, say that relations with the Muslims under the Italians were good, or correct, but also assert that often this was a surface phenomenon below which lay complex feelings. A number of individuals reported instances of physical harassment by Muslim youths on the way to school, and there also seem to have been quasi-institutionalized expressions of the hostility cum attachment which linked the two communities. It was common for groups of Jewish youngsters and Muslim youngsters to encounter one another in the area outside *bab el-jdid*[19] on Sabbath afternoons and engage in mutual stone throwing (Khalfon 1986:71). One man described this activity as partially fighting and partially sport. Thus, while on a daily basis there was much Muslim-Jewish interaction that was uneventful, and even included instances of positive mutual involvement, the time-honored ambivalences remained an immanent feature of social intercourse.

These attitudes and cultural forms were perpetually available for mobilization in changing political circumstances. This may be seen in the reactions of Muslim onlookers to the flogging of Jews, which took place in December 1936. Balbo, the governor of Libya, in pursuing his vigorous policy of modernizing the local Jews, ordered the public flogging of two Jews for refusing to open their shops on the Sabbath, in the new city that had been developed by the Italians (De Felice 1985:162). This incident has left a deep impression on the memory of the Jews of Tripoli, and a number of eyewitnesses testify to the pleased reaction within the crowd of Muslim spectators (Nahum 1974). One report cites the Muslim youths there as commenting on *al-yahud al-kuffar,* the infidel Jews (Khalfon 1986:74).

Among both Jews and Muslims there was a tendency to frame contemporary events in modes of discourse linked to traditional religion. The episode of the flogging is remembered by Jews more as a challenge, internally, to Jewish life, than because of the vindictive reaction of some Muslims.[20] In popular lore Balbo appears as an oppressor, and it is claimed that the plane crash which took his life occurred on a Saturday as retribution for his attempt to force Jews to desecrate the Sabbath. Folk memory is, to a large extent, ignorant of the fact that it was Balbo who successfully restrained the immediate application of the racial laws, enacted in Italy in 1938, to the Jews of Libya, resisting Mussolini's pressure in this direction (De Felice 1985:171ff.; Segrè 1987:348–49).

It is therefore necessary to keep in mind prevailing cultural orientations which structured perceptions and explanations of political events that affected the population at large. Such events were not lacking in the life of Libya's Jews from the mid-1930s onward. In the following section, various episodes are briefly mentioned to provide background to the anti-Jewish riots of November 1945, concerning which I attempt to show the role of traditional religious notions within current political situations.

Political Events up to World War II and the Riots

Italo Balbo, appointed governor of Libya in 1934 (De Felice 1985: 143ff; Segrè 1987), was committed to an energetic program of developing the colony, and the advance of the local Jewish community, modeled after emancipated Italian Jewry, was a significant component in his program. Fascist rule meant that the ancient religious sensibilities of the Jews could be respected only insofar as they did not stand in the way of state-promoted modernization. Balbo's predecessor, in 1932, took a clear stand that children in intermediate schools, in which both Italians and Jews were enrolled, be required to attend on the Sabbath, and expelled those attempting to circumvent this rule (De Felice 1985:136–40). As already discussed, when Balbo was confronted with the issue of opening stores on the Sabbath in 1936, he pursued his policy unequivocally and vigorously.

By the late thirties the pressures emanating from Italy's alliance with Nazi Germany became more of a factor exerting pressure on the Jewish community than did the issue of modernization. In fact, it was by citing the importance of the Jews in the local economy that Balbo convinced Mussolini not to demand immediate application in Libya of the racial laws passed in Italy. Nevertheless, anti-Jewish policies affected Jewish life in a number of ways. Beginning in 1938, Jews were not allowed to study along with Italians in secondary schools, and attempts by the Jewish community to organize its own secondary education were successful for only a brief period of time.

In 1940 Balbo was killed in a plane crash, and during the next year German troops entered Libya to reinforce the Italians fighting in North Africa. These events brought even greater hardship to the Jewish community, and restrictions, expressed in various measures, affected economic and other daily activities in Libya.[21] Jews holding foreign passports were deported. Those of French nationality were sent to Tunisia which was under the control of Vichy France. British nationals were shipped to Italy, and eventually to concentration camps in Bergen-Belsen and Innsbruck, where ultimately they were exchanged for German prisoners of war held by the English. During the war, the enthusiasm shown by the Jews of Benghazi for the British forces who took the city (which changed hands five times) led to an order by Mussolini to transfer most of the Jews of that city to a concentration camp in Tripolitania (in Jado), after Benghazi had been temporarily retaken by the Italians (De Felice 1985:179–80). In mid-1942 the male Jews of Libya became subject to civilian mobilization, and about one thousand of them were sent to a camp about 150 miles east of Tripoli, from whence some were delegated to labor behind the front in Cyrenaica (De Felice 1985:181). Because of the wartime situation, many of the economic laws passed to restrict Jews did not have much practical effect and became void with the final fall of Tripoli to the British in January 1943.[22]

The war itself, particularly the bombings of the city of Tripoli by the French and British in 1940 and thereafter, led to a special form of Jewish-Muslim cooperation. Many of the Jews of Tripoli sought refuge outside the city and rented rooms in Arab villages in the area. There was also an organized effort on the part of the Jewish community to find rooms for poor Jewish families (De Felice 1985:177–78). It appears that some of the Jews, with their commercial connections, were able to obtain black market supplies for their Muslim hosts living under wartime conditions. This period is mentioned by many Jews as an era of life together, in contrast to the tension and tragedy of the 1945 riots; perhaps the legislation and partial enforcement of racial laws provided the impetus to some Jews to consider more carefully their ties to the Muslims.

Given the overall suffering during the war, it does not appear that the Muslims took heart at the special plight of the Jews. De Felice suggests that some of the more politically conscious Arabs were concerned that racial measures might eventually be adopted that would be applied to Muslims as well. For both different and overlapping reasons, Jews and Muslims alike initially perceived the British victory as their liberation. In the case of the Muslims, the British conquest brought the end of Italian rule and the departure of some of the colonists. As for the Jews, the British forces included the Palestine Brigade, soldiers who had volunteered so that there would be Jewish participation in the war. Members of the brigade made special efforts, insofar as permitted by the British, to establish contact with Jewish communities freed from Axis control. Their presence in Libya further catalyzed Zionist sentiment and activities (Gelber 1983).

The period immediately after the war is described by De Felice as one of "euphoria" in which "Arab-Jewish relations (especially in small towns and among elites) seemed to be settling down and were characterized by a sincere desire to work together peacefully" (1985:186). Within the city of Tripoli some Jews joined the police force, something that had not taken place under the Italians, and patrolled together with Muslims. Many Jews, expecting an improved situation, moved into apartments in the new city, renting them at low prices from Italians who had returned to the mainland. While the immediate euphoria declined, and postwar economic dislocation set in, at an everyday level there was a sense of normalcy. However, with the conclusion of World War II, the question of the ultimate political disposition of Libya arose, and for the Jews this was a particularly perplexing question. Against the background of hope for the future, coupled with a great deal of uncertainty, the riots occurred in November 1945, and it is to their description and interpretation that we now turn.

An Account of the Riots

The riots, according to almost all official accounts and most informants, were totally unexpected. As is common in similar situations, some oral reports recorded at the time pointed to a "precipitating incident," such as rumors that the Jews had attacked the qadi of Tripoli whose office was near the Jewish quarters, or that the Jews in Palestine had murdered Muslims praying at the Aqsa mosque (see also De Felice 1985:204). British inquiries after the event discovered a fight that had taken place between a Jew and a Muslim, and apparently brawling between youths of the two communities had become a standard feature in new city life on Sunday evenings. On the other hand, the report of the Jewish community (a version that is accepted by De Felice) stresses that the initial rioting which took place on Sunday evening, November 4, 1945, occurred simultaneously at various places within the city of Tripoli, suggesting that some planned instigation was involved.

At that juncture, the head of the Jewish community went to the headquarters of the British police. He was unable to find a single officer and was told that one could not be located. Things quieted down that evening. The following morning rioting resumed, and many Muslims from the neighboring villages converged on the city. The leaders of the Jewish community again went to the police and requested that the military intervene because the police force, which included many local Muslims, would be unable to handle the situation. They were received by a colonel who promised to look into the situation immediately.

The rioting, which involved shop looting, arson, and physical attacks, grew in intensity. In the city of Tripoli the Jews who lived outside the Jewish quarters suffered most, while the majority of the population was able to close itself off in the old Jewish section. Informants report that mostly poorer Muslims of all ages participated in the riots, while wealthier notables stood by and watched. Women also took part by cheering on the rioters with high-shrilled cries (*zgharit*). The most common shout of the rioters was the phrase *jihad fil-kuffar*, a holy war against the infidels. Not infrequently, Jews recognized some of the participants. In some cases a glance from a Jewish friend was sufficient to make a Muslim acquaintance leave the crowd, while in other instances mutual recognition was not accorded. There are also numerous stories of Jews who were helped to safety, spontaneously, by individual Muslims. One person helped by a Muslim he did not know said the Muslim's motivation seemed to be deeply personal and religious, as if through this act he would earn his place in the world to come.

The only official action taken on Monday, November 5, was the announcement of a curfew and the appearance of a few troops in the streets who did not react against the mobs. During Tuesday the rioting continued, and, while a headline of the *London Times* on November 8 read "Firm British Action," the report of the Jewish community states that no effective measures were taken until the evening of November 6 and the morning of November 7. During this period thirty-eight Jews and one Muslim were killed in the city of Tripoli.[23]

The riots also spread from Tripoli to other towns with Jewish populations, sometimes starting a few days later than in Tripoli. In several cases the Jews were thereby forewarned, but appeals to the police and local Muslim leaders were not always effective. At the same time, informants from the villages also tell of instances in which Muslims invited Jewish families to stay with them until the rioting was over, or in which notables used their influence to forestall outbreaks.[24] The toll in lives in the villages (all Jews) was as follows: Amrus—40; Zanzur—34; Tajura—7; Zawia—13; Qusabat—3. In this last town there was also a forced conversion to Islam, and similar episodes might have occurred elsewhere. Throughout the province nine synagogues were burned and thirty-five Torah scrolls ruined. In addition to heavy injuries, there was a loss in property, from looting and burning, estimated at 268 million military authority lire.

Explaining the Riots

The riots have been given various emphases by those attempting to understand and explain them. Each of these can be linked to the analyst's outlook on the events, but may also be placed in the context of general concepts concerning "collective behavior." One crucial line of divide is between theories that view such events as outbursts which are essentially disorganized and guided by emotionality, and more recent propositions that "collective action" (including mass violence) is rational, organized, and geared toward attaining the political ends of the participants.[25] I show, building on De Felice's analysis, that in interpreting the riots these perspectives can complement one another, particularly if they are supplemented by attention to culture and symbolic action.

It is useful to start with a hypothesis widely held by Libyan Jews—that the riots were instigated by the British. Those who hold this view attribute various motives to the British, for example, that they were attempting to show that native Libyans were incapable of ruling themselves, or that they were seeking to warn Jewish activists in Palestine who were militantly opposing the British mandate there (Nunes-Vais 1982:130). De Felice weighs the evidence carefully, coming to the conclusion that the claim cannot be substantiated, but he does agree (as do all observers) that the British were inordinately slow in quelling the riots and that this might have reflected some policy seeking to court favor with the Libyan Arabs (1985:207–8).

In contrast to this explanation, official British reports, which also underline that the riots were unexpected, tend to point to a variety of factors, without singling out a major cause or assigning responsibility. Such background factors are not difficult to locate. Economically, the province of Tripolitania was still struggling with the dislocations of war. Many people had come to the city from the countryside seeking employment, which was not to be found. Along with the economic stress[26] was considerable political anomie. Tripolitania had been freed from Italian rule by the British, but its political future was uncertain. Promises of independence had been made to the neighboring province of Cyrenaica, where Sanusi forces actively had abetted the Allied effort, but no commitments had been made to Tripolitania. Various proposals about the political future had been offered, including return to colonial status under Italy and, later, a trusteeship under the Soviet Union.

In Tripolitania, after the British occupation of the province, political émigrés from the time of the Italian regime were allowed to return home. Many of these had been educated abroad, learning techniques of nationalist agitation in Beirut, Damascus, and Cairo (Khadduri 1963:51–52). These activists organized various political groups. Rennel (1948:466) reports frequent demonstrations during 1945 and claims that the pogroms were a spillover from these political protests. A Jewish informant, who was a member of the British police force, remembers demonstrations demanding the release of jailed nationalist activists. More immediately, the local (government-controlled) newspaper, *Trablus el Gharb*, carried a report of anti-Jewish riots that had broken out in Alexandria and Cairo on November 2, the anniversary of the Balfour Declaration (Comunità 1945:21). The same report had been heard on the radio. This unstable political situation in the province is a plausible setting for the riots, but does not do justice to the specific course of the disturbances.

The general tenor of official British explanation thus points to political uncertainty, and a diffuse sense of unrest and frustration, easily "ignited" by a simple incident such as suggested by Rennel (above), or by a brawl between Jewish and Muslim youths. This approach, as I have hinted, is consonant with a view of "collective behavior," classically expressed in Le Bon's *The Crowd* (1896) and restated fifty years later in the following terms: "not having a body of definitions or rules to guide its behavior, and instead, acting on the basis of impulse, the crowd is fickle, suggestible and irresponsible" (Blumer 1946:168). Grasping the situation in these terms obviates the search for more specific and purposeful causes.

De Felice, as I noted, takes issue with this view, not in the name of social science theory, but because he focuses on evidence, ignored by earlier writers, concerning the existence of organizers who directed the rioters' actions. Not only did the outbreaks begin simultaneously in different parts of the city, but it appears that in the new city marks were intentionally painted on houses, enabling rioters to differentiate between Jewish, Italian, and Muslim homes. Also, clubs and bludgeons were consciously distributed to the participants in the pogrom. De Felice concludes that this was the work of a newly emergent nationalist elite, organized into the Hizb al-Watani in which the returning émigrés were prominent, that was seeking political expression.

The arguments marshaled by De Felice are persuasive, although the data available are less ample than one would wish. As has been intimated, the search for an organizing agent fits into recent approaches to the study of "collective action," which, rather than seeing such events as unstructured, attaches "great importance to the social structures which link the actors to each other, as well as to their rivals, enemies and exploiters" (Tilly and Tilly 1981:15). This avenue of research relates primarily to conflicts growing out of class situations, in which it is not difficult to diagnose the interests of the participants and study how they are organized and mobilized, engaging in various forms of "rational" collective action in a defined political context (Tilly 1978). Studies show that many such eruptions are political. They do not lash out randomly as a result of deprivation, but are aimed at specifiable gains from a social adversary. Such a view, however, is only partially appropriate to the Tripolitanian riots.

Granting that there was more organization and direction by the Hizb al-Watani (Nationalist party) than previously appreciated, what was to be gained by selecting the Jews as the target of heightened nationalist feelings? The remaining Italian community, some of whom advocated Libya's reestablishment as an Italian colony (Rennel 1948: 466), would be a more likely target (Khadduri 1963:84, 104). Moreover, it could be claimed that a riot against the Jews served to discredit demands for self-rule. In addition, why could not a strong nationalist claim seek to include the Jews? Indeed, at later stages of pressure and negotiations toward independence, approaches were made to the Jewish community, by Muslim leaders, to support the nationalist effort. Some informants remember participating in an anti-Italian demonstration with Muslims while chanting together, "Snusi wamakabi watalyan yil'an weldhi" (Sanusi and Maccabee curse the father of the Italians). If collective behavior has a logic linking it to a political end, then there is room for making this logic fully explicit and trying to understand, in cultural context, the anti-Jewish form that the riots took.

Modern Nationalism and Traditional Rhetoric

It appears correct to claim that the riots were political in nature, but it also must be remembered that they took place in an inchoate political setting. The Nationalist party was small, its activities were clandestine, and the British were focused on negotiations with the Sanusi leadership based in Cyrenaica, rather than on Tripolitania. In addition, who was the political enemy and what were the demands? Was it the immediate British Military Administration, the Italians who still retained hopes of returning to Libya, or the Big Powers whose jostling among themselves would eventually determine the direction of the country's future? The most natural answer is that all of these were targets of the riot, which appears to have been the case. The same answer implies, however, that the riots were a generalized cry regarding issues of power, rather than an action aimed at a specific political goal. Thus the overall "message" of the riots looms large in comparison to the pressure they exerted for definable concessions. In such a setting, explicit attention to ritualized communication warrants further exploration.

Researchers in collective behavior have, in fact, become more attune to ritual aspects of the phenomena they study. In Smelser's systematization of the theory of riots as disorganization, he at first contrasts riots to festivals, because the former seek social change while the latter preserve the status quo, but later he admits that it is difficult to maintain this as a clear-cut distinction (1962:73). More recent work asserts this directly, as in the generalization that earlier (eighteenth-century) forms of collective action "have exotic features, costumes and disguises, symbols of the crowd's enemies, ritual sacking of wrong-doer's dwellings" (Tilly and Tilly 1981:20). In recognizing this trend it is also possible to utilize anthropological advances in the study of ritual, in particular the work of Turner in *The Ritual Process* (1969).

Riots as Rituals: Decoding Collective Behavior

The analyses of Turner bear relevance to the study of the ritual aspects of collective behavior from several points of view.[27] In particular, his focus on the liminal phase of ritual activities, bridging the moves out from and back into more clearly defined and established social structures, helps salvage or, more precisely, specifies the "disorganization" aspect of collective behavior. It is not necessary to ignore the more recent understandings of collective action as purposeful to recognize that events such as riots signal a "time out" from normal social routine and are, institutionally, "betwixt and between" standard social arrangements. On occasions such as these, when regularized structure is submerged, we find "an amplification of structure in Lévi-Strauss' sense" (Turner 1969:133). Thus, during "in-between periods," which is one way to describe the political situation in Libya of 1945, we may expect to witness a proliferation and embellishment of symbolic acts. Thus a theory of symbolic action can provide a positive characterization of a phase of collective behavior previously explained by concepts such as "uninstitutionalized."[28]

Traditional Components of the Tripolitanian Pogrom

If riots are occasions when symbolic statements are made with great force and precision, what was being pointed to by the 1945 outbreaks? While the current political situation provided the most immediate context of the "message," its contents are most fully grasped when traditional worldview and rhetoric are taken into account. At this juncture, it is important to indicate a fact about the riots which has not been discussed in the literature, but was told to me by several informants, namely, that the riots took place several days before the Muslim Great Festival, the celebration of which, throughout the world of Islam, parallels the conclusion of the pilgrimage to Mecca. In chapter 6, aspects of this celebration in the Tripolitanian setting were discussed, and it was argued that one of the themes emerging during the festival is Muslim-Jewish religious rivalry. While that analysis pertains to the turn of the century, there is every reason to believe that the same symbolic associations persisted, albeit muted in expression, throughout the period of Italian and British rule. It is not farfetched to assume that preparations for the holiday brought along with them religious connotations emphasizing the difference between Judaism and Islam. As noted earlier, in the villages Jewish notables would be called upon to skin the animals slaughtered on this holiday, the "Festival of the Sacrifice," and in the days preceding the festival, Jewish smiths would be requested to sharpen the knives of the Muslim clients. The constellation of circumstances allowed the mutual mobilization of traditional ideas and contemporary goals.[29]

But what are traditional Muslim ideas concerning Jews? As has been stressed from the outset,[30] Muslim-Jewish interaction in Libya was guided by competing models. In one, Muslims interact with Jews as they would with other town dwellers, attending to their Jewishness as *an* element, but not necessarily *the* central element of their social persona; in the other, there is a requirement to distinguish vividly between Muslim and Jew, and assure that the former dominates the latter. From this point of view, the riots were clearly an occasion when the second model, in its starkness and simplicity, became the regnant principle.

To emphasize the sharpness of the choice on occasions such as these, we quote from Rosen's study of the town of Sefrou, during the 1967 Israeli-Arab War, when there was danger of anti-Jewish riots breaking out in Morocco. During those tense days, Rosen sought to understand the nature of links between the various elements of the population and received the following explanation from a Muslim shopkeeper:

> You have to understand the custom in this country. People do whatever some big man tells them to do. *What* they are told to do doesn't matter nearly so much as the fact that someone takes hold of things and tells them how they should act. If the government does nothing and someone tells us to kill the Jews that is what we will do. If the government tells us to be good to the Jews we will follow their directions. (Rosen 1968:392–93)

Here, in an undefined situation, the alternatives are clearly posed: Jews are entitled to protection *or* Jews forfeit the right to life and property. There is no middle ground. Each is a recognized cultural pattern, and it is the right and obligation of those who hold power to determine which view will hold sway.

Political Messages of the Riots

In the case of Libya, in contrast to Morocco, someone did give the go-ahead to kill the Jews (according to De Felice, the leaders of the Hizb al-Watani), but what was the meaning of this action and what was to be gained by it? Jewish informants, when asked to explain the riots, show a clear tendency to speak in political or quasi-political terms. One common response is to contrast the Italian period, during which the Muslims were ruled "with a strong hand," with the period of British rule when they were given "independence" and "parties." Often the position of the Jews in Libya is explicitly mentioned as part of this comparison. Under the Italians, it is said, the Jews were "like kings" (cf. chap. 5, "Social and Symbolic Aspects of Peddling")—"no one could tell them what to do." Under the British, however, the Muslims began to act "as if they were the lords of the land." In brief, the perceived situation was that Italian rule had raised the status of the Jews, and, within the social-symbolic universe we are discussing, this implies the lowering of the position of the Muslims.

We stress *perceived* situation because the definition and symbolization of reality are crucial here. At the time of the riots, the Jews did not enjoy any noticeable improvement in status vis-à-vis the Muslims. The most recent Jewish experience under the Italians had been the imposition of racial laws, and while Britain had freed the Jews from the Nazi-inspired threat, they were very evenhanded in relating to the two communities and extremely careful about allowing expressions of Jewish prominence, particularly Zionist activity.[31] It seems, therefore, that one of the issues constituting the rhetoric of the riot was the "equal" status accorded to the Jewish community under the previous Italian regime—a policy culturally synonymous with the Muslims' domination by a foreign (European-Christian) power.[32] The riots are thus to be understood as a generalized call to eliminate foreign rule in terms that resonate with the traditional religio-political order.

Religious Aspects of the Political Messages

There is ample evidence that the riots should be viewed in the context of a religious worldview and not only as political in a narrow sense. Most of the participants in the riots were workers and peasants, among whom political notions were intermixed with religious ideas and sentiments. A number of facts cited support this assessment: the timing of the outbreak (several days before the Great Festival), the cries of the phrase *jihad fil kuffar* (jihad against the infidels),[33] the women's high-pitched cheers (which normally are features of festive occasions, but also may accompany the brave feats of warriors), the desecration of Jewish religious shrines, and the forced conversions to Islam. Appearing at a time of "political liminality," the rioting highlighted a clearly defined and desired conceptual order opposing Muslim and Infidel, with the latter subordinated to the former, expressed in an untrammeled attack upon Jewish life, property, and religion.

While there certainly is "disorder" during riots, they are also occasions of heightened structuring at symbolic levels and can be illuminated by reference to aspects of "the ritual process." The focus on the "Muslim versus (over) Infidel" conception suppresses the more differentiated view of Jews as part of the local population. Just as many rituals involve the feigned anonymity of the participants, created by masks and painted faces, so anonymity is required by riots. People who enjoyed the relationships of friend, neighbor, and customer/shopkeeper, and who after the riot continued to be friends and neighbors, ceased, temporarily, to be recognized by one another and turned into stereotyped objects. Transformed into symbolic representations, Infidel versus Muslim, they could be robbed, beaten, and deprived of life in a manner removed from the daily social realities obtaining among the same set of individuals. The "ritual" tenor of this attitude, that riots are a "normal" interlude in the course of social life, is perhaps indicated by the fact that in some instances Jewish women, after the riots, noticed articles of clothing stolen from their homes being worn by Muslim women in the neighborhood, and asked them to return them.[34] The emergent political motivations behind the riots called for one symbolization of reality, and everyday life called for another.

If the Jews, as victims of the riots, unwittingly became players in a macabre "social drama" (see below), whose contents broadly may be decoded as "power to the local Muslim community," one of the important audiences of the message was constituted by the British, both as the current ruler of the land and as signifying foreign European domination in general. As stressed in chapter 3, a major test of political legitimacy in this tradition is the ability to protect the weak. Although content and conditions had changed, the riots follow a logic similar to the "discourse" between the peasants and pasha at the end of the Ottoman period, when the governor's resolve to protect the Jews was seen as a test of his political strength in general. The British, when faced with a challenge expressing the same logic, did not meet the test very well (whatever political motives may have been involved). While in European Big Power thinking, a riot of such scope could be cited as evidence of Tripolitania's political immaturity, to the Muslims, whether instigators or active participants in the pogrom, it most likely was perceived as a direct challenge to Britain's right to rule.

The Riots and Other Social Dramas

The concept of "social drama" was developed by Turner (1957:92–93) to help understand critical episodes in the life of a society which highlight central, but conflicting, cultural principles underlying conflictual situations. These episodes might lead to either redressive action or the open recognition of a communal schism. This adds another dimension to our comprehension of the riots, which, in some local instances, became the occasion of expressions of solidarity, but in a larger historical perspective marked the beginning of Libyan Jewry's separating itself from its long-standing social milieu.

Recalling once again that the riots took place shortly before the Great Festival, we should appreciate that the remembrance of Abraham which appears as a theme in this festival can also suggest kinship between Muslims and Jews (cf. chap. 6, "Customs in Debate"). The legendary genealogical traditions shared partially by Jews and Muslims, that Isaac and Ishmael both are the sons of Abraham, can either be a recognition of unity *or* figure in the dispute over which of these sons is his rightful spiritual heir. If the latter trope set the tone for the destructive impetus of the riots, it is instructive to consider a case in which tension developed but rioting did not result.

As news of the riots spread from the city of Tripoli, a situation developed, in almost all the towns of the region, in which groups of Muslims began milling about and speaking of attacking the Jews. In the community of Tighrinna in the Gharian,[35] about seventy miles south of Tripoli, communal relations were maintained with the help of ceremonial action. Local Muslim notables told the leaders of the Jewish community to hold a kind of "open house" in which food and drinks were lavishly served to all comers. For twenty-four consecutive hours Muslim and Jewish guests came in and out of the house of the Jewish sheikh. People reiterated pat phrases such as "we are brothers," "we have lived together for thousands of years," "your father is our father," and "each man has his own religion." All of these statements, in contrast to the riot situation, celebrate the sameness of Jew and Muslim, and deemphasize the distinctions between the communities. The complementary distribution of riots and rituals of solidarity both suggests the usefulness of viewing collective behavior in its symbolic dimension and underlines the social power of the traditional metaphors.

After the riots, allusions to age-old religious imagery continued to play a part at the highest level of "peace-making" efforts. The administration appointed a committee of Arab and Jewish leaders to convene to find ways of repairing the breach between the communities (De Felice 1985:197ff.). Part of this process was the preparation of an official report by the Jewish community concerning the events during, and consequences of, the riots. The report (Comunità 1945: 17–18) emphasizes a seemingly "trivial" incident under the heading "Arab-Jewish Relationships Throughout the Centuries." It tells of a theatrical presentation, earlier in the year, of the biblical story *Joseph and His Brothers*, by the Maccabee Organization, stressing that the play was rendered in the local Arabic vernacular to an audience that included Muslim notables and representatives of the British administration. The choice of the tale of Joseph was not accidental and has significance to both internal Jewish life and Muslim onlookers. For the Jews, Joseph is the prototype of Jewish success in a potentially dangerous "land of exile," and his contribution to the welfare of the land is recognized by the highest echelons of society. For the Muslims, the story emphasizes how brothers, despite bitter incidents of antagonism, can be reconciled.[36] In its Islamic version, the story of Joseph is a favorite Muslim tale (Heller 1931). That this was true in Libya is confirmed by an anecdote reporting that on the night of the performance some young Muslim "toughs" appeared outside, objecting that the Jews were "using Joseph, who belongs to us." This account concludes that the youths were placated by diplomatically assuring them that "we do not claim to own Joseph, we only wish to borrow him for one night" (Khalfon 1986:97). Jews and Muslims understood well, even if this was not appreciated by the British, that politics could not be carried on divorced from local cultural moorings.

The Pogrom and Jewish Departure from Libya

The riots, as a social drama, clearly were a turning point in the matrix of relationships which included Muslims, Jews, and Britons. One informant, close to the circles of the Libyan Jewish elite, claims that after the riots the Jewish leaders were not given as easy access to the heads of the administration as they had enjoyed before. More broadly, I cite De Felice's assessment that the riots became the watershed in the Jews' relation to Libyan Muslim society: "From a historian's perspective, the deep and decisive significance of the 1945 pogroms is that a radical change took place not only in Arab-Jewish relations, but in the relation of the Jews to Libya itself" (1985:206). De Felice then quotes a report, written about a year later, by the director of the Alliance Israélite Universelle schools in Libya: "An unprecedented blow has been dealt to the Jews' sense of security and any illusions they had for taking initiatives: there is terror, poverty, disease, and

suffering, without a glimmer of hope to brighten the dark future.
Should they go away? If so, how? And where?" He adds that this description summarizes, "without exaggeration or flourish," the whole
drama of Libyan Jews brought about by the 1945 pogroms" (p. 209).

A number of years, and additional political upheavals, were to
pass before the state of Israel emerged as a reality, and not until spring
1949 did the British administration give permission to the Jewish
Agency to organize immigration to Israel. There is little doubt however that the riots, separated from the mass immigration[37] by about
four years, were a central factor in bringing it about. Although Jews
probably would eventually have left an independent Libya, as they
have the other countries of the Maghrib, under different circumstances the emigration might have been more gradual, as in the cases
of Morocco or Tunisia. As one man teasingly explained to me (an eth-
nographer from the United States toting a camera): "If it were not for
the riots we would have come here [to Israel] as tourists, looking
around and taking pictures."

But even as the Jews were severing ties with their ancestral
abode, there were those who saw the event as a chapter in the continuing saga of Muslim-Jewish religious interchanges. A curious but
understandable story comes from the town Zuara, in which there was
a predominant Berber population and in which the Berber qaimaqam
was known for his friendship toward, and protection of, the Jews.
With the establishment of Israel, and the preparations of the Jews to
move there, he commented on these developments in a positive light:
"The Muslims know that the Jews are supposed to return to their
land," he is reported to have said; "it was written in their Qur'an, but
they changed that part of it."[38]

8 History and Cultural Process: Change and Stability in the Meaning of Jews in Libyan Society

Religious Differences and Social Life

One of the first comprehensive portraits of Middle Eastern society and culture from an anthropological perspective was Coon's *Caravan* (1951), which proposed the metaphor of a "mosaic" in describing the "ethnic" (cultural, religious, linguistic) diversity of the Middle East. The argument linked to this metaphor was that the medley of ethnic differences reflected the internal religious and social life of the distinct communities, but was neutralized in the "market place," where groups came into daily contact. One outcome of the present study has been to demonstrate how oversimplified Coon's model is. I have shown how Muslim-Jewish cultural interchange (including rivalry seeking to fend off the results of such interchange) and a general concern with the structure of the boundaries separating and linking the two religions were endemic cultural processes at work in social settings as diverse as leisure, politics, and peddling. In the present chapter, the major themes recurring in the study of these processes are summarized.

Anthropological analysis commonly isolates a set of phenomena, temporally, in order to concentrate on a given "slice of time," treated as the "ethnographic present." This strategy has been followed in each chapter of the present work, but it now must be asked whether the individual cases, spanning well over a century of political developments and social change, can be woven into a dynamic perspective, and whether the cultural and religious forms and features that have been stressed played a significant role in the unfolding patterns of historical change and stability.

In approaching these questions, three themes are briefly recapitulated: (1) that Muslim-Jewish interchange percolated into many different realms of social life; (2) that an important aspect of this interchange was rivalry, albeit muted rivalry; and (3) that an ap-

123

preciation of these processes must take into consideration textual-based culture as an influence on daily action. After surveying these aspects of a broadly based cultural realm in which Jewish and Muslim life partially overlapped and met, we return to the theme of the differing *models* concerning Jews in a Muslim society, and I attempt to provide an overview linking the various facets of this issue that we have considered. The discussion will also relate to general anthropological concerns seeking to understand the dynamics of long-term cultural stability coupled with social or political change.

Religious Identity and Daily Life

Being a Jew or Muslim was first of all a matter of religion, but had direct and indirect implications for many other spheres of behavior. Jews, for example, would want to reside within easy access of a synagogue, and much of a person's "social life" was confined to members of his or her own religious community. Religion did not carry with it extensive instructions for economic activity, but echoes of religious affiliation were also present in the realm of work. The peddler in the countryside is an example of how being Jewish was central to the carrying out of an economic role, and even in the city of Tripoli, crafts such as tailoring were not free of cultural and communal associations. In addition to the data already presented, a final example is offered—that of a coppersmith, the father of one of my informants, who fashioned brass vessels to serve the needs of both Muslim and Jewish clients. When someone came to order a pot or similar utensil, the coppersmith would ask about its purpose, that is, what types of dishes would be prepared or served in it. There was some overlap in the kitchenware of Jews and Muslims, but early in the twentieth century the kitchenware of both was fairly distinct from that of the Italians, who used imported enamelware, which also was adopted by the wealthier Jews. At the same time, there were distinctive types of vessels for foods linked to festivals and celebrations of the two local groups. The Jewish coppersmith knew how to make vessels for both groups, so he had some degree of familiarity with domestic practices that were part of the Muslim holidays. More generally, the matter of "religion" and religious differences was not confined to institutional contexts organized for religious aims, but filtered into a myriad of social terrains, including the "marketplace."

Religious Rivalry

Contact between Jews and Muslims, and mutual knowledge of religious practices, even if partial, opened the way for influence, including comparison and rivalry, between the groups. While it is not surprising that minority Jews would imitate the majority Muslims, our data show that the opposite process sometimes occurred as well (see, in particular, chap. 6). This was a matter of great sensitivity. When I once asked a Jewish man from the Gharian if, when in Libya, he had known the Muslim "call to prayer," which one obviously could hear several times a day, he at first acted as if he did not understand the question; only later did he explain to me that the first part of the call (concerning God's uniqueness) was not a problem for Jews, while the second (Muhammad as a prophet) was. Attention to these matters probably was more widespread than suspected. Often it was camouflaged, even to those engaging in it, in various ways.

One further extensive example may be given, from the Jewish side, concerning the season of the High Holidays. The most solemn period of the Jewish calendar consists of the ten days in autumn that link Rosh ha-Shanah (the New Year) and Yom Kippur (the Day of Atonement). Religiously speaking, this is a period in which God sits in judgment over individuals, examining their past deeds and deciding their fate for the coming year. One liturgic feature of this period is the lengthy penitential prayers, known a *selihot*, which are chanted in the synagogue before dawn and before the standard morning prayers. In both the Ashkenazi and Sephardi rites, the period of reading selihot has been extended, creating a prelude to the intense High Holiday season, with the Ashkenazim beginning to read them on the Saturday night before the New Year and the Sephardim beginning a whole month before the holiday.

In Tripoli (as elsewhere in North Africa), Jewish males would arise in the early hours of the morning during this season and go to the synagogue. In the barely lit darkness, the subdued and refined tones of the penitential chanting could be heard throughout the Jewish quarters. The solemn mood was not without its attraction and conviviality, as in each synagogue, to help promote wakefulness and stimulate participation in the prayers, a beadle would warm up coffee and distribute cakes baked by women of the community. One informant, in describing the selihot of the month of Elul (the month preceding Rosh ha-Shanah), reminisced with a mixture of nostalgia and awe, declaring: "What a month that was!" It does not demand much imagination for us to add the gloss: "and *our* month was no less impressive than *their* month," for Ramadan, too, is characterized by a combination of solemnity and festivity during hours of darkness, before and after the required daylight fasting.

Field-workers will appreciate that one cannot always follow through with explicit questioning such as, "Did you perceive Elul as standing in contrast, or being an answer to, Ramadan?" although at times sensitive informants volunteer such insights. Such a query, as likely as not, would yield the (historically correct) response insisting that the selihot of Elul are anchored anciently in Jewish tradition. But instances such as these, coupled with parallel incidents from other spheres of life, produce a picture of active Muslim-Jewish mutual referencing, usually constructed with cultural materials from the past but fully tuned into, and carried farther by, current social dynamics.

The point is that viewing the selihot of Elul as *either* formal Jewish tradition *or* a response to the Muslim environment would do injustice to the pulse of life in Tripoli, animated by a distinct combination produced by these dual cultural thrusts. While for the purpose of analysis, attention to each might be carried out separately, it is also critical to sense (following Bourdieu 1977) that *misrecognition* of the "Muslim" input to selihot (alongside the impulse to rivalry) may have been a prerequisite for their importance to most members of the Jewish community.[1] Perhaps another form of misrecognition, from the Muslim side, is provided by the Moroccan example of record keeping in which a list of notables visiting a regional qadi omitted the name of the local rabbi who was a frequent guest in the qadi's house (Eickelman 1985:121). Given current sensitivity to the question of links between "knowledge and power," it is possible to interpret cases such as these not only as reflecting the "unimportance" of Jews in Muslim eyes (the standard historical explanation), but as the active "putting down" of a rival in a manner that succeeds in attracting a minimum of attention to the very possibility of competition.

The view of Jewish (or Muslim) practice as consisting of an arena in which one tradition both merges with and submerges external rival influences may be relevant to other historical facts, which, at present, can only be presented in terms of their structural juxtaposition. It is striking, for example, that the major pilgrimage shrine for Jews in Tripolitania was found in the town of Zliten, which is also the site of an important Muslim marabout (Goldberg 1980:52). At the same time, it is not without interest that a large new synagogue was erected at the Tripolitanian shrine at about the same time that a similar project was undertaken by the Jews of the island of Jerba, in Tunisia (a pilgrimage site also visited by Jews from Libya; see Udovitch and Valensi 1984:123–24). Another example, about which one can only speculate at the moment, concerns the possible mutual influence between Arab and Jewish nationalism. It may not be incidental that the Maccabee club, which called itself Zionist, but which functioned primarily as a cultural and sports organization, was established (in 1920) about one year after the formation of a literary club that was a rallying point for Libyan nationalist sentiment (Khadduri 1963:81, n. 1). This similarly raises the question as to what extent cultural activities among the Jews, such as the teaching of modern Hebrew, were perceived as "political" by Arab nationalists. I have no doubt that further probing into the internal life of the two communities would show that, culturally and religiously, Jews and Muslims were important reference groups for one another (cf. Shinar 1982 on the Jews in North African Ibadi settings). Such a probe would require a greater understanding of the specific nature of Tripolitanian Islam than is currently available.

Texts and Social Life

The example of selihot in Jewish tradition brings us to the topic of texts. At various points in these analyses, I have attempted to show the influence or use of aspects of the "great traditions" of Islam and Judaism. While the question of the impact of these traditions (in which texts are central) on local life was formulated three decades ago (Redfield 1955), relatively few studies concerning the Middle East conceptualize the problem in a detailed fashion and bring adequate data to provide answers.[2] In the present study I have, for the most part, only been able to point to correspondences between aspects of classic religious culture and contemporary life in Tripoli, but these are striking enough to demand further work in this area.

It is indeed difficult not to fall into one of two traps—either studying contemporary ethnographic settings without reference to written sources or treating social life as if the entire Muslim population were preoccupied exclusively with the teachings of the Qur'an and the Hadith. For example, Udovitch and Valensi, in their study of Jerba, point to the fact that in choosing similar names for children, Jews will select Avraham, and Muslims Ibrahim (1984:28), but they do not mention a prohibition against non-Muslims giving their children distinctive Muslim names (Lewis 1984:33). Perhaps this is a reaction to an overly textual bias of some historians and students of religion, and indeed there is room to wonder whether each time a stone was thrown at Jews by a Muslim child if there was an awareness that this was "a form of amusement recorded in many places from early to modern times" (Lewis 1984:36).[3] But the issue cannot be ignored, for in Judaism and Islam the hallowed texts not only provide guidance internal to each tradition, but set off one religion from the other. They define the place of non-Muslims in Muslim society (see below), while they provide for the Jews an interpretation of their dependent position in terms of "exile." No consideration of these questions, even if based on direct observation of a community in situ, can ignore the central values and conceptions of these matters found in written religious works.

In the present study I have shown certain correspondences between popular notions and classical conceptions, and also have pointed to contexts, outside of regular religious settings, in which reference to texts is invoked (e.g., the play *Joseph and His Brothers*, which carried messages to both Jews and Muslims). It was common, of course, to use traditional texts as the basis of preaching in the synagogue, or on other occasions (such as in the home of a mourner). Rabbi Khamus Agiv, one of the most popular preachers in Tripoli, told me how he utilized preaching for current purposes shortly after the 1945 riots in Tripoli, when he was serving as rabbi in the Cyrenaican town of Derna. He arrived in the synagogue on the Sabbath in which the Torah portion named *va-yishlaḥ* (Genesis 32:3ff.) is read—a section describing the reconciliation of Jacob and Esau. Upon seeing the Sudanese soldiers (who could understand Arabic) placed to guard the synagogue by the British army, he immediately changed the topic of his sermon-lesson and stressed the amity between the two brothers in the biblical story.[4] I can only agree with Smith (1980) that ways must be developed to appreciate "scripture" as a force in history, and recommend foci of research, such as that outlined by Tambiah (1970, chap. 21), which seeks to understand channels of transmission of textual culture within the political structure of society.

Culture Dynamics and Historical Change

I have argued that cultural interchange between Muslims and Jews was extensive and complex, and that the textual sources of both Judaism and Islam deserve attention in studying these processes as part of everyday life. At the same time, it must be pointed out that the comparisons, contrasts, and rivalries on which I have focused did not take place on an equal footing. The Muslim call to prayer reverberated in the streets and impinged on Jewish ears, while the reverse was not true. Both Muslims and Jews might use epithets likening the "other" to an animal, but while Muslim donkey drivers could do this publicly, as part of daily humor, Jews would hide their insults in pseudo-learned textual play, in which they themselves were the only audience (chap. 7, "Jews, Italians, and Religious Aspects"). The official view of the Jews' subordinate place in Muslim society was always accessible, so we therefore return to the topic of the Jews in Libyan society examined as a question concerning *cultural* process.

One implication of the theoretical focus on culture is the insistence that the realm of culture may be subdivided and internally organized in a fashion that does not neatly correspond to institutional divisions at a sociological level.[5] In principle, anthropological work may be carried out from two different angles. A skilled "social" anthropologist conventionally concentrates on a given field of interaction and documents different cultural threads which become intertwined in the field; alternatively, a researcher might take a cultural realm (consisting of customs, rituals, myths, "semantic fields," or whatever) and attempt to reveal all the social situations in which this symbolic realm proves relevant. The organization of this work has followed the second strategy.

The approach advocated is somewhat akin to that taken in two recent studies of ritual stability and change in historical perspective—Bloch's (1986) research into the circumcision ritual in the history of the Merina of Madagascar, and Ohnuki-Tierney's (1987) analysis of monkey symbolism in Japanese culture and history. Bloch's study wrestles with reconciling the ritual, which showed great stability in the form of its performance and in the meanings attributed to it over a period of two hundred years, with the society, which during the same time span underwent far-reaching political changes and "used" the ritual in different ways. Ohnuki-Tierney demonstrates the continuity of structural principles in monkey rituals and performances over a millennium of history in Japan, while viewing differences in specific forms of ritual and myth as transformations of those principles that were related to central societal changes.

Our study of Jewish-Muslim interchange in Libya has not been concerned with a single ritual or ceremony, but has dealt with an area of religion and culture which might be labeled, most broadly, "non-Muslims in Muslim society." This realm of culture, which has relevance not only for the formal status of non-Muslims in Libya, but for a variety of social settings ranging from daily etiquette to political rhetoric, also has shown striking lines of continuity from the early nineteenth to the mid-twentieth centuries, despite several changes of regime and other powerful impacts from external sources.

In Bloch's (1986) study he devotes detailed analysis to Merina circumcision and to the understanding of ritual in general, reaching the conclusion that it is in the nature of ritual to create and define a world apart from mundane conceptions and sentiments, so that the impingement of "society" on ritual (and the reverse) is indirect and allows ritual forms to perdure in the face of extensive social change. It may be argued that this is characteristic of "culture" in general, as clearly distinguished analytically from "social structure."[6] Ohnuki-Tierney (1987:232–38) shares this perspective, studying stability and transformations within a symbolic realm and independently correlating these shifts in meaning with historical change. A similar assumption serves as our point of departure in examining some of the internal dynamics of culture with regard to Jews (non-Muslims) in Muslim Libyan society and their interdigitation with other historical developments. As indicated, this examination does not zero in on a single cultural form, but takes into account (as does Ohnuki-Tierney 1987:210–18) that a cultural realm may be inherently internally diverse, including oppositions and contradictions.

The starting point of this study is the late medieval period, or the end of the Qaramanli regime. The analysis presented in chapter 2 shows that the life of the Jewish community was shaped both by its official status as separated and subjugated in terms of the dhimma and by the competing notion that Jews were "the creatures of the handiwork of the Blessed," that is, members of society like other residents of Tripoli. The social configuration in that period was a direct continuation of the medieval situation in the Muslim Mediterranean, described succinctly by Goitein on the basis of geniza documents: "The Muslim, Christian, and Jewish communities each formed a nation, *umma*, in itself, but in every country they shared a homeland, *watan*, in common. Both concepts were of highest practical and emotional significance" (1971b:274). Thus while the Jews as a religious community in Tripoli were required to be below the Muslim umma, as members of the "homeland" (the everyday term for the same notion in modern Tripoli is *balad* rather than *watan*), they were enmeshed in an extensive set of ties with Muslims, and many of these relationships did not directly flow from their religious status as Jews.

These two ancient and clearly different models[7] (in dialectic relation to one another) provide the starting point for our analysis, but must be elaborated and qualified in several ways to appreciate their interpenetration with the shifting social and political conditions in Libyan society. It is possible to see these two ideal stances as the main elements in a cultural "code" which also has a "grammar," or possibility of different combinations, that may be applied to the changing social realities of non-Muslims in society. To this notion of a set of general principles or rules, the perspective of Bourdieu (1977) should be added, that formal rules do not directly generate behavior but that concrete social forms arise from a "practical logic" in which symbolic and instrumental elements are tightly knitted together. Another modification of the initial theoretical position is that the original terms of the cultural code are sometimes used in rhetorical patterns of great refinement, justifying "close readings" which reveal several layers of signification in relation to current social developments. With these perspectives in mind, I trace the uses and elaboration of the code within the context of historical movement, which did not lack in reversals and paradoxes, affecting Libya and its Jewish community over the past century and a half.

At the outset, it is useful to look more closely at the two major terms of the model, beginning with the assignment of the Jews to the official status of a protected people. As noted, this status, in Muslim law, is accorded to all non-Muslims who are "people of the book," but historical developments in North Africa have made the Jews the prime example of dhimmi in immediate experience. The potential exists, however, of perceiving the Jews in terms of the more general category, and thereby associating them with other non-Muslims, namely, Christians/Europeans. It is not accidental from this point of view that foreign consuls from Europe, during the Qaramanli regime, took up residence inside the Jewish quarters or nearby. The perception of the Jews as non-Muslims thus has built into it an ambiguity, which, according to the analysis of the Sabbath games, was precisely expressed in the weekly sports contest. The Jewish community, split down the middle into the two quarters, could stand for either local Tripolitan society or for its opponents. This ambiguity became crucial in the twentieth century, as will be discussed shortly.

With regard to the second model, that of Jews as part of the "homeland" along with other local residents, the social implications of this outlook have been emphasized by Rosen (1972, 1984) in his work on Moroccan society. He shows that there is much about Muslim-Jewish interaction (or Arab-Berber ties) which cannot be explained in terms of ethnic or religious groupings. "Muslim" or "Jew" appear as one set of social categories that guide interaction, alongside other ways of defining relationships such as rich/poor or influential/weak. Two quotes give the gist of his argument: "Ethnic identities do not . . . constitute all-embracing stereotypes which define the ways in which persons of different backgrounds must view and relate to one another in virtually all circumstances" (1972:443), but "in a way which is as typical in its underlying principles as it is distinctive in its resultant patterning. Jews are indeed treated as members of the community of men though they are obviously not members of the community of Believers" (p. 446).

This characterization of the tone and dynamics of interaction between Muslims and Jews appears appropriate to the "sons of the homeland" frame of interaction in Tripoli, but should, we have seen, be modified in one respect. While being a Jew or Muslim is not always a "master status," governing interaction in all spheres of life, it has been shown to be a *pervasive* status, reaching into a multitude of behavioral realms, often in minor key, but nevertheless ubiquitous. While as a pure model there may have existed a conception of Jews as undifferentiated from other Tripolitans, in everyday life, networks of interaction were rarely totally free of ethnic and religious accretions.

This observation suggests the utility of the notion of "practical logic," stressed by Bourdieu (1977). Alongside the two principal models discussed, there is a third, explicitly part of daily discourse and action, which stood between, and perhaps mediated, the pure precepts guiding contacts with Jews. Reference here is to the emphasis on honor, implying manliness (in a variety of senses), in which Jews could partially partake but clearly were not full participants. This mode of conceptualizing Jewish-Muslim ties was prominent and institutionalized in the rural areas (see chap. 5), but undoubtedly colored interaction in the urban context as well. It allowed Jews to play crucial roles in the local economy, while marking the differences between them and the Muslim. The code of honor, not explicitly derivative of religious dictates relating to nonbelievers, could absorb both the demand to keep the Jews distinct and allow extensive interaction with them on an everyday basis. It was "logical" in bringing together both of the time-honored traditions and "practical" in enhancing everyday exchange between members of different religious communities.

The cultural logic of honor, in which all relationships are suffused with a concern over who is stronger and who is weaker, does not coexist easily with principles of strict equality. It probably first began to be challenged in the nineteenth century under Ottoman rule and underwent further "deterioration" with the coming of the Italians. The experience of the Jews under Ottoman rule, however, was conditioned by a situation in which "modernization" was initially associated with a Muslim regime, rather than with a European power. This entailed the emergence of Jews into a society in which the government sought to make all its inhabitants, regardless of religion, equal, but which was still bound to popular rhetoric in which it was taken for granted that Jews should be subordinate to Muslims. One feature of this constellation of political and social factors was the surprising demand to conscript Jews to the army first, to create pressure on the Muslims (chap. 3). This ploy, which did not succeed, expressed a unique combination of the cultural principles I have discussed, probably marking one of the outer limits, logically and sociologically, of Jewish life in a Muslim land.

Italian colonization promoted further steps toward moving the

Jews as a whole in the direction of full civic participation. The main thrust of Italian policy was to remold the Jews of Libya to resemble the Jews of Italy, even though this goal was compromised by political developments from the 1930s onward. One way of assessing the effect of Italian rule on relations between Muslims and Jews is to view it as undermining the workability of the practical logic that had enabled Jewish-Muslim interaction. When informants claim that under the Italians, "Jews were like kings," it is not to be understood that many Jews exercised power or influence over Muslims (although this happened occasionally too), but that the former conventions, whereby Jews, in daily interaction with Muslims, acknowledged their own special and less honorable position, could be ignored with impunity. The dissolution of the practical model brought into sharper focus the two plainly opposed principles—Jews as protected nonbelievers *or* Jews as "the creatures of the handiwork of the Blessed"—neither of which, in their naked simplicity, was a satisfactory guide to daily life in the new reality.

One of the expressions of the practical logic wherein Jews had maintained an active place in society, even while somewhat lacking in honor, was the equation of Jews and women (chap. 5). Both are weak, both need protection, both provide important services and are therefore part of the "natural" scene. In traditional circumstances, the removal of Jews from society was "unthinkable." Indeed, there is an account from the late eighteenth century in which the Jews, harassed by a notable in the town of Zawia, all moved out of that small market town to Tripoli, and their absence from the area brought about economic retribution (Goldberg 1980:145–46). A further implication, then, of the withering away of the practical logic of Jews as less honorable is the raising of the possibility that they are not a fixed natural ingredient in the order of things, but that their presence is conditional.

The growing conceptual split between the two cardinal, but opposite, conceptions of Jews in Muslim society, concomitant with the weakening of a plausible model in which Jews were a taken for granted element of local reality, provided the background for the pogrom cum social drama, in which rioters opted for the alternative—placing Jews below Muslims—with no mitigating clauses offering them protection.

This uncompromising definition of the situation, leaving little room for maneuver by the Jews, or on their behalf, can be linked, culturally, not only to the weakening of formerly serviceable models by Italian policies, but to the logic of Libyan nationalism. It was during the Italian period that groundwork was laid among Libyan Muslims for the acceptance of nationalist loyalties, although it is difficult to estimate to what extent explicit nationalist conceptions diffused to different segments of the Libyan population. Nationalism, while building on older religious symbols and sentiments, represents a new formulation concerning the relationship linking individual citizen and national state, requiring a homogeneity between the two. If we attempt to formulate the idea of nationalism in terms of the cultural conceptions we have been discussing, it may be seen as involving the expansion of the notion of "homeland" (*watan*) from a kind of "local patriotism," to an exhaustive political loyalty (*wataniyya* means nationalism in modern Arabic). Muslims and non-Muslims could share in the sense of local patriotism,[8] but modern wataniyya often excludes those who do not partake in its defining characteristics. To the extent that religion serves to catalyze such a conceptual expansion, the reformulation involves a merging of *umma* and *watan*, in Goitein's terms (above), and leaves little room for those who do not fit into the emergent political category.[9]

It thus was the erosion of the cultural basis of the ancient workaday arrangements which combined with nascent nationalist symbolism to extrude the Jews, conceptually, from their place in the "homeland." From this point of view the riots consisted of taking actions that brought these notions to their logical conclusion in the given cultural context. Assigning Jews to the category of infidels (*kuffar*), the cry heard most often during the riots, turned Jews into total enemies of the homeland cum nation, making possible their separation from the "life blood"[10] of Libyan society.

Placing Jews under the rubric of infidels in the context of the riots may be elaborated in yet another way. Jews technically should not be treated as infidels, and certainly not after they have accepted the terms of their subordinate position in Muslim society as dhimmi. The cry "jihad fi dimmi" (a jihad against the protected nonbeliever), however, was not heard and is, of course, self-contradictory, both from the point of view of official Islamic doctrine and by virtue of the meanings associated with the term *dimmi* in local Tripolitanian culture (see previous note). A dhimmi may be subjugated and humiliated, but not murdered![11] The terminology of the riot, thus, was not accidental. The attachment of the epithet *kuffar* to the Jews opens the way for treating them as absolute enemies, devoid of all rights or claims for consideration. This was a response more appropriate to infidel foreigners seeking to dominate Libyan society than to the Jews in its midst. The equation of the Jews with the foreigners then, in accordance with the interpretation in chapter 7, permitted the nationalist activists to utilize the Jews to "make a statement" challenging non-Muslim rule. From this point of view the issue is not the Jews per se, but the enemies of Islam,[12] of whom the Jews were constituted as the most immediate representation.[13]

It may be claimed that the total identification of Jews with the enemies of Libyan Muslim society, which held sway during the course of the riots, was eminently predictable, being brought about by Italian colonization and the Jews' tendency to see their future as linked to Italy. Without denying that the Italian presence benefited many Jews and that some of the elite enthusiastically cultivated ties with Italians, the majority of Jews continued to live a traditional lifestyle (including dress), spoke Arabic, and remained in contact with Muslim customers and clients. Thus the conceptual linking of the Jews to the Italians was only partially required by the "objective" situation and reflected, in part, the existence of such an identification in current cultural paradigms. Even in the precolonial setting, when in everyday common sense Jews were very much a part of the local scene, the ability to see them as "outsiders," as those who threatened the fabric of society, was always a potentiality. Reference already has been made to the Qaramanli period, when it was considered natural for European consuls to take up residence in the Jewish quarter, and if my analysis of the Sabbath games is correct, the symbolic use of the Jews to represent the struggle of Tripolitan society against European states was predicated precisely on the ambiguity that Jews could stand for local society and/or could represent an intrusive threat. Casting the Jews into the camp of the infidels, as was done during the riot, obviously reflects the political pressures of post–World War II Libya, but also draws on an inherited cultural repertoire and represents one possible configuration generated by the images and syntax of preexisting conceptions.

At the most general level, this study has shown the interweaving of mundane practices, and "curious" customs, with the historical movement of Libyan society as described through political and social analysis. Investigating the links between these normally distinct approaches to societal understanding is a challenge to anthropology as a discipline, which should, and will, I hope, exercise researchers in the future. A few studies have pointed to questions and data parallel to those discussed here. Turner and Turner (1978:136) point to the fact that pilgrimage rituals preserve sentiments that, under given circumstances, may be shaped in nationalist terms. In a different setting, Nash (1979:168–69) has speculated about the role of ancient rites, reworked into rituals of protest, in triggering political rebellion—a connection that seems to have occurred more than once in Bolivian history. Her hypothesis is that if a ritual is seen "as a rehearsal that keeps alive the sentiment of rebellion until a historically appropriate moment, it may reinforce political movements."[14] Bloch's (1986) historically oriented study has emphasized the ideological function of ritual, in the Marxist tradition, as a factor stifling creativity and blinding participants to their participation in suppression. Closer to our region of concern, Khuri (1987:311) concludes that with regard to Shia Islam, opposition is a "religious constant expressed repetitively and continuously in ritual." The precise place of ritual in historical development is notoriously difficult to prove, particularly if one aspires to causal explanation, but the data on Libyan society indicate the importance of research in this direction.

The 1945 riots, which for most Libyan Jews proved to be the critical turning point in their relationship to Libyan society, can best be understood when an appreciation of symbolic processes is wed to more conventional political analysis. Using Nash's terminology, some of the scenes of the riots, or more precisely, the meanings that animated them, had been "rehearsed" over the years in countless interpersonal interactions, celebrations of festivals, and political rhetoric, all drawing on the cultural realm we have sought to unravel. This does not mean that the riots were an inevitable outcome of traditional views of non-Muslims or Jews in Libyan society. The claim is rather that this cultural realm, with its internal tensions, combinations, and modes of transformation into action, was flexible and "productive" enough to comprehend and express the extensive changes experienced by Libyan society in the past century and a half, and the effect of these developments on the Jewish minority dwelling within it.

From this point of view, the decision of the overwhelming majority of the Jews to leave Libya was one of the scenarios "built into" the historical cultural paradigm, although not necessarily the only one possible, and certainly not necessarily in the wake of a pogrom. Our interpretation has stressed the alternatives existing within Muslim tradition for viewing the place of non-Muslims, and also has pointed to the options within Libyan society for perceiving Jews more as part of the "homeland" or as associated with external enemies. In either instance, one aspect of the political weakness of the Jews was that they had little influence as to which perception of them would prevail at any given moment. That they could become a trope in the rhetoric of the Muslims' political struggle was an eloquent statement of their powerlessness. Our "unpacking" of the actions of the riot has highlighted the implications that there was little room for the Jews in the emergent symbolic constitution of Libyan society. Whether the planners and perpetrators of the riots sensed that the response of the Jews would be to take these "statements" seriously, and separate themselves from their erstwhile homeland at the first opportunity, can only be guessed, but there is little doubt that both the message and its reception built upon a set of shared meanings growing out of a long history together. The riots, signaling the beginning of a permanent rupture, represented the reworking of cultural principles that had linked Jews to the wider society over preceding generations.

Notes

Chapter 1

1. See Chouraqui 1952:135, which cites the *American Jewish Yearbook* (Shapiro 1951:195–200). For more recent figures, see Schmelz and DellaPergola 1986.

2. In addition to the works cited see Goitein 1955, Fattal 1958, M. Cohen 1986, and the latter's bibliography (1981). Shinar 1980 focuses on studies of North Africa. Continuing attention to the question is reflected in Patai's recent book (1986), in the collection Cohen and Udovitch 1989, and in recent reviews such as Rosen 1985, Gellner 1986, and Rejwan 1986. See also Schroeter 1988, Stillman 1988, and Deshen 1989 on Morocco.

3. A general view of Libyan history is provided by Wright 1969 and 1981. The history of Tripolitania is the subject of books by Féraud (1927) and Rossi (1968), while Cyrenaica, particularly the Sanusi order, is dealt with by Evans-Pritchard 1949 and Martin 1976. See Dearden 1976 on the Qaramanli period, Simon 1987 on the Turkish-Italian war, and Anderson 1986 for a comparative analysis of state bureaucracy beginning with the Ottoman regime and leading up to the present political period. Khadduri 1963 and Roumani 1987 discuss political developments in detail. Various aspects of Bedouin social structure in eastern Libya have been described by Peters (e.g., 1965, 1968, and 1977), and Mason 1977 depicts religion in the life of an oasis community there. Segrè 1974 provides an analysis of the colonizing efforts under the Italians, and the collections by Albergoni (1975), Joffe and McLachlan (1982), and Allan (1982) give a rounded perspective on social and economic developments from the nineteenth century to the present. Davis 1987 discusses the major features of Libyan society after the 1969 revolution.

4. The main works dealing with the Jews of Libya are Slouschz 1908, 1927; Zuaretz et al. 1960; Goldberg 1972, 1980; Kahalon 1972; Ha-Cohen 1978; Hirschberg 1981; De Felice 1985; and Simon 1979, 1982, 1984, 1986. These items are primarily in English, while some are available in Hebrew and/or Italian. Bibliographies are provided by Attal 1973 and Attal and Tobi 1980.

5. Methodological aspects of this work are discussed in Goldberg 1974, 1982, and 1983. As indicated later in this chapter, a central document in the study of Jewish life in Libya is the book *Highid Mordekhai* (Ha-Cohen 1978), and several of the subsequent chapters in this work are built upon analyses that relate materials provided by Ha-Cohen to ethnographic data gathered by the writer. In addition, many of the editor's notes in *The Book of Mordechai* (Goldberg 1980, which is a partial translation of Ha-Cohen 1978) are based on this combination of approaches. The importance of utilizing both written sources and interview-observation when researching non-Muslims in Muslim societies is underlined by Eickelman's (1985:121) account of the record keeping by a qadi in rural Morocco during the period of the protectorate. A list was kept of men of learning who visited the qadi's distinguished brother, but the list did not include the local rabbi who was a frequent and respected guest (see below, chap. 8, "Religious Life").

6. Tripolitania is the smallest but most populated region of Libya, its capital being Tripoli. Residents of the region are referred to as Tripolitanians, and of the town as Tripolitans. Most of the material in this study is derived from Tripoli and Tripolitania, but there is some reference to the region of Cyrenaica, to the east, and the Jewish community in its capital, Benghazi. There was no permanent Jewish settlement in the southern region of Libya, the Fezzan.

7. Examples of attempts to link textual-based studies with field research may be found in Dumont 1970, Gombrich 1971, and Marriot and Inden 1977 with regard to South Asia; Tambiah 1970 provides an important methodological discussion. In Middle Eastern anthropology, Antoun 1976 has argued the point persuasively and recently has published an in-depth exemplary study (1989); other examples from that region may be found in Meeker 1979, in Geertz's analysis of bazaar activities in terms of classic Islamic conceptions (Geertz, Geertz, and Rosen 1979), and in Abu-Zahra 1988. The collection by Jain (1977) addresses the question, as does Goldberg's (1987a) consideration of the importance of texts in Jewish culture and religion.

8. The term *Torah* in Jewish culture refers not only to the Pentateuch but to the whole tradition of the "written law" and "oral law" (which also came to be written) stemming from divine revelation (see Rabinowitz 1971b). While the Qur'an may be considered holy scripture, Islam has its own special conceptions of the relation of the written text to the recited text, the theological significance of the book, and the importance of the oral rendition of the book in the life of Muslims (see Welch 1986). This latter topic has recently been explored in detail by Nelson 1985.

9. A *geniza* is a storage place, usually within a synagogue, where sacred texts, and other texts and documents written in Hebrew characters, are preserved because of the rabbinic law forbidding their destruction (they may be disposed of by burial parallel to the way a person is buried). In the last century, it was discovered that one of the ancient synagogues in Old

Cairo contained a geniza with materials going back over one thousand years. This geniza formed the basis of Goitein's studies of the Islamic high Middle Ages which center on the city of Cairo, but reflect commercial and cultural ties extending both east and west. The different parts of his multivolume work deal with economic foundations (1967), the community (1971b), the family (1978), daily life (1983), and the individual (1988).

10. M. Cohen (1980), also basing his work on materials in the Cairo geniza, has shown the importance of studying the Christians and Jews of medieval Egypt in comparative perspective.

11. Later editions of *Jews and Arabs* do not present this introduction.

12. Maraboutic groups are those which claim descent from pious individuals who often functioned as mediators and were believed to have performed miracles. Their powers were connected to the possession of *baraka* as discussed by various writers, particularly with regard to Moroccan society (e.g., Westermarck 1926; Geertz 1968). Peters (1968, 1977) discusses some of the sociological characteristics of maraboutic groups in eastern Libya, and Agostini's survey (1917) shows their distribution in traditional Tripolitanian society.

13. See the Babylonian Talmud, Tractate *Keritut* 6a. The prescription in the Shulhan 'Arukh (see Rabinowitz 1971a) is in the division *Orah Hayyim,* cap. 583, with the more recent gloss in the *Mishna Berura* of R. Yisrael Meir Ha-Cohen (many editions). Herzog (1965:32–33, n. 48) documents a custom of this genre among Yiddish speakers of northern Poland involving the preparation of sweet carrots (*mern,* which also means "to multiply"). He notes the absence of a parallel custom among the coterritorial non-Jewish population, but his discussion ignores the basis of the custom in the "great tradition."

14. See the "Editor's Introduction" and "Author's Introduction" to *The Book of Mordechai* (Goldberg 1980). Part of Ha-Cohen's work has appeared in Italian (Moreno 1924, n.d.).

15. The following excerpt is translated from Ha-Cohen 1978:43–45. All material quoted from Ha-Cohen 1978 has been translated into English by the author for this volume.

16. A note by Ha-Cohen provides an example of a dispute in which he was involved, which illustrates the point, citing both the biblical book of Ecclesiastes and the Qur'an. See Goldberg 1980:60–61, n. 3.

17. Ha-Cohen uses the terms "Muhammadan" and "Muslim" interchangeably.

18. The saying is an almost direct citation of Proverbs 27:19, meaning that just as a face is reflected in water, so one man's feeling toward another reflects the other's feeling toward him.

19. See chapter 2, "Popular Anti-Jewish Sentiment."

20. See Goldberg 1980:69–73.

Chapter 2

1. With regard to the period of Shim'on Lavi, see Ha-Cohen 1978:82–83, Hirschberg 1981:149, and Goldberg 1983. On the Spanish exiles in general, see Baer 1966, and the Sabbatean period is analyzed by Scholem 1973.

2. See Slouschz 1908, 1927:18–33; Féraud 1927; Dearden 1976; and Folayan 1979 cited by Pennell 1982.

3. The consul Richard Tully was born in Leghorn, where he must have been familiar with the Jewish commercial activities. In Tripoli, Jews were among his creditors (Dearden 1976:96–97). Miss Tully was his sister.

4. See the work on Moroccan (and by implication North African) social structure by Geertz 1976; Rosen 1972, 1984; Eickelman 1976; and Brown 1977.

5. I use the term *individualized*, rather than *individual* or *personal*, because, in my understanding, the fact of a person's Jewishness was a consideration that framed the development of the personal relationship (Goldberg 1980:41–61).

6. Technically the Tripoli-based buccaneers were corsairs (not pirates) because they were officially supported by the government, but I use the terms interchangeably. This was an important activity for several southern European states as well (see Dearden 1976:16; Valensi 1977:47ff.; and Laroui 1977:253 and n. 21).

7. Guweta eventually moved to Palestine and donated large sums of money to rebuild synagogues after the 1837 earthquake in Safed (see Goldberg 1985). One may surmise that his adventure with the pasha took place toward the end of the latter's reign when his position had been severely weakened (see below).

8. On Khalfon see Hirschberg 1981:154ff., 180.

9. The role of so-called Queen Esther is given prominence by Vallière (Féraud 1927:277, 282 and n., 284 and n.) and is also mentioned often by Tully (1957:180, 268). Slouschz (1937:248), basing himself on a manuscript of A. Khalfon's poetry in his possession, surmises that she was the mother of Khalfon's wife. Ha-Cohen (from whom Slouschz claims to have acquired the manuscript), while appreciative of the importance of Jewish influence in the harem, makes no mention of this particular woman.

10. A similar comment, that one cannot distinguish the Jews from the Muslims, is made by an African traveler in Tripoli in the nineteenth century (Norris 1977). This most likely referred to the well-off. The majority of Jews wore something that indicated their difference from Muslims (De Felice 1985:7).

11. Dearden, in summarizing the organization of the Qaramanli administration, states: "the Pasha's chief minister was the chamberlain or Grand Kehya who controlled the administration of internal affairs and the Pasha's Secretariat, and headed the Divan. He was aided by the Little, or

Piccolo, Kehya who supervised, among other matters, the system of Protocol, the secretariat for foreign affairs, and the pay of the Pasha's Palace guards" (1976:6). Ha-Cohen's story simply presents one "el-Kehya."

12. Even if it is assumed that these were symbolic lashes, such as are administered yearly at the eve of the Day of Atonement, the message of submission to the rabbinic law and authority is clear.

13. The official named was Rahamim Barda, who died, according to Ha-Cohen 1978:147, in 1807. This would place the incident in the early part of the nineteenth century.

14. This incident, like the one described by Ha-Cohen regarding Benghazi (Goldberg 1980:173–77), began with the Jews celebrating a springtime custom of going out to the fields and reciting a blessing over the blossoming trees.

15. This is an example of the existence of an "ethnic" stereotype somewhat independent of the religious framework that was the major basis of differentiation of the communities (cf. Stillman 1975:20–21).

16. Ha-Cohen (1978:120n.) learned of the activities of the biryonim through the oral accounts given him by one Shabbetai Nahum, who was the second most influential "tough" and who passed away in 1872 at a ripe old age. See Lapidus' (1967:143–84) discussion of the *zu'ar* linked to different quarters in late medieval Mamluk cities.

17. Accounts of Tripoli (and of other North African towns; see in particular Schroeter 1988:81–90) stress that the Sabbath was a rest day "forced" upon the Muslims, because of the Jews' cessation from commerce and crafts. A similar situation in the Qaramanli period would be congruent with the assumption that Muslims had the leisure to watch the Jewish games. If the inference is correct, that Muslims were among the onlookers, the text, by ignoring this fact, may represent an inversion of a typical (or stereotypical) Muslim perception of the Jews: either they "do not count" or they are assimilated to "women and children."

18. Later in the nineteenth century, a new gate was opened in the western wall, allowing the Jews, who lived in that part of the city, more direct access to the Jewish cemetery. This gate was known as Bab el-Jdid (see chap. 3, introduction). Informants from the present century report that this gate was the site of stone throwing between groups of Muslim youngsters and Jewish youngsters, and one man stated that this stone throwing was "half a fight and half sport" (see chap. 7, "Jews, Muslims, and Italians"). Dare one seek lines of continuity linking this recent contest, in which, under Italian and British rule, Jews were pitted against Muslims, with the games of close to a century and a half ago, in the very same spot, where under Muslim rule one group of Jews "fought" another (see chap. 8, "Culture, Dynamics, and Historical Change")?

Chapter 3

1. On the Ottoman takeover, see Rossi 1968:289ff.; Dearden 1976, chap. 5; and Anderson 1984:326–27.

2. See Anderson 1984:325–26 on the Hamidian period. See also the reference to Ahmed Razem Pasha, who was named minister of war after the Young Turk revolt, and note 10, below.

3. Two of the important landmarks in giving non-Muslims a greater official place in Ottoman society were the Imperial Rescript of Gulhane (Shaw and Shaw 1977:60ff.) and the Reform Decree of 1856 (p. 124).

4. Many of the articles sent by Ha-Cohen to the press are listed in Appendix II of *The Book of Mordechai* (Goldberg 1980:198–99), and other press items dispatched by Ha-Cohen are found in the notes to Simon 1979.

5. The association of Jew and woman in popular culture in Tripolitania is discussed in chapter 5.

6. See Goldberg 1980:43–45 on Ha-Cohen's use of this term.

7. The fact that Jews traveling outside the areas of their tribal protectors were identified by the name of their "lord" probably explains why Berber patronyms were common among North African Jews (Goldberg 1980: 26–27).

8. Ha-Cohen calls the rebel pasha by the name Ahmed Bey. Ahmed, who was Muhammad Bey's brother, was the bey du camp and, according to Féraud 1927, was the more forceful of the two personalities.

9. As in the stories concerning the Jewish toughs, discussed in the previous chapter, Ha-Cohen's narrative of these events has many folkloristic characteristics. This does not mean the facticity of the events he recounts should automatically be rejected.

10. This is the same ruler who opened a gate in the western wall of the town (see above). He later became grand vezir of the empire.

11. On the Alliance in Tripoli see Ha-Cohen 1978:238–40, Kahalon 1972, and De Felice 1985:12–13. Dumont 1982:226–27 discusses the Alliance's educational efforts in Turkey, and an extensive discussion of the Alliance's importance in a North African country may be found in Laskier 1983. A general view of the Alliance's educational activities as reflected in its documents is provided by Rodrigue 1989.

12. On Camondo, see Hirschberg 1969:199–200 and Rosenthal 1982:374, 376.

13. In the previous chapter, Lyon's account of an incident of this nature is cited in "Popular Anti-Jewish Sentiment."

14. On Hazzan, see Hirschberg 1981:182 and Zohar 1981. His innovations in the realm of education and his decision regarding European languages are found in Hazzan 1879:14a–16b.

15. For example, Ha-Cohen, in discussing the influence of R. Ya'acov Mimun (above), reports favorably how he was able to ostracize a Tunisian Jew of French nationality when the latter came to Tripoli and publicly flouted religious rules (lewd behavior and the violation of the Sabbath). The young man complained to the French consul, saying: "Freedom has spread throughout the world. How can R. Ya'acov publicly ostracize me?

He has forbidden the Jews from speaking to me on account of deeds which are only between me and heaven." Despite this argument, R. Ya'acov was able to convince the consul of the correctness of his stance, so the consul did not defend the young man's rights (1978:151). Ha-Cohen reports another incident in which the right of rabbinical authority is upheld in Benghazi (pp. 335–36). In section 66 of his work (pp. 188–89) he states briefly but clearly that those who reject religion in the name of secular knowledge have only a superficial understanding of the latter. He thus envisions the individual Jew (and one assumes the individual Muslim as well) as part of a religious *community*, with the community exercising control over the individual's religious behavior.

16. On the introduction of local councils, see Shaw and Shaw 1977:83ff. and Anderson 1984:331. Representatives of the *millets*, or non-Muslim communities, sat on these councils.

17. There was a traditional exemption of the inhabitants of Tripoli and Benghazi (along with some other major cities in the empire) from serving in the army (Shaw and Shaw 1977:245–46). During the nineteenth-century reforms, an attempt was made to enlist more subjects of the empire to serve. However, it was still possible for many to pay a military exemption tax. For non-Muslims, payment of this tax became automatic, after 1876, when it replaced the older head tax, anchored in Islamic law (p. 100), to be paid by dhimmis.

18. See Hirschberg 1981:182–83 on Rabbi Shabbetai. Beginning with the appointment of Rabbi Hazzan (above), chief rabbis were appointed from Istanbul (Simon 1979:7) and were expected to fit into the overall policies regarding the province.

Chapter 4

1. The word *Allah* for God was also used in Jewish speech.

2. Ha-Cohen states that the Jews of the Gharian have the same customs for weddings, circumcisions, and so forth as do the Jews of the Jebel Nefusa (Goldberg 1980:140). References to other descriptions of Libyan Muslim weddings are found in Goldberg 1980:119, n.1.

3. Detailed comments on several aspects of the wedding may be found in Goldberg 1980:122–26. Most of the comments included here relate to the theme of our analysis.

4. The Jewish marriage contract is the *ketubbah*. The reference is to the Babylonian Talmud.

5. This is the Hebrew word. The local Arabic term is *shuash*.

6. The parallel journey in the Muslim ceremony of Bin 'abbas is called *jah-fa*. See al-Ahmar 1976:130. There are many partially similar and partially different parallels, only a few of which are discussed here.

7. I have not previously explained this custom. Perhaps it is connected with the fact that cotton wicks burn in oil lamps which can "stand for" the individual members of a family (Goldberg 1989:146). In this case, the

bride's incorporation of the wicks may be an attempt to portend fertility.

8. This is a fourth prayer service in addition to the three services normal on weekdays. See Idelsohn 1960:xvi.

9. See the Mishnah, Tractate *Qiddushin* 1:1.

10. The evolution of the forms of marriage payments in Judaism is a complex and imperfectly understood matter. See, for example, Falk 1966 and Friedman 1976:15–48.

11. See Schereschewsky 1971.

12. This was not the case in all Jewish communities. See the medieval Egyptian materials discussed by Friedman 1976. The Cairo geniza materials from the Middle Ages provide many examples of Muslim influence on Jewish practice, coupled with attempts to resist that influence. For example, Goitein 1967:146 discusses how Muslim law recognizes a formal status between a freed slave and his or her former owner, the latter being known as the *mawla* of the former. Jewish law concerning freed slaves recognizes no such continuing official status, but practice was clearly influenced by the prevailing Muslim norms. "In a court record from Fustat, dated June 28, 1080, the freedman Mubarak (who had become a successful businessman) was first characterized as the mawla of Joseph b. Joshiah, a person known from other documents, then the Arabic term was deleted and replaced by the Hebrew 'freed by' " (Goitein 1967:146).

13. Leach 1958 provides a general study of "magical hair" and deals with issues of the interrelated levels of analysis in the interpretation of symbols.

14. See the Mishnah, Tractate *Ketubbot* 2:1.

15. In a folklore documentary produced in Israel, this form of head movement is depicted among Jews originating from a small community outside of Tripoli. Jews from the city of Tripoli have expressed indignation at the film, claiming that no such dancing took place.

16. Hebrew: *ke-ilu dafaqta otah.*

17. Babylonian Talmud, Tractate *Qiddushin*, 2b.

18. The Mishnah (Tractate *Qiddushin* 1:1) states that there are three (different) ways of acquiring a wife—payment of money, delivery of a contract of transfer, and sexual congress. Later, Jewish law incorporated all these items into a standard marriage.

19. Goitein may have later modified his views somewhat, as in *A Mediterranean Society: The Family* (1978), where he stresses the importance of brother-sister ties as opposed to husband-wife ties.

20. See R. Rosen 1981.

21. See Mishnah *Ta'anit*, chap. 4.

Chapter 5

1. A description of the Jewish communities in the market towns of Tri-

politania is found in Mordechai Ha-Cohen's book (Goldberg 1980). Studies of specific market towns may be found in Khuja's paper on Gharian town (1960) and Blake's monograph on Misurata (1968).

2. Féraud 1927:276–77; Rossi 1968; and Pennell 1982.

3. Frequently, in Ha-Cohen's (1978) text, the term "merchant" implies being Jewish (Goldberg 1980:59).

4. See Anderson 1984 on economic development under Ottoman rule. In Morocco, too, foreign rule brought new categories of people from traditional sectors of the society into the field of commerce (Waterbury 1972).

5. The attainment of religious majority (*bar-mitzvah*) standardly takes place at the age of thirteen. Accounts rendered by former peddlers from the Gharian region (Goldberg 1972) indicate that there was a sense that travel away from home also signaled a move out of the family circle and into manhood.

6. In Tripolitania, as in the Sefrou area (Rosen 1984:155–56), Jews often bought the unripe fruit or field produce of Muslim farmers.

7. In discussing the Jews of Sefrou, Morocco, C. Geertz (Geertz, Geertz, and Rosen 1979:164) states that they were "in no way marginal." It is not my intention to quibble over the use of a term, but in Rosen's (1984:159) discussion of the same community he, while exploring the conceptual similarity of Jews and women, asserts that they were both "only half seen."

8. See Rosen 1984:156–60, and the discussion below on Jews and women for an appreciation of some of the complexities of the place of the Jews in Morocco. Among other points, Rosen indicates that urban Muslims view the Jews as having nothing to guide them in overcoming their passions. In structuralist parlance, this may be seen as placing the Jews closer to "nature." On the other hand, in rural areas Jews were often ambivalently respected by Berbers for their association with learning, being "the people of the book." See Goldberg 1978 and note 14 below on the ritual expression of this ambivalence.

9. See Peristiany 1965 and Gilmore 1987.

10. See the Babylonian Talmud, Tractate *'Avodah Zarah,* 38.

11. See Bourdieu 1973, Zarka 1975, and the chapter by H. Geertz in Geertz, Geertz, and Rosen 1979.

12. See McClure 1913:277–78 for another version of this saying.

13. Bourdieu 1962:28–29 gives a North African example. There is more discussion of this matter with regard to the Middle East. See Antoun 1968a and Meeker 1976. Abu-Lughod 1986:103–17 discusses honor and shame in the context of gender and sexuality in a Bedouin society, but also shows how these concepts are linked to more general notions concerning the relationships between those who are powerful and those who are dependent on them.

14. The parallelism between *Muslim/Jew* and *man/woman* may be seen as problematic, as the former contrast, in Lévi-Straussian terms, is the product of culture while the other is of the order of nature. On the other hand, it is possible to see the link in terms of a structuralist "reduction" (Sperber 1975:55), wherein people are divided according to those closer to culture (men) and those closer to nature (women), and men are further divided in accordance with the same principle, yielding Muslim men and Jewish men. In analyzing the status of Jews in Morocco, as expressed in local rituals, Goldberg 1978 has shown how they are a problematic category, viewed both at the cultural and "natural" level. Culturally, they share with the Muslims a belief in scriptural religion, but are outside the community of believers. "Naturally," they are seen as "autochthones" and show a closeness to the soil, but have ceded physical control of the land to the Muslims. Thus the Jews' cultural status, religion, and relative scriptural erudition are linked to their natural status, historical primacy in the region, and the observance of festivals linked to the solar agricultural cycle. In other words, the Jew is at once a "spiritual" (cultural) and natural autochthone (see n. 8).

Chapter 6

1. While there certainly were Muslim religious leaders in Tripoli, the town did not have a special reputation as important in this regard (Goldberg 1980:33, n. 31). The discussion that follows stresses the role of religion in the separation of and rivalry between Jews and Muslims, but there is no intention of overlooking that Judaism and/or Islam could also be invoked to promote solidarity and commonality between the two religions (see chap. 7). Heightened rivalry between the groups in a city may also reflect the dynamics of urban ethnic relations (Fischer 1976:125–36).

2. Ha-Cohen cites two incidents, both involving him personally, in which religious debate was initiated in rural towns (Goldberg 1980:11, 60–61).

3. John Davis, who did fieldwork in southeastern Libya (Davis 1987), commented to me that often as not when he first met a family, they would, knowing him to be a European/Christian, ask whether or not he believed in the virgin birth.

4. Other tales are found in Panetta 1943:176–78, and 1977:35. While the analogue is not precise, it may be that Jewish abhorrence of the camel, a prominent animal in the Middle Eastern setting which Jews were forbidden to eat, can be likened to Jewish aversion to the pig in Europe. Jews, of course, shared with Muslims an aversion to the pig.

5. This title is given in Zuaretz et al. 1960:405–6.

6. See the discussion of this genre by D. Cohen 1964:126, Zafrani 1968, and Ben-Ami 1971.

7. The following is part of a footnote provided by Ha-Cohen:

> Rabbi Yosef Agib is a signator on the decision accepting the conversion of the aforementioned proselyte to the Jewish religion. The communal ledger

in which this decision is recorded is presently found in the hands of the Learned Rabbi Yehudah Jarmon [cf. Saraf 1982:xii–xiv] in Tunis. The aforementioned Rabbi Yosef passed away in the year 1710, as is inscribed on his grave. The present story could not be copied from the manuscript of Rabbi Avraham Khalfon [cf. Goldberg 1980:3; Hirschberg 1981:154ff., 180], because the relevant page was in the hands of Rabbi Ya'aqov Raqah [cf. Zuaretz et al. 1960:73–74] and was then lost. However the said proselyte composed a poem in Arabic concerning the event, and some of the stanzas have survived among the sacred songs of the elderly women. I composed the story from these surviving stanzas, but from this version of the story it appears that the name of the proselyte was Abraham Aditor, and I do not know how to interpret the word *aditor*. According to what has been passed on orally, the Jewish notables met his request, for one is duty bound to honour the request of the deceased. After great effort, using cunning and sparing no expense, they obtained his corpse and buried him among the Jews. The members of his family left Tripoli with their wealth, and mingled with the Jews elsewhere. (1978:95)

8. The Sabbath is distinguished by the serving of three meals instead of two, based on the pattern of meals in Talmudic times.

9. The phrase used here is taken from a legend embellishing the biblical narrative of Jacob's competition with Esau over the birthright, a theme which, according to our interpretation, is evoked later on. See *Midrash Rabbah* 1951:570 on Genesis 25:34.

10. The story of the special taste of Sabbath food which cannot be duplicated by Gentiles is widespread. Its prototype is in the Babylonian Talmud, *Shabbat* 119a.

11. The phrase refers to an incident in which a proselyte asked the sage Hillel to teach him all the Torah while standing on one foot (Babylonian Talmud, *Shabbat* 31a).

12. Maimonides' thirteen principles. See Hertz 1948:6.

13. Traditional rabbinic law is reluctant to accept the desire to marry a Jewish woman as a reason for conversion to Judaism.

14. Ha-Cohen utilizes a classic phrase describing what a proselyte is to be taught (Babylonian Talmud, *Yebamot* 47a).

15. When a proselyte previously has been circumcised, rabbinic law requires that a minor incision be made to the extent that some blood is let.

16. Abraham too was not born of "Jewish" parents, and it is widespread Jewish practice to name a (male) Jewish convert "Abraham" or "so-and-so, the son of Abraham."

17. According to Ha-Cohen's history (1978:85), this pasha ruled in Tripoli during 1687–1704.

18. Tishri is the seventh month of the Jewish year and occurs in the fall (September/October). It is the month during which the High Holy Days (Rosh ha-Shanah and Yom Kippur) and the Festival of Sukkot (Tabernacles) are celebrated.

19. These sections are normally distributed within the family (Cesàro 1939:170) or given to the poor. It is noteworthy that there is a Jewish celebration, taking place on the twenty-first of Tishri (see the previous note), with the canonical Hebrew name of Hosha'nah Rabbah, but which was known in Tripoli as the "night of liver and lung" (Zuaretz et al. 1960:371) because those parts of a slaughtered animal were grilled and eaten during a nocturnal study session.

20. Jason 1965 provides an index of "Jewish-Oriental Tales," wherein stories of disputes between Jews and Gentiles are given a classification (AT 922 *C).

21. See, for example, Marcus 1983, Ben-Ami 1984:166–84, and Meged and Goldberg 1986.

22. The tale reflects the seriousness with which religious matters were taken in the medieval world, but, at the same time, the depiction of the local "inquisition," in which the governor inspects Hmayid's *kuskus* dish, is not without its humor.

23. Yemenite *kubaneh;* Ashkenazi *cholent;* Moroccan *skhina.*

24. This is indicated in Adadi's work (1865); he opposed the practice in terms of rabbinic law.

25. Stories circulating in Israel about Jews leaving Morocco to immigrate to Israel stress that some left in a manner that allowed them to depart suddenly, without any interference. They accomplished this by leaving on a Friday night (the Sabbath), when they normally were at home and were forbidden to travel. How did the Muslims know they left? On the morrow, no Jews came to take their *skhina* from the communal ovens. The abandoned Sabbath meal was a multilayered statement of the rupture of ancient and complex social ties.

26. The Arabic term is *ihalfu l-ihud,* which has the technical meaning of not following the ways of the nonbeliever (Vajda 1960:265).

27. Both of these figures are incorrect. Jews circumcise on the eighth day, although festivities begin on the eve of the eighth day, that is, the end of the seventh. There is also a Tripolitanian custom of holding a small celebration for the mother forty days after giving birth to a boy (Zuaretz et al. 1960:390–91; Khalfon 1986:209). At this time she terminates the impurity of parturition. In both these instances a partial familiarity with Jewish practice is shown by the Muslim informant and is interpreted in terms of the Muslim's own understandings. It is interesting that some Islamic scholars believe that one should circumcise on the seventh day, and that this is interpreted by some as the seventh day not counting the day of birth, that is, the eighth day (Wensinck 1986).

28. *Midrash Rabbah* 1951:484, on Genesis 22:1.

29. Ha-Cohen uses the Hebrew phrase *yesh 'omrim,* which is very characteristic in rabbinic discourse when an alternate opinion is offered. He has

no difficulty formulating a diversity of opinion within Muslim tradition in the framework of Jewish halakhic terminology.

30. The following is given in an account of the Great Sacrifice in Tripoli at the end of the last century:

> Ma, a questo proposito, non si può lasciare sotto silenzio una stravagantissima usanza di taluni di questi ebrei della *Hara*. Gelosi, per cosi dire, dell'omaggio che gl'islamiti fanno ad uno de' più grandi loro patriarchi, trepidi quasi che il Signore Iddio benedetto, tratto in abbaglio da quel caro nome, accetti come moneta corrente il sacrificio de' miscredenti, si affrettano di nottetempo, o prima che spunti il sole, a scannare anch'essi un montone, affine d'accaparrarsi, pei primi, le grazie del signore. (Milano 1912:142)

> But with regard to this subject, one cannot help but mention an extraordinary custom of some of the Jews of the *hara*. Jealous, so to speak, of the homage paid by the Muslims to one of their greatest patriarchs, and almost trembling that the Lord God, blessed-be-He, dazzled by his dear name, might accept as current coinage the sacrifice of the miscreants, they hasten at night, or before the dawn, to slaughter a sheep in order to preempt for themselves the grace of the Lord.

One Tripolitan informant claimed that Muslims slaughtered without reciting a (Jewish) blessing, so the Jews turned the occasion into a sacrifice offered by them. I have also recently been told that among the Libyan Jews in Rome, who emigrated from Tripoli after the 1967 war, are individuals who continue to maintain this practice.

31. In a settlement of Israeli Bedouins there are a number of families originating from Tripolitania. This group has been studied by Kressel (1975), who relates (pers. comm.) that in oral renditions of the story of Ishmael's sacrifice, the "sacrifice" is usually followed by the boy's circumcision. He also noticed that little boys frequently hold their genitals while observing the slaughter of the victim during the holiday.

32. Such a decision by Hazzan takes into account debate on the topic as reflected in rabbinic decisions and discussion over the ages (cf. Levinsky 1947).

Chapter 7

1. The use of the term *pogrom* (also appearing in the English translation of De Felice's book), taken from the historical experience of eastern Europe, particularly the Ukraine, is intentional, because the anti-Jewish outbreaks there also frequently took place in the background of nascent nationalist sentiment.

2. Here, as in the chapter generally, we rely considerably on De Felice's assessment of the pogrom (1985:188–208), which draws on archival materials not previously subject to analysis. On several points my discussion attempts to go beyond an earlier essay on the riots (see Goldberg 1977),

and in particular to relate to De Felice's conclusion that the riots were consciously promoted by nationalist organizers.

3. The source cited by De Felice is from a 1926 article by I. Sciaky (De Felice 1985:320, nn. 3, 4).

4. Le Tourneau's characterization of the Jews of Fez (Morocco) on the eve of the French protectorate as a "population étrangère" (1949:86) would be very inappropriate in the Tripolitan context. The Libyan case also differs in that Italian domination did not loosen the traditional cultural moorings of the Jews of Libya to the extent that French influence did among some of the Jews of Morocco. As indicated in chapter 3, the Jews had experience in "managing" cultural influence from a variety of directions. See the discussion by Simon (1979) concerning the cooperation between the Jewish elite and the modernizing Turkish administration in Tripoli. Even when Jews were quick to take advantage of new opportunities provided by the Italian presence and profit from their ability to be middlemen between the local Muslims and Italian institutions (Del Boca 1986:42), this was seen as their normal role in the society.

5. Additional information on the Sabbath as an issue of confrontation between the government and the Jewish community is given below, in "Jews, Muslims, and Italians."

6. See, for example, Memmi 1965 and Sivan 1985:189–207.

7. While the Italian presence in Libya may have widened the economic gap between the well-to-do and the rank and file among Tripoli's Jews, the basic patterns linking (and separating) the different elements of the population may have been similar to those which obtained during Ottoman rule (Goldberg 1984).

8. See Nunes-Vais 1982 and Simon 1986.

9. John Wright (pers. comm.) relates that during his first visit to Tripoli, he on one occasion realized that he was walking in an area of the city where he could not hear the cry of the *muezzin*. He then realized he was standing in what had been the former Jewish quarter. The comparison of Tripoli to Tel Aviv may be an echo of the rhetoric used in a fascist publication as part of the campaign requiring Jews to open their shops on the Sabbath (see below, and De Felice 1985:161).

10. See De Felice 1985:321, n. 15. The schools of the Alliance Israélite Universelle, in the years before the Italian takeover, sometimes attracted more female than male students. Some girls attended school for the first time in the framework of Hebrew classes organized by the Ben Yehudah organization in the early 1930s (Zuaretz et al. 1960:142ff.).

11. Lists of synagogues and descriptions of them are found in Ha-Cohen 1978 and Zuaretz et al. 1960:103–22.

12. The figure is based on my interviews. The definition of a synagogue, if one takes into account local practice, could include a room set aside for prayer in a private building. During two days a week (exclusive of Sab-

baths and festivals) it would be necessary to have a Torah scroll in the room, but otherwise no other paraphernalia is required. Jews living in the new city were often less punctilious in observance than those in the Jewish quarters, but attendance at Sabbath worship continued to be very widespread. Some new city denizens went to old city synagogues on Sabbaths, and particularly on the festivals.

13. It was common practice for Jews, after Sabbath morning worship, to enter the coffeehouse of a Muslim acquaintance and be served, without ordering a drink and without paying for it. Payment would be made during the week, thereby circumventing Sabbath prohibitions. See chapter 6.

14. See De Felice 1985:184 and below.

15. On the 'Isawiyya, see Trimingham 1971:86.

16. The Jews of Tripoli see Rabbi Shim'on Lavi, a Spanish exile and well-known kabbalist, as having revived Jewish life in the city in the mid-sixteenth century after it had been captured by Spain, handed over to the Knights of Malta, and ultimately retaken by corsairs operating under Ottoman protection. See chapter 2, introduction.

17. A sense of rivalry was not necessarily confined to the lower classes. It was expressed in soccer matches between Jewish and Muslim teams, matches that were limited by Balbo in the 1930s (De Felice 1985:355, n. 92).

18. Reference here is to *gematria*, in which each Hebrew letter is assigned a numerical value, and larger numbers can be composed through combinations of letters in which order is not important.

19. See chapter 2, n. 18. The open area at the entrance of the new gate (*fum al-bab*) linked the Jewish quarter with the lower-class area mentioned earlier. Is it possible to see in these games/fights an instance in which youths engage in activities valued by their respective communities, but which cannot be carried out by more responsible adults? Cf. Peters 1972.

20. Hebrew accounts of this episode (Zuaretz et al. 1960:194–96; Khalfon 1986:74–75) use the term *gezerah*, which means a decree concerning the Jewish community which is difficult to bear but carries the connotation that there is an inexplicable theological reason behind the arbitrary suffering.

21. Khalfon 1986:85 cites a popular verse which describes how, during the rationing in the course of the war, Jews were forced to stand at the end of the line.

22. De Felice (1985, chap. 6) documents the successive implementation of racial legislation. His analysis is supplemented by Simon's article (1986) which, basing itself on oral accounts that recently have been collected, helps see the events of World War II from the perspectives of the Libyan Jews involved in them.

23. There are some small differences in the numbers presented by various documents.

24. See the case from Gharian, discussed below, in "The Riots and Other Social Dramas."

25. This point of view has been put forth notably by Charles Tilly. See Tilly, Tilly, and Tilly 1975; Tilly 1978; and Tilly and Tilly 1981. A similar point of view is implied in Lapidus' (1967:143–84) discussion of urban violence in late medieval Muslim cities. See also the review article by Marx and Wood (1975). In the introduction to a recent collection on the "anthropology of violence," Riches (1987) states that violence can be both strategic and meaningful. The papers in the collection do not contain a case study of a riot.

26. Although the investigation of the British found that some wealthy Jews in Tripoli had been a focus of the crowd's attack (C. Daniels, *New York Times*, Nov. 14, 1945), no informants attributed economic motives or resentment to the rioters and looters.

27. Viewing a riot in ritual mode places a different perspective on the claim, voiced by Muslim leaders, Jews, and the British, that the riots were "unexpected." Granted that this specific outburst was unexpected, it is surprising how quickly the Jews reacted to the first hints of rioting, almost as if a well-rehearsed scene were about to be enacted, or how the Muslim and Jewish leaders in the Gharian knew to forestall trouble through ceremony (below, "The Riots and Other Social Dramas"). From the point of view of the participants, it similarly is surprising how quickly the notions of what is expected and acceptable riotous behavior spread throughout the city and the countryside. Put more generally, if rioting consists of unstructured behavior, how can we explain the high degree of regularity in the kinds of acts that occur during riots? Riots appear to draw upon some sort of tradition of how one acts in such circumstances. Compare the following quote regarding eastern Europe: "Most Jews knew, by experience or by eyewitness accounts, of pogroms. They had direct evidence of the strange fashion in which their neighbors might suddenly become pillagers and murderers. They knew equally well the reverse transition when, the pogrom over, these same killers once again became neighbors, customers" (Zborowski and Herzog 1962:152).

28. Other aspects of Turner's approach to ritual may help interpret behavior during collective outbreaks (see Goldberg 1977). The thematics of a hostile riot appear to be directly opposite to the experience of *communitas*, a "generic human bond without which there could be no society," which Turner 1969 sees as characteristic of the liminal phase in rituals of reversal. In riot behavior, in contrast, structural categorizations (e.g., Muslim versus Infidel), which separate people one from another, are given great prominence. The two experiences may be closely interlinked, however (cf. Bilu 1988). Turner has written of ritual in general that "powerful drives and emotions . . . are divested in the ritual process of their antisocial quality and attached to components of the normative order, energizing the latter with a borrowed vitality and thus making the Durkheimian obligatory desirable" (1969:52–53). In riots, the normative

and affective remain attached, but society is portrayed in simplified and condensed representations, so that what is "anti-social" in an everyday setting may be entirely appropriate within a riot frame of reference. Turner, in arguing for communitas, says that the breakdown of social structure does not necessarily mean the Hobbesian war of every man against every man, but may lead instead to "the experience of mankind." Viewing riots from a ritual point of view suggests that the boundary separating communitas from Hobbes is at times easily traversed.

29. A few informants discounted the connection between the festival and the rioting, but a man from Zawia remembers a client who picked up his knife on the afternoon before the outbreak and, pointing it at the Jew's heart, said, "This is for you." A smith from Amrus, hearing about the riots, ran and threw all the knives in his possession down a well. Earlier, mention was made of Jewish-Muslim hostilities which took place on the mulid, and not infrequently outbreaks against Jews in the Ukraine coincided with the Easter season. In very different contexts, Nash (1979:168–69) has stressed how rebellions of Bolivian mine workers occurred on the festive days of ancient pre-Columbian traditions, and Bloch (1986:31) links an anti-French rebellion in Madagascar to the date of one of the central traditional rituals.

30. See chapter 2, "Popular Anti-Jewish Sentiments."

31. While Zionist activity among the Jews is one of the factors cited in an official British report as part of the background of the riots, a number of sources ignore this factor (e.g., Rennel 1948 and Khadduri 1963), and De Felice explicitly rejects it (1985:202–3; see n. 33 below). While Zionism, whether in traditional religious, cultural, or modern political terms, was more widespread in the Jewish community than was appreciated by outsiders, the leadership of the Jewish community, at the time, did not give it prominence (see C. Daniels, *New York Times*, Nov. 8, 1945) and attempted publicly to emphasize what it had in common with other native Libyans. To the extent that De Felice is correct that the younger nationalists instigated the riots, he is referring to individuals who had become exposed to political issues throughout the Arab world, including the question of Palestine. However, it was not a central concern of the average Libyan Muslim at the time. The 1945 pogroms may be contrasted with the June 1948 riot (De Felice 1985:223ff.), in which Palestine was an explicit rallying cry. This contrast also was made by my informants. See n. 33, below.

32. An example of the identification of Italian rule with the well-being of the Jews "at the expense" of the Muslims, transposed into the realm of personal history, is provided in an account given me by a man whose store was looted during the riots. When asked if he knew any of the looters personally, he told of an incident that had brought him into conflict with a Muslim. The Jewish merchant had sent his son on an errand to another store; while the boy was inside the store, some Muslim youths slashed the tire of his bicycle. Upon hearing of the incident the merchant went to

the (Italian) police, who helped him locate the culprit. Through the intervention of the police, the merchant was able to force the father of the lad to pay for a new tire. The Muslim vowed to get even with the Jew, and the latter surmises that perhaps it was this same man who looted his store a number of years later during the riots. Another "symbolic" hypothesis may be ventured that the Jews who moved into the new city apartments (where Italians had resided), after the British takeover of Tripoli, were not only more physically vulnerable during the rioting but became identified with Italians in the course of the pogrom.

33. When asked how the Muslims referred to the riots, when they talked about the events, some of my informants said that they did not know, while several said that the Muslims referred to the outbreaks as *jihad*. De Felice 1985:203 notes that during the pogroms, no one ever heard any shouts against Zionism. See note 31, above.

34. After the riots, the mufti of Tripoli issued a *fetwa* and exhorted Muslims to return what had been stolen from the Jews.

35. On the Jewish community in the Gharian region, see Goldberg 1972.

36. The orientation to Muslim ears is also indicated by the fact that within Jewish tradition the image of Joseph is frequently encapsulated in the phrase "Joseph the Righteous," rather than "Joseph and His Brothers." The staging of the play in Arabic can also be placed in counterpoint to Hebrew plays, which were a major feature of Zionist efforts within the community to teach modern Hebrew. This of course is the type of activity which would not have been flouted in front of the British and Muslim leaders (see n. 31).

37. Close to 90 percent of the Jews of Libya, who numbered over thirty-five thousand (Goldberg 1971), immigrated to Israel between the spring of 1949 and the end of 1951 when Libya became independent. Immigration began when the British authorities granted permission to the Jewish Agency to set up an office in Tripoli and organize the operation. As an indication of how the causes of events can be reinterpreted in terms of their results, a number of Libyan Jews have told me that their guess is that the Jewish Agency was behind the riots, for they clearly had the effect of bringing the Jews to Israel.

38. The Berber, while Muslim himself, distances his stance from that of the "Arabs" and flips over the age-old accusation of Muslims that the Jews falsified the Torah, erasing references proving the truth of Islam.

Chapter 8

1. There are other forms of "cultural management" of outside influences on Jewish life. Hasidic tradition, for example, has an explicit justification for utilizing non-Jewish tunes applied to songs of religious content. It uses kabbalistic concepts to claim that the appropriation of these melodies from non-Jews redeems divine sparks which have been scattered around the world and brings them closer to their original source.

2. Antoun 1976 has argued that anthropologists should have greater familiarity with classical languages and texts (see Meeker 1976:421). Geertz's
   study of bazaar life in a Moroccan town views some of the central activities in terms of classic Islamic conceptions (Geertz, Geertz, and
   Rosen 1979), and Rosen 1984 has made similar connections to concepts
   that inform social relations and their perception. Deshen's study of
   southern Tunisian Jews (1975) shows how the "ritualization of literacy"
   underlines the importance of texts in their lives. Still, with few excep-
   tions (see Antoun 1968b), these studies do not focus on the concrete
   settings in which textual-based ideas and values are transmitted to a
   wider community.

3. See Goitein 1971b:285 and Stillman 1979:84, 201–3, 304–5. The "textual basis" of this practice might be linked to the notion, derived from the
   tradition of the Pact of 'Omar, that Jews are to refrain from public processions. The harassment of Jewish funerals that was avoided by building
   the new gate in Tripoli (chap. 3) may have included the throwing of
   stones.

4. In both Muslim and Jewish weekly public worship there are conventional references to the existing political power. With regard to the
   former, during the *khutba* the name of the ruler is mentioned—an act
   that is probably routine but which can become very sensitive at times of
   political instability. There are prayers (in different versions) in Jewish tradition, recited after the conclusion of the reading of the Torah, for God's
   blessing on the ruler(s) of the country. In the remote Jewish community
   of Yefren, in the tense period of the 1945 riots, the name of the local British commanding officer was inserted into that prayer.

5. See Schneider 1976.

6. Schneider 1976:199ff. distinguishes between general conceptions concerning social relations which are part of culture and more defined
   norms which are part of the "social system." Distinctions such as these
   obviously raise the question of how the levels interrelate, but that is also
   part of their usefulness, to allow such problems to be formulated clearly.
   In the context of the discussion, Bloch 1986:194 makes the related point
   that different aspects of culture may exhibit varying degrees of fixity in
   relation to social and political events.

7. Lewis 1984:30 indicates that the distinction with which we are concerned was often made in practice in medieval Islam, but was rarely
   expressed in principle.

8. See chapter 3 and Simon 1979 for examples of the well-being of the Jews
   being linked to the good of the city of Tripoli as a whole. A clear expression of such sentiment is found in Ha-Cohen's book (1978) on the
   Jews of Libya, which includes a great deal of information on the society
   in general. In an introduction he gives several reasons for writing the
   book and then states: "In addition, it will answer [the] complaint against
   Tripoli: 'How shall we look upon her, for even though she is one of Af-

rica's cities, no spirited man in her has risen up to gather and organize her history and customs?'" (Goldberg 1980:36). It should further be noted that Ha-Cohen came from a family that held Italian nationality.

9. The Tripolitanian pogrom may be compared with the anti-Jewish *farhud* in Baghdad in 1941, which clearly involved a nationalistic anti-British reaction and also reflected modern forms of political anti-Semitism. See Kedourie 1974; Glitzenstein-Meir 1981; Taggar 1981. It would also be of interest to comparatively weigh the factors that figured in other anti-Jewish riots in the late 1940s, such as those in Aleppo and in Aden during December 1947 (H. Cohen 1973:46, 67), or in Morocco in June 1948 (Chouraqui 1952:128).

10. We refer to the folk interpretation of *dimmi*, as Jews being the blood of the Muslims, mentioned in the introduction. The play on words reflects the fact that the classical Arabic term *dhimmi* is pronounced *dimmi* in local Tripolitanian Arabic (and other dialects), so that the term for "member of the people of the *dhimma*" is homophonic with the term meaning "my blood." The semiotic transformations that allow the Jews to be "the blood" of Muslim society in one context and totally extruded from it in another may not be unlike the phenomenon, analyzed by Ohnuki-Tierney 1987, whereby "monkeys" and "special status people" appear as mediators with the divine in one set of circumstances and devalued scapegoats in another. See, also, the next paragraph.

11. It should be remembered that during the riots some Muslims protected Jews by taking them into their homes or guiding them off the street to safety.

12. It may be a more general phenomenon in ritual that even when participants do not wear masks or costumes, they are "playing" another social or cultural category. In Bloch's study (1986:173) he concludes that women in ritual are treated very differently than in everyday life (in which they have considerable social influence), but that their place in ritual is not connected to issues of gender.

13. It is not difficult to see how, via the various Peircian modalities, the Jews could stand for the Italians. The Jews who dressed like Italians created an iconic resemblance, and their proximity in residence and work established an indexical link. Given that many (in fact most) Jews did not have these characteristics, the relationship was also "symbolic," that is, arbitrary, and based on one of the received conventional notions in which Jews and Christians were part of the same overall category. See the next paragraph.

14. In discussions of liminality and the ritual process, Turner (1969, 1982) has argued that in addition to the accepted view of ritual reinforcing the status quo, symbolic representations emerging in ritual action provide the opportunity for a society to regard and become aware of itself, and thereby may also contain transformative potential. See also the discussion on communitas (chap. 7, n. 28). The general question of ritual and politics recently has been given extensive treatment by Kertzer 1988.

References

Abu-Lughod, L. 1986. *Veiled Sentiments: Honor and Poetry in a Bedouin Society.* Berkeley: University of California Press.

Abu-Zahra, N. 1988. "The Rain Rituals as Rites of Spiritual Passage." *International Journal of Middle East Studies* 20:507–29.

Adadi, A. 1849. *Ha-shomer emet.* Leghorn: Ben Amozag.

———. 1865. "Quntres maqom shenahagu." In *Vayigra avraham.* Leghorn: Ben Amozag.

Agostini, E. de. 1917. *Le popolazioni della Tripolitania: Notizie etniche e storiche.* Tripoli: tip., Pirotta and Bresciano.

Ahmar, A. S. al-. 1976. "The Changing Social Organization of a Libyan Village." Ph.D. diss., University of Leeds.

Albergoni, G., ed. 1975. *La Libye nouvelle: Rupture et continuité.* Paris: CNRS.

Allan, J. A., ed. 1982. *Libya since Independence: Economic and Political Development.* London: Croom Helm.

Alliance Israélite Universelle. 1870–73. *Bulletin d'alliance israélite universelle.* Paris.

Anderson, L. 1984. "Nineteenth Century Reform in Ottoman Libya." *International Journal of Middle East Studies* 16:325–48.

———. 1986. *The State and Social Transformation in Tunisia and Libya, 1830–1980.* Princeton: Princeton University Press.

Antoun, R. 1968a. "On the Modesty of Women in Arab Muslim Villages: A Study in the Accommodation of Tradition." *American Anthropologist* 70:671–97.

———. 1968b. "The Social Significance of Ramadan in an Arab Village." *Muslim World* 58:36–42, 95–104.

———. 1976. "The State of the Art in Middle Eastern Anthropology." In L. Binder, ed., *The Study of the Middle East: Research and Scholarship in the Humanities and Social Sciences,* 137–228. New York: Wiley.

———. 1989. *Muslim Preacher in the Modern World: A Jordanian Case Study in Comparative Perspective.* Princeton: Princeton University Press.

Appleton, L. 1979. "The Question of Nationalism and Education under Italian Rule." *Libyan Studies* 10:29–33.

Atkinson, J. 1832. *Customs and Manners of the Women of Persia and Their Domestic Superstitions.* London: J. Murray. Translated from the Persian.

Attal, R. 1973. *Les Juifs d'Afrique du nord: Bibliographie.* Jerusalem: Institut Ben-Zvi.

Attal, R., and Y. Tobi. 1980. "Oriental and North-African Jewry—An Annotated Bibliography." *Sefunot* 1 (16):401–93.

Babylonian Talmud. 1935–48. Trans. (into English) and ed. I. Epstein. London: Soncino.

Baer, Y. 1966. *A History of the Jews in Christian Spain.* Trans. L. Schoffman. Philadelphia: Jewish Publication Society.

Bar-Asher, S. 1981. "The Jewish Community in Morocco in the 18th Century: Studies in the History of the Social Status and Self-Government of the Jews of Fes, Meknes and Sefrou" (in Hebrew; English summary). Ph.D. diss., Hebrew University of Jerusalem.

Baron, S. W. 1957. *A Social and Religious History of the Jews.* Vol. 5. New York: Columbia University Press.

Ben-Ami, I. 1971. "La qṣida chez les Juifs marocains." *Scripta Hierosolymitana* 22:1–17.

———. 1974. "Le mariage traditionnel chez les Juifs marocains." In I. Ben-Ami and D. Noy, eds., *Studies in Marriage Customs,* 9–116. Folklore Research Center Studies, no. 4. Jerusalem: Magnes.

———. 1984. *Saint Veneration among the Jews in Morocco* (in Hebrew). Folklore Research Center Studies, no. 8. Jerusalem: Magnes.

Bilu, Y. 1988. "The Inner Limits of Communitas: A Covert Dimension of Pilgrimage Experience." *Ethos* 16:302–25.

Blake, G. 1968. *Misurata: A Market Town in Tripolitania.* Durham Research Papers, no. 9. Department of Geography, Durham College, University of Durham, England.

Bloch, M. 1986. *From Blessing to Violence: History and Ideology in the Circumcision Ritual of the Merina of Madagascar.* Cambridge: Cambridge University Press.

Blumer, H. 1946. "Collective Behavior." In A. M. Lee, ed., *Principles of Sociology,* 167–224. New York: Barnes and Noble.

Bourdieu, P. 1962. *The Algerians.* Trans. A. C. M. Ross. Boston: Beacon Press.

———. 1973. "The Berber House." In M. Douglas, ed., *Rules and Meanings,* 98–110. Harmondsworth, England: Penguin.

———. 1977. *Outline of a Theory of Practice.* Trans. R. Nice. Cambridge: Cambridge University Press.

Bowie, L. 1976. "An Aspect of Muslim-Jewish Relations in Late Nineteenth-Century Morocco: A European Diplomatic View." *International Journal of Middle East Studies* 7:3–19.

Briggs, L. C., and N. Guède. 1964. *No More Forever: A Saharan Jewish Town.* Papers of the Peabody Museum of Archaeology and Ethnology, 55(1). Cambridge: Harvard University Press.

Brown, K. 1977. "Changing Forms of Patronage in a Moroccan City." In E. Gellner and J. Waterbury, eds., *Patrons and Clients in Mediterranean Societies,* 304–28. London: Duckworth.

Bulliet, R. 1976. Review of *A Mediterranean Society: The Jewish Communities of the Arab World as Portrayed in the Documents of the Cairo Geniza.* Vol. 2: *The Community,* by S. D. Goitein. *International Journal of Middle East Studies* 7:457–59.

Cesàro, A. 1939. *L'arabo parlato a Tripoli.* Roma: Mondadori.

Chouraqui, A. 1952. *Marche vers l'Occident: Les Juifs d'Afrique du Nord.* Paris: Presses Universitaires de France.

Cohen, A. 1979. "Interview" of C. Geertz (in Hebrew). *Mahshavot* 48: 19–29.

Cohen, D. 1964. *Le parler arabe des Juifs de Tunis.* Paris: Mouton.

Cohen, H. 1973. *The Jews of the Middle East, 1860–1972.* New York: Wiley.

Cohen, M. 1980. *Jewish Self-Government in Medieval Egypt: The Origins of the Office of the Head of the Jews, ca. 1065–1126.* Princeton: Princeton University Press.

———. 1981. *The Jews under Islam: From the Rise of Islam to Sabbatai Zvi.* Princeton Near East Paper, no. 32. Princeton University: Program in Near Eastern Studies. Reproduced from *Bibliographical Essays in Medieval Jewish Studies* (New York: Ktav, 1976), 169–229, with a supplement for the years 1973–80.

———. 1986. "Islam and the Jews: Myth, Counter-Myth, History." *Jerusalem Quarterly* 38:125–37.

Cohen, M., and A. Udovitch, eds. 1989. *Jews and Arabs: Contacts and Boundaries.* Princeton: Darwin Press.

Comunità Israelitica della Tripolitania. 1945. *I tumulti antiebraici in Tripolitania: 4, 5, 6, e 7 Novembre 1945.* Tripoli: Ben-Zvi Institute Collection 1724.

Coon, C. 1951. *Caravan: The Story of the Middle East.* New York: Holt.

Davis, J. 1987. *Libyan Politics: Tribe and Revolution.* Berkeley: University of California Press.

Dearden, S. 1976. *A Nest of Corsairs: The Fighting Karamanlis of Tripoli.* London: John Murray.

De Felice, R. 1985. *Jews in an Arab Land: Libya, 1835–1970.* Trans. J. Roumani. Austin: University of Texas Press.

Del Boca, A. 1986. *Gli Italiani in Libia: Tripoli bel suol d'amore, 1860–1922.* Rome: Laterza.

Deshen, S. 1975. "The Ritualization of Literacy: The Works of Tunisian Scholars in Israel." *American Ethnologist* 2:251–60.

———. 1983. *Individuals and the Community: The Social Life of 18th–19th Century Moroccan Jewry* (in Hebrew). Tel Aviv: Misrad HaBitahon.

———. 1989. *The Mellah Society: Jewish Community Life in Sherifian Morocco.* Chicago: University of Chicago Press.

Dumont, L. 1970. *Homo Hierarchicus.* Chicago: University of Chicago Press.

Dumont, P. 1982. "Jewish Communities in Turkey during the Last Decade of the Nineteenth Century in the Light of the Archives of the Alliance Israélite Universelle." In B. Braude and B. Lewis, eds., *Christians and Jews in the Ottoman Empire,* 1:209–42. New York: Holmes and Meier.

Eickelman, D. 1976. *Moroccan Islam.* Austin: University of Texas Press.

———. 1985. *Knowledge and Power in Morocco: The Education of a Twentieth-Century Notable.* Princeton: Princeton University Press.

Eisenberg, J. 1927. "Isḥaḳ." In *Encyclopedia of Islam,* 2:532–33. Leiden: Brill.

Encyclopaedia Judaica. 1971. Jerusalem: Keter.

Evans-Pritchard, E. E. 1949. *The Sanusi of Cyrenaica.* London: Oxford University Press.

Falk, Z. 1966. *Jewish Matrimonial Law in the Middle Ages.* London: Oxford University Press.

Fattal, A. 1958. *Le statut légal des non-Musulmans en pays d'Islam.* Beirut: Imprimerie Catholique.

Féraud, L. C. 1927. *Annales tripolitaine.* Paris and Tunis: Librarie Vuibert.

Fischer, C. 1976. *The Urban Experience.* New York: Harcourt Brace Jovanovich.

Folayan, K. 1979. *Tripoli during the Reign of Yusuf Pasha Qaramanli.* Ife-Ife: University of Ife Press.

Fox, R. G. 1977. *Urban Anthropology: Cities in Their Cultural Settings.* Englewood-Cliffs, N.J.: Prentice-Hall.

Friedman, M. 1976. "The Minimum *Mohar* Payment as Reflected in Genizah Documents: Marriage Gift or Endowment Pledge?" *Proceedings of the American Academy for Jewish Research* 43:15–48.

Geertz, C. 1968. *Islam Observed.* New Haven: Yale University Press.

———. 1973. *Interpreting Cultures.* New York: Basic Books.

———. 1976. "From the Native's Point of View: On the Nature of Anthropological Understanding." In K. H. Basso and H. A. Selby, eds., *Meaning in Anthropology,* 221–37. Albuquerque: University of New Mexico.

Geertz, C., H. Geertz, and L. Rosen. 1979. *Meaning and Order in Moroccan Society: Three Essays in Cultural Analysis.* Cambridge: Cambridge University Press.

Gelber, Y. 1983. *Jewish Palestinian Volunteering in the British Army during the Second World War* (in Hebrew). Vol. 3. Jerusalem: Yad Ishak Ben-Zvi.

Gellner, E. 1983. *Muslim Society.* Cambridge: Cambridge University Press.

———. 1986. "Prejudicial Encounters." Review of *Semites and Anti-Semites,* by B. Lewis. *Times Literary Supplement,* 22 August, p. 903.

Gilmore, D., ed. 1987. *Honor and Shame and the Unity of the Mediterranean.* Special Publication of the American Anthropological Association, no. 22.

Glitzenstein-Meir, E. 1981. "The Baghdad Pogrom—June 1–2, 1942" (in Hebrew). *Pe'amim* 8:21–37.

Goitein, S. D. 1955. *Jews and Arabs: Their Contacts through the Ages.* New York: Schocken.

———. 1965. "Djum'a." In *Encyclopaedia of Islam,* 2:592–94. Leiden: Brill.

———. 1967. *A Mediterranean Society: The Jewish Communities of the Arab World as Portrayed in the Documents of the Cairo Geniza,* Vol. 1: *Economic Foundations.* Berkeley: University of California Press.

———. 1971a. "The Concept of Mankind in Islam." In W. Wagar, ed., *History and the Idea of Mankind,* 72–91. Albuquerque: University of New Mexico Press.

———. 1971b. *A Mediterranean Society: The Jewish Communities of the Arab World as Portrayed in the Documents of the Cairo Geniza.* Vol. 2: *The Community.* Berkeley: University of California Press.

———. 1978. *A Mediterranean Society: The Jewish Communities of the Arab World as Portrayed in the Documents of the Cairo Geniza.* Vol. 3: *The Family.* Berkeley: University of California Press.

———. 1983. *A Mediterranean Society: The Jewish Communities of the Arab World as Portrayed in the Documents of the Cairo Geniza.* Vol. 4: *Daily Life.* Berkeley: University of California Press.

———. 1988. *A Mediterranean Society: The Jewish Communities of the Arab World as Portrayed in the Documents of the Cairo Geniza.* Vol. 5: *The Individual.* Berkeley: University of California Press.

Goldberg, H. 1967. "Patronymic Groups in a Tripolitanian Jewish Village: Reconstruction and Interpretation." *Jewish Journal of Sociology* 9:209–26.

———. 1971. "Ecologic and Demographic Aspects of Rural Tripolitanian Jewry: 1853–1949." *International Journal of Middle East Studies* 2:245–65.

———. 1972. *Cave Dwellers and Citrus Growers: A Jewish Community in Libya and Israel.* Cambridge: Cambridge University Press.

———. 1973. "Culture Change in an Israeli Immigrant Village: How the Twist Came to Even Yosef." *Middle Eastern Studies* 9:73–80.

———. 1974. "Tripolitanian Jewish Communities: Cultural Boundaries and Hypothesis-Testing." *American Ethnologist* 1:619–34.

———. 1975. "The Relations of the Jews of Tripolitania with Their Neighbors." *Proceedings of the VIth World Congress of Jewish Studies* 2:123–30.

———. 1977. "Rites and Riots: The Tripolitanian Pogrom of 1945." *Plural Societies* 8:35–56.

———. 1978. "The Mimuna and the Minority Status of Moroccan Jews." *Ethnology* 17:75–87.

———, trans. and ed. 1980. *The Book of Mordechai: A Study of the Jews of Libya.* Philadelphia: Institute for the Study of Human Issues.

———. 1982. "Tailors in Tripoli in the Colonial Period." In E. G. H. Joffe and K. S. McLachlan, eds., *Studies in the Social and Economic History of Libya: The Colonial Period,* 161–72. Wisbech, Cambridgeshire: MENAS Press.

———. 1983. "Language and Culture of the Jews of Tripolitania: A Preliminary View." *Mediterranean Language Review* 1:85–102.

———. 1984. "The Jewish Community in Tripoli in Relation to Italian Jewry and Italians in Tripoli." In J.-L. Miège, ed., *Les relations intercommunautaires juives en Méditerranée occidentale, XIIIe–XIXe siècles,* 79–89. Paris: CNRS.

———. 1985. "Between Tripolitania and Eretz Israel in the Nineteenth Century" (in Hebrew). *Pe'amim.* 24:87–92.

———, ed. 1987a. *Judaism Viewed from Within and from Without: Anthropological Studies.* Albany: SUNY Press.

———. 1987b. "Ottoman Tripoli" (in Hebrew). In Y. Dan, ed., *Culture and*

History: Ino Sciacky Memorial Volume, 171–84. Jerusalem: Misgav Yerushalayim.

———. 1989. "Family and Community in Sephardic North Africa: Historical and Anthropological Perspectives." In D. Kraemer, ed., *The Jewish Family: Metaphor and Memory*, 133–51. Oxford: Oxford University Press.

Gombrich, R. 1971. *Precept and Practice: Traditional Buddhism in the Rural Highlands of Ceylon*. Oxford: Clarendon Press.

Ha-Cohen, Mordecai. 1978. *Higgid Mordecai: Histoire de la Libye et de ses Juifs, lieux d'habitation et coutumes* (in Hebrew). Ed. and annotated by H. Goldberg. Jerusalem: Institut Ben-Zvi.

Handelman, D. 1989. "The Madonna and the Mare: Symbolic Organization in the Palio of Siena." In *Models and Mirrors: Towards an Anthropology of Public Events*, 116–35. Cambridge: Cambridge University Press.

Hazan, E. 1982. "Rabbi Musa Bujnah: Paytan of South Libyan Jewry" (in Hebrew). In M. Abitbol, ed., *Communautés juives des marges sahariennes du Maghreb*, 453–568. Jerusalem: Institut Ben Zvi.

Hazzan, E. B. 1879. *Ta'alumot Lev*. Part I. Leghorn: Ben-Amozag.

Heller, B. 1931. "Yusuf b. Ya'ḳub." In *Encyclopaedia of Islam*, 4:1178–79. Leiden: Brill.

Hermassi, E. 1975. *Leadership and Development in North Africa: A Comparative Study*. Berkeley: University of California Press.

Herr, M. D. 1971. "Intermediate Days." In *Encyclopaedia Judaica*, Jerusalem: Keter. 6:1244.

Hertz, J. 1948. *The Authorized Daily Prayer Book*. Rev. ed. New York: Bloch Publishing.

Herzog, M. 1965. "The Yiddish Language in Northern Poland." *International Journal of American Linguistics* 31 (2, pt. 3).

Hesse-Warteg, E. 1882. *Tunis: The Land and the People*. London: Chattas and Windus.

Hirschberg, H. Z. (J. W.) 1965. *A History of the Jews in North Africa*. Vol. 2. *From the Ottoman Conquests to the Present Times* (in Hebrew). Jerusalem: Mosad Bialik.

———. 1969. "The Oriental Jewish Communities." In A. J. Arberry, ed., *Religion in the Middle East: Three Religions in Concord and Conflict*, 1:119–225. Cambridge: Cambridge University Press.

———. 1981. *A History of the Jews in North Africa*. Vol. 2. *From the Ottoman Conquests to the Present Time*. Leiden: Brill.

Idelsohn, A. 1960. *Jewish Liturgy and Its Development*. New York: Schocken.

Jain, R. K., ed. 1977. *Text and Context: The Social Anthropology of Tradition*. Philadelphia: Institute for the Study of Human Issues.

Jason, H. 1965. "Types of Jewish-Oriental Oral Tales." *Fabula* 7:115–224.

———. 1975. *Studies in Jewish Ethnopoetry*. Asian Folklore and Social Life Monographs, no. 72. Taipei.

Joffe, E., and K. McLachlan, eds. 1982. *Studies in the Social and Economic History of Libya: The Colonial Period*. Wisbech, Cambridgeshire: MENAS Press.

Kahalon, Y. 1972. "La lutte pour l'image spirituelle de la communauté de Libye au XIXe siècle" (in Hebrew; French summary). In H. Z. Hirschberg, ed., *Zakhor le-Abraham: Mélanges Abraham Elmaleh*, 79–122. Jerusalem: Comité de la communauté marocaine.

Katz, J. 1962. *Exclusiveness and Tolerance: Studies in Jewish-Gentile Relations in Medieval and Modern Times*. Oxford: Oxford University Press.

Kedourie, E. 1974. "The Sack of Basra and the *Farhud* in Baghdad." In *Arabic Political Memoirs and Other Studies*, 283–314. London: F. Cass.

Kertzer, D. 1988. *Ritual, Politics, and Power*. New Haven: Yale University Press.

Khadduri, M. 1963. *Modern Libya: A Study in Political Development*. Baltimore: Johns Hopkins University Press.

Khalfon, H. 1986. *Lanu u-Levanenu* (For our children after us): *The Life of the Libyan Jewish Community* (in Hebrew). Netanya: Published by the author.

Khuja, M. 1960. "Garian Town." In S. G. Willimot and J. I. Clarke, eds., *Field Studies in Libya*, 120–24. Durham Research Papers, no. 4. Department of Geography, Durham College, University of Durham, England.

Khuri, F. 1987. "The Ulama: A Comparative Study of Sunni and Shi'a Religious Officials." *Middle Eastern Studies* 23:291–312.

Kressel, G. 1975. *Individuality and Tribalism: The Dynamics of an Israeli Bedouin Community in the Process of Urbanization* (in Hebrew). Tel Aviv: Hakibbutz Hameuhad.

Lapidus, I. 1967. *Muslim Cities in the Late Middle Ages*. Cambridge: Harvard University Press.

Laroui, A. 1977. *The History of the Maghrib: An Interpretive Essay*. Princeton: Princeton University Press.

Laskier, M. 1983. *The Alliance Israélite Universelle and the Jewish Communities of Morocco, 1862–1962*. Albany: SUNY Press.

Leach, E. 1958. "Magical Hair." *Journal of the Royal Anthropological Institute* 88:147–64.

Le Bon, G. 1896. *The Crowd*. London: Unwin.

Le Tourneau, R. 1949. *Fès avant le protectorat*. Casablanca: Société Marocaine de Librarie et l'Édition.

Levinsky, Y. T. 1947. *The Striking of Haman in Jewish Communities: A Purim Folklore Anthology* (in Hebrew). Tel Aviv: Yeda Am.

Levy, R. 1957. *The Social Structure of Islam*. Cambridge: Cambridge University Press.

Lewis, B. 1968. "The Pro-Islamic Jews." *Judaism* 17:391–404.

———. 1971. *Race and Color in Islam*. New York: Harper and Row.

———. 1984. *The Jews of Islam*. Princeton: Princeton University Press.

Loeb, L. 1976. "Dhimmi Status and Jewish Roles in Iranian Society." *Ethnic Groups* 1:89–105.

Lyon, G. F. 1821. *A Narrative of Travels in North Africa in the Years 1818, 1819 and 1820*. London: John Murray.

McClure, W. 1913. *Italy in North Africa: An Account of the Tripoli Enterprise*. London: Constable.

Marcus, E. 1983. "The Oicotype of the Desecrator's Punishment (AT*771)" (in Hebrew; English summary). In I. Ben-Ami and J. Dan, eds., *Studies in Aggadah and Jewish Folklore,* 337–67. Folklore Research Center Studies, no. 7. Jerusalem: Magnes Press.

Marriot, M., and R. Inden. 1977. "Toward an Ethnosociology of South Asian Caste Systems." In K. David, ed., *The New Wind: Changing Identities in South Asia,* 227–38. The Hague: Mouton.

Martin, B. G. 1976. *Muslim Brotherhoods in Nineteenth Century Africa.* Cambridge: Cambridge University Press.

———. 1985. "Ahmed Raṣim Pasha and the Suppression of the Slave Trade, 1881–1896." In J. R. Willis, ed., *Slaves and Slavery in Muslim Africa,* 2:51–82. London: F. Cass.

Marx, G. T., and J. L. Wood. 1975. "Strands of Theory and Research in Collective Behavior." *Annual Review of Sociology* 1:363–428.

Mason, J. 1975. "Sex and Symbol in the Treatment of Women: The Wedding Rite in a Libyan Oasis Community." *American Ethnologist* 2:649–61.

———. 1977. *Island of the Blest: Islam in a Libyan Oasis Community.* Ohio University, Center for International Studies, no. 31. Athens, Ohio.

Meeker, M. 1976. "Meaning and Society in the Middle East: Examples from the Black Sea Turks and the Levantine Arabs." *International Journal of Middle East Studies* 7:243–70, 383–422.

———. 1979. *Literature and Violence in North Arabia.* Cambridge: Cambridge University Press.

Meged, A., and H. Goldberg. 1986. "Rabbi Saʿadia Adati: The Legend of a Saint in the Rif of Spanish Morocco and Its Social Context" (in Hebrew, English summary). *Jerusalem Studies in Jewish Folklore* 9:89–103.

Memmi, A. 1965. *The Colonizer and Colonized.* Trans. H. Greenfield. New York: Orion Books.

Midrash Rabbah. 1951. Ed. H. Freedman and M. Simon. London: Soncino.

Milano. 1912. *Pionieri italiani in Libia. Relazioni dei delegati della Societa Italiana di Esplorazioni Geographiche e Commerciali di Milano, 1880– 1896.* Milano: Francesco Vallardi.

Moreno, M., ed. and trans. 1924. *Usi, costumi e istituti degli Ebrei libici, fascicolo 1: Religione e magia, feste e cerimonie, vita e morte,* by M. Cohen [Mordechai Ha-Cohen]. Official study, Government of Cyrenaica; colonial reports and monographs. Benghazi: Unione tipografia editrice.

———. N.d. [1928]. *Gli Ebrei in Libia: Usi e costumi,* by M. Cohen [Mordechai Ha-Cohen]. Collection of work and monographs published by the Ministry of Colonies. Rome: Sindicato italiano arti grafiche.

Nachtigal, G. 1971. *Sahara and Sudan.* Vol. 1: *Tripoli and Fezzan.* Trans. A. G. B. Fisher and H. J. Fisher. London: C. Hurst.

Nahum, E. 1974. "Salonica and Tripoli" (letter to the editor). *Jerusalem Post,* 25 October, p. 12.

Nash, J. 1979. *We Eat Mines and Mines Eat Us: Dependence and Exploitation in Bolivian Tin Mines.* New York: Columbia University Press.

Nelson, K. 1985. *The Art of Reciting the Qur'an.* Austin: University of Texas Press.

Noah, M. M. 1819. *Travels in England, France, Spain and the Barbary States in the Years 1813–14 and 15.* New York: Kirk and Mercein.

Norris, H. T. 1977. *The Pilgrimage of Ahmad: Son of the Little Bird of Paradise.* Warminster, England: Aris and Phillips.

Nunes-Vais, R. 1982. *Reminiscenze tripoline.* Rome: Uaddan.

Ohel, M. 1973. "The Circumcision Ceremony among Immigrants from Tripolitania in the Israeli Village of Dalton." *Israel Annals of Psychiatry and Related Disciplines* 11:66–71.

Ohnuki-Tierney, E. 1987. *The Monkey as Mirror: Symbolic Transformations in Japanese History and Ritual.* Princeton: Princeton University Press.

Panetta, E. 1943. *L'Arabo parlato a Bengasi.* Vol. 1: *Testi con traduzione e note.* Rome: Libreria dello Stato.

———. 1977. *La donna nel folklore della Libia.* Rome: Accademia Nazionale dei Lincei.

Paret, R. 1971. "Ibrahim." In *Encyclopaedia of Islam,* 3:980–81. Leiden: Brill.

Pascon, P., and D. Schroeter. 1982. "Le cimetière juif d'Iligh (1751–1955): Étude des épitaphes comme documents d'histoire sociale (Tazerwalt, Sud-Quest Marocain)." *Revue de l'Occident Musulman et de la Méditerranée* 34:34–67.

Patai, R. 1971. *Tents of Jacob: The Diaspora Today and Yesterday.* Englewood Cliffs, N.J.: Prentice-Hall.

———. 1986. *The Seed of Abraham: Jews and Arabs in Contact and Conflict.* Salt Lake City: University of Utah Press.

Pennell, C. R. 1982. Review of *Tripoli during the Reign of Yusuf Pasha Qaramanli,* by K. Folayan. *Libyan Studies* 13:113–14.

Peristiany, J. G., ed. 1965. *Honour and Shame.* Chicago: Chicago University Press.

Perlmann, M. 1974. "The Medieval Polemics between Islam and Judaism." In S. D. Goitein, ed., *Religion in a Religious Age,* 103–38. Cambridge, Mass.: Association for Jewish Studies. Proceedings of Regional Conferences held at the University of California, Los Angeles, and Brandeis University in April 1973.

Peters, E. 1965. "Aspects of the Family among the Bedouin of Cyrenaica." In M. Nimkoff, ed., *Comparative Family Systems,* 121–46. Boston: Houghton Mifflin.

———. 1968. "The Tied and the Free." In J. Peristiany, ed., *Contributions to Mediterranean Sociology,* 167–90. The Hague: Mouton.

———. 1972. "Aspects of the Control of Moral Ambiguities: A Comparative Analysis of Two Culturally Disparate Modes of Control." In M. Gluckman, ed., *The Allocation of Responsibility,* 109–62. Manchester: Manchester University Press.

———. 1977. "Patronage in Cyrenaica." In E. Gellner and J. Waterbury, eds., *Patrons and Clients in Mediterranean Societies,* 275–90. London: Duckworth.

Piccioli, A. 1935. *The Magic Gate of the Sahara.* Trans. A. Davidson. London: Methuen.

Pollack, H. 1971. *Jewish Folkways in Germanic Lands (1548–1806): Studies in Aspects of Daily Life.* Cambridge: MIT Press.

Rabinowitz, L. 1971a. "Shulhan 'Arukh." In *Encyclopaedia Judaica,* 14: 1475–77. Jerusalem: Keter.

———. 1971b. "Torah." In *Encyclopaedia Judaica,* 15:1235–36. Jerusalem: Keter.

Redfield, R. 1955. "The Social Organization of Tradition." *Far Eastern Quarterly* 15:13–22.

Rejwan, N. 1986. "The Continuing Controversy." *Midstream* 32:20–25.

Rennel, F. 1948. *British Military Administration of the Occupied Territories of Africa.* London: His Majesty's Stationery Office.

Richardson, J. 1848. *Travel in the Great Desert Sahara in the Years 1845 and 1846.* 2 vols. London: Bentley.

———. 1853. *Narrative of a Mission to Central Africa Performed in the Years 1850–51.* 2 vols. London: Chapman and Hall.

Riches, D., ed. 1987. *The Anthropology of Violence.* Oxford: Blackwell.

Rodrigue, A. 1989. *De l'instruction a l'émancipation: Les enseignants de l'alliance israélite universelle et les Juifs d'Orient, 1860–1939.* Paris: Calmann-Levy.

Rosen, L. 1968. "A Moroccan Jewish Community during the Middle East Crisis." In L. Sweet, ed., *Peoples and Cultures of the Middle East,* 2:388–404. Garden City, N.Y.: Natural History Press.

———. 1972. "Muslim-Jewish Relations in a Moroccan City." *International Journal of Middle East Studies* 3:435–49.

———. 1984. *Bargaining for Reality: The Construction of Social Relations in a Muslim Community.* Chicago: University of Chicago Press.

———. 1985. "Communities Enmeshed." Review of S. D. Goitein, *A Mediterranean Society: The Jewish Communities of the Arab World as Portrayed in the Documents of the Cairo Geniza,* vol. 4; A. Cohen, *Jewish Life under Islam: Jerusalem in the Sixteenth Century;* B. Lewis, *The Jews of Islam;* A. L. Udovitch and L. Valensi, *The Last Arab Jews: The Communities of Jerba, Tunisia. Times Literary Supplement,* 7 June, p. 648.

Rosen, R. 1981. "Le symbolisme feminin ou la femme dans le système de représentation judéo-marocain, dans un mochav en Israël" (in Hebrew). M.A. thesis, Department of Sociology and Social Anthropology, Hebrew University of Jerusalem.

Rosenthal, S. 1982. "Minorities and Municipal Reform in Istanbul." In B. Braude and B. Lewis, eds., *Christians and Jews in the Ottoman Empire,* 1:369–86. New York: Holmes and Meier.

Rossi, E., 1929. "Tripoli." In *Encyclopaedia of Islam,* 4:814–18. Leiden: Brill.

———, trans. and annotator. 1936. *La cronaca arab tripolini di Ibn Ghalbun. sec. XVII.* Bologna: Licinio Capello.

———. 1968. *Storia di Tripoli e della Tripolitania della conquista araba al 1911.* Ed. M. Nallino. Rome: Istituto per l'Oriente.

Roumani, J. 1987. "The Emergence of Modern Libya: Political Conditions and Colonial Change." Ph.D. diss., Princeton University.

Rubin, B.-Z., ed. 1988. *Luv, hedim min ha-yoman* (Libya, echoes from the diary): *Selected Chapters of Zionist Activity among Libyan Jews* (in Hebrew). Jerusalem: Association for Libyan Jewish Heritage and the Libyan Jewish Cultural Center.

Saint-Paul, G. 1902. "Réflexions sur les moeurs et sur la caractère des indigènes Tunisiens." *Bulletins et Memoires de la Société d'Anthropologie de Paris* 3 (5th ser.):296–308.

Saraf, M. 1982. *Nehorai: Rabbi Nehorai Garmon of Tunisia and His Poetry* (in Hebrew, English summary). Tel Aviv: Tel Aviv University.

Schereschewsky, B.-Z. 1971. "Betrothal." In *Encyclopedia Judaica*, 4:753–57. Jerusalem: Keter.

Schmelz, U., and S. DellaPergola. 1986. "World Jewish Population." *American Jewish Year Book* 86:350–64.

Schneider, D. 1976. "Notes towards a Theory of Culture." In K. Basso and H. Selby, eds., *Meaning in Anthropology*, 197–221. Albuquerque: University of New Mexico Press.

Scholem, G. 1973. *Sabbatai Sevi: The Mystical Messiah*. Trans. R. J. Z. Werblowsky. Princeton: Princeton University Press.

Schroeter, D. J. 1988. *Merchants of Essaouira: Urban Society and Imperialism in Southwestern Morocco, 1844–1886*. Cambridge: Cambridge University Press.

Segrè, C. 1974. *Fourth Shore: The Italian Colonization of Libya*. Chicago: University of Chicago Press.

———. 1987. *Italo Balbo: A Fascist Life*. Berkeley: University of California Press.

Shapiro, L. 1951. "North Africa." *American Jewish Year Book* 52:425–36.

Shaw, S., and E. K. Shaw. 1977. *History of the Ottoman Empire and Modern Turkey*. Vol. 2, *Reform, Revolution and Republic*. Cambridge: Cambridge University Press.

Shinar, P. 1980. "La recherche relative aux rapports judéo-musulmans dans le Maghreb contemporain." In J.-L. Miège, ed., *Les relations entre Juifs et Musulmans en Afrique du Nord, XIXe–XXe siècles*, 1–31. Paris: CNRS.

———. 1982. "Réflexions sur la symbiose judéo-ibadite en Afrique du Nord." In M. Abitbol, ed., *Communautés juives des marges sahariennes du Maghreb*, 81–114. Jerusalem: Institut Ben Zvi.

Simon, R. 1979. "The Jews of Libya and Their Gentile Environment in the Late Ottoman Period" (in Hebrew). *Pe'amin* 3:5–36.

———. 1982. "The Socio-economic Role of the Tripolitan Jews in the Late Ottoman Period." In M. Abitbol, ed., *Communautés juives des marges sahariennes du Maghreb*, 321–28. Jerusalem: Institut Ben Zvi.

———. 1984. "The Relations of the Jewish Community of Libya with Europe in the Late Ottoman Period." In J.-L. Miège, ed., *Les relations intercommunautaires juives en méditerranée occidentale, XIIIe–XXe siècles*, 70–78. Paris: CNRS.

———. 1986. "The Jews of Libya on the Verge of Holocaust" (in Hebrew). *Pe'amim* 28:44–77.

———. 1987. *Libya between Ottomanism and Nationalism: The Ottoman*

Involvement in Libya during the War with Italy (1911–1919). Islam-kundliche Untersuchugen, no. 105. Berlin: Klaus Schwarz Verlag.

Sivan, E. 1985. *Interpretations of Islam*. Princeton: Darwin Press.

Slouschz, N. 1908. "La Tripolitaine sous la domination des Karamanlis." *Revue du Monde Musulman* 6:58–84, 211–32, 433–53.

———. 1927. *Travels in North Africa*. Philadelphia: Jewish Publication Society of America.

———. 1937. *Livre des voyages: Mes voyages en Lybie* (in Hebrew). Tel Aviv: Comité Jubilaire.

Smelser, N. 1962. *Theory of Collective Behavior*. New York: Free Press.

Smith, W. C. 1980. "The True Meaning of Scripture: An Empirical Historian's Non-reductionist Interpretation of the Qur'an." *International Journal of Middle East Studies* 11:487–505.

Sperber, D. 1975. *Rethinking Symbolism*. Cambridge: Cambridge University Press.

Spies, O. 1936. "Mahr." In *Encyclopaedia of Islam*, 3:137–38. Leiden: Brill.

Stillman, N. 1975. "Muslims and Jews in North Africa: Perceptions, Images, Stereotypes." In *Proceedings of the Seminar on Muslim-Jewish Relations in North Africa*, 13–27. New York: World Jewish Congress.

———. 1979. *The Jews of Arab Lands: A History and Source Book*. Philadelphia: Jewish Publication Society of America.

———. 1988. *The Language and Culture of the Jews of Sefrou, Morocco: An Ethnolinguistic Study*. Manchester: Manchester University Press.

Streicker, A. 1970. "Government and Revolt in Tripoli Regency, 1795–1855." M.A. thesis, Northwestern University.

Taggar, Y. 1981. "The Farhud in the Arabic Writings of Iraqi Statesmen and Writers" (in Hebrew). *Pe'amim* 8:38–45.

Tambiah, S. 1970. *Buddhism and the Spirit Cults in North-East Thailand*. Cambridge: Cambridge University Press.

Tilly, C. 1978. *From Mobilization to Revolution*. Reading, Mass.: Addison-Wesley.

Tilly, C., L. Tilly, and R. Tilly. 1975. *The Rebellious Century: 1830–1930*. London: J. M. Dent.

Tilly, L., and C. Tilly, eds. 1981. *Class Conflict and Collective Action*. Beverly Hills, Calif.: Sage.

Trimingham, J. 1971. *The Sufi Orders in Islam*. Oxford: Clarendon.

Tully, R. 1957. *Letters Written during a Ten Years' Residence at the Court of Tripoli*. Introduction and notes by S. Dearden. London: Arthur Baker.

Turner, V. 1957. *Schism and Continuity in an African Society*. Manchester: Manchester University Press.

———. 1969. *The Ritual Process: Structure and Anti-Structure*. Chicago: Aldine.

———. 1979. *Process, Performance, and Pilgrimage: A Study in Comparative Symbology*. Ranchi Anthropology Series, no. 1. New Delhi: Concept Publishers.

———. 1982. *From Ritual to Theatre: The Human Seriousness of Play*. New York: Performing Arts Journal Publications.

Turner, V., and E. Turner. 1978. *Image and Pilgrimage in Christian Culture: Anthropological Perspectives.* New York: Columbia University Press.

Udovitch, A. L., and L. Valensi. 1984. *The Last Arab Jews: The Communities of Jerba, Tunisia.* New York: Harwood.

Vajda, G. 1960. "Ahl al-Kitab." In *Encyclopaedia of Islam,* 1:264–66. Leiden: Brill.

Valensi, L. 1977. *On the Eve of Colonialism: North Africa before the French Conquest, 1790–1830.* Trans. K. J. Perkins. New York: Africana Publishing.

Von Grunebaum, G. 1951. *Mohammedan Festivals.* New York: Henry Schuman.

Wansbrough, J. 1977. Review of *A History of the Jews in North Africa,* vol. 1: *From Antiquity to the Sixteenth Century,* by H. Z. Hirschberg. *Maghreb Review* 2(3):41.

Waterbury, J. 1972. *North for the Trade: The Life and Times of a Berber Merchant.* Berkeley: University of California Press.

Welch, A. 1986. "Al-Ḳuran." In *Encyclopaedia of Islam,* 5:400–429. Leiden: Brill.

Wensinck, E. 1986. *Ritual and Belief in Morocco.* 2 vols. London: Macmillan.

Wright, J. 1969. *Libya.* New York: Praeger.

———. 1981. *Libya, a Modern History.* Baltimore: Johns Hopkins University Press.

Zafrani, H. 1968. "Une qaṣṣa de Tingir: Hymne à Bar Yoḥay." *Revue des Études Juives* 127:366–82.

Zarka, C. 1975. "Maison et société dans le monde arabe." *L'Homme* 16:87–102.

Zborowski, M., and H. Herzog. 1962. *Life Is with People.* New York: Schocken.

Zenner, W. P. 1972. "Some Aspects of Ethnic Stereotype Content in the Galilee: A Trial Formulation." *Middle Eastern Studies* 8:405–16.

Zohar, Z. 1981. "Halacha and Modernization: Responses of the Rabbis of Egypt to the Challenges of Modernization, 1882–1922" (in Hebrew). M. A. thesis, Hebrew University of Jerusalem.

———. 1983. "The Halakhic Teaching of Egyptian Rabbis in Modern Times" (in Hebrew). *Pe'amim* 16:65–88.

Zuaretz, F., A. Guweta, Ts. Shaked, G. Arbib, and F. Tayer, eds. 1960. *Libyan Jewry* (in Hebrew). Tel Aviv: Committee of Libyan Jewish Communities in Israel.

Index

'Abd a-Jalil, 41
'Abd al-Hamid, Sultan, 36, 144 n. 2
Abraham (biblical figure), 92, 93, 96, 120; distinguished from Ibrahim, 127; as name of proselyte, 149 n. 16
Abu-Jinah. *See* Bujnah
Adadi, Avraham Hai, 39
Aden, 158n
Agib, Yosef, 84, 86, 148–49 n. 7
Agiv, Khamus, 128
Agriculture, 11, 36, 70, 72, 74, 78; in relation to weddings and festivals, 56, 57, 61, 148 n. 14
Ahmed Bey, 24, 144 n. 8
Ahmed Razem Pasha, 44, 144 n. 2
Ahsan Husni Pasha, 48–50
Aleppo, 158 n. 9
Alexandria, 46, 114
Algeria, 10, 35, 79. *See also* Mzab
Ali Burghul. *See* el-Jezairli, Ali
Ali Pasha Qaramanli, 23, 25
Alliance Israelite Universelle, 42, 44, 121, 144 n. 11, 152 n. 10
Almohads, 5
Amrus, 48, 69, 112, 155 n. 29
Arabic: Hebrew word play related to, 9–10, 107; Jews speaking, 20, 53, 105, 121, 128, 135, 144–45 n. 15. *See also* Geniza, Cairo; Hebrew script
Army: exemption of residents of Tripoli and Benghazi, 145 n. 17; Jews recruited to Turkish, 13–14,

38, 45, 48–50, 132; soldiers of Yusef Pasha Qaramanli, 30, 33
Ashkenazim, 10, 21, 61, 67, 94, 125. *See also* Music: Hasidic; Yiddish
'Atiya, Sa'adan, 47

Baghdad, 158 n. 9
Balad, 130
Balbo, Italo, 16, 108, 109, 153 n. 17
Baraka, 141 n. 12. *See also* Marabouts
Barda, Rahamim, 24, 143 n. 13
Bar-mitzvah, 71, 147 n. 5
Bedouin, 72, 74, 76, 81, 87, 89, 139 n.3, 147 n. 13, 151 n. 31
Beirut, 113
Benghazi, 72, 83, 109, 110, 140 n. 6, 143 n. 14, 144–45 n. 15
Ben Yehudah Organization. *See* Hebrew; Zionism
Berbers, 53, 81, 122, 144 n. 7, 156 n. 38; in Algeria, 79; in Jebel Nefusa, 33, 39–40, 70; in Morocco, 34, 131, 147 n. 8
Bin'abbas, 54, 58, 60–61, 64
Blacks, 19, 38
Bride-price. *See* Marriage: and betrothal payments
Bujnah, Musa, 18, 83, 85–86, 88

Cairo, 113, 114. *See also* Geniza, Cairo

173

Camondo, Abraham, 42
Caravan trade, 24, 68–70
Cemeteries and tombstones, 20, 36, 87, 106, 143 n. 18
Charity, 57, 60–61, 104
Chief Rabbi. *See* Hakham Bashi
Christianity, 5, 85, 94
Christians, 37, 44, 96, 100, 101, 105, 131, 158 n. 13; attitudes of Libyan Muslims toward, 11, 107, 118, 148 n. 3; in Middle Ages, 4, 5, 6, 94, 130, 141. *See also* Dhimmi; Infidels; Non-Muslims
Circumcision, 7, 15, 86, 91–92, 93–94, 129, 149 n. 15, 150 n. 27, 151 n. 31
Clothing and headdress: distinguishing Jews from Muslims, 25, 26, 27–28, 40, 106, 142 n. 10; looted during riots, 119; in Jewish-Muslim commerce, 72, 73, 74, 93; wedding finery, 56, 60, 65
Collective Behavior, 112–16. *See also* Riots, anti-Jewish; Ritual: aspect of riots
Colonial rule, 97, 99, 103, 104, 110, 113, 115, 135, 139 n. 3
Commerce. *See* Economy; Peddlers
Communitas. *See* Ritual: aspect of riots
Concentration camps, 16, 109–10
Consuls, 44, 131, 135; American, 33; British, 24, 45; French, 24, 45, 144 n. 15; Italian, 44. *See also* Noah, Mordechai
Conversion, 94; to Islam, 12, 21–22, 83, 90, 112; to Judaism, 15, 83–88, 91, 148 n. 7, 149 n. 13
Corsairs, 13, 22, 23, 29, 33, 142 n. 6. *See also* Ransom of captives
Cosmetics, 56, 60, 70, 72–73, 75, 79
Courts, 41–42. *See also* Rabbinic courts and authority
Crafts. *See* Economy
Cultural borrowing: between Jews and Muslims, 2, 52–55, 61, 98; and distinctiveness, 14–15, 54–55, 57–67, 91–92, 125, 150 n. 27; dynamics of, 14, 52–55, 66, 124–27
Culture: anthropology and history, 4, 6, 17, 123–24; everyday rehearsal of, 135–37; and practical logic, 132–33. *See also* Ritual; Structural analysis
Cyrenaica, 62, 104, 110, 113, 115, 128. *See also* Benghazi

Damascus, 113
Dance, 62. *See also* Music
Day of Atonement. *See* Yom Kippur
Derna, 128
Dhikr. See 'Isawiyya
Dhimma, 39, 47, 130
Dhimmi, 5, 11, 82, 95, 96; classic meaning, 4, 7; and *dimmi*, 7, 134, 158 n. 10; synonymous with Jew, 7, 38, 131. *See also* Christians; Infidels; Non-Muslims; Pact of 'Omar, 157 n. 3; Protection
Dhu-l-ḥijja, 87, 92
Divorce, 59, 85
Dowry. *See* Marriage: and betrothal payments
Drinking. *See* Food and drink

Economy: craft specialization, 39, 73, 74, 79, 93, 101–2, 117, 124; commerce in countryside, 39, 48, 57, 147 n. 4; development under Ottomans, 36–37, 44, 71; importance of Jews during Italian period, 16, 100, 109; occupations ranked by honor, 81; during Qaramanli period, 19, 22, 25–26, 27; affected by religious days, 28, 43, 89, 143 n. 15; affected by strikes, 45, 47, 49; technical change, 100, 101–2. *See also* Caravan trade; Corsairs; Peddlers; Women: traditional work and roles

Education: during Italian period, 16, 99, 100, 102–3, 109; during Ottoman period, 36, 46, 144 nn. 11, 14

Egypt, 35. *See also* Cairo

Elul, 125–26

England, 45; British Military Administration, 16, 111–15, 117, 118, 119, 121, 122; conquest of Libya, 15, 109–10; subjects in Libya, 26, 109. *See also* Consuls: British

Esau (biblical figure). *See* Jacob and Esau

Ethnicity: Jews and Muslims under Italians, 72, 100, 107; principle of social structure in North Africa and Middle East, 20, 81, 123, 131; in Qaramanli Tripoli, 19, 31, 143 n. 17. See also *Hara*; Christians; Dhimmi; Italy; Maltese; New City; Non-Muslims

Europe, 69; eastern, 67, 141 n. 13, 151 n. 1, 154 n. 27, 155 n. 29. *See also* Ashkenazim; Yiddish

European influence: on Libya, 11, 13, 35, 44–45, 95, 105; on Libyan Jews, 15–16, 42–43, 45–46, 98–99, 102–4; on Middle East and North Africa, 4, 37. *See also* Colonial rule; Education; France; Italy

European languages, Jews' knowledge of, 22, 44, 46, 102

Exile, 30, 121, 128

Family, 15, 21, 63–66, 71, 145

Fascism, 16, 99, 103, 109. *See also* Concentration camps; Germany; Mussolini; Italy: racial laws

Fasting, 125

Festivals, 59, 72, 107, 124, 148 n. 14, 152–53 n. 12. *See also names of individual holidays*

Fez, 18, 152 n. 4

Fezzan, 15, 140 n. 6

Fifteenth of Ab, 65

Folklore: linked to literate culture and tradition, 8, 15; linked to society and politics, 2–3, 23, 108, 153 n. 21; Muslims vs. Jews in, 30–31, 82–83, 84–87, 90, 96, 107; oral literature and customs, 87–89; wedding customs, 59–63. *See also* Cultural borrowing; Dance; Magic; Music; Religious rules and laws; Ritual; Sabbath: Jewish games on the; Structural analysis; Texts

Food and drink: differences in Muslim and Jewish rules, 8–9, 96, 124, 148 n. 4; Muslim-Jewish commensuality, 15, 76–78, 153 n. 13; and word play, 9, 141 n. 13. *See also* Sabbath: food practices on the; Slaughtering

France: influence on North Africa, 35, 44, 53; nationals in Libya, 19, 119; during World War II, 109, 110. *See also* Alliance Israelite Universelle; Consuls: French; Paris

Friendship. *See* Ṣaḥbi

Funerals and mourning, 104, 157 n. 3. *See also* Cemeteries and tombstones

Games. *See* Sabbath, Jewish games on the; Sports

Garabulli, 72, 73

Garagush, 107

Gematria, 153 n. 18

Gender. *See* Wedding ceremonies and betrothal customs; Women

Geniza, Cairo, 6, 130, 141 n. 10, 146 n. 12

Germany, 109, 118

Ghardaia. *See* Mzab

Gharian, 39, 53, 60–65, 69, 90, 120, 125, 147 n. 5. *See also* Bin'abbas; Tighrinna

Ghoma, 40, 51

Governor, 106. *See also* Balbo, Italo;
  Ottoman: governors of Libya;
  *names of individual Ottoman
  governors*
Great Festival, 87, 89, 92–94, 116–
  17, 118, 120, 151 n. 30
Guweta, Yitzhaq, 22, 142 n. 7

Ha-Cohen, Mordechai, 49, 88–90,
  157–58 n. 8; personal background,
  10–11, 22, 45, 69–70, 157–58 n.
  8; sources of his book, 11, 37, 144
  n. 4; views of social and religious
  change, 38, 43, 45, 46
Hafez Pasha, 48–49, 51
Hagar (biblical figure), 93
Ḥajj, 93. *See also* Pilgrimages
Hakham Bashi, 46, 50. *See also*
  Hazzan, Eliyahu Bekhor;
  Shabbetai, Hizqiya
Halakha. See Religious rules and
  laws
Haman (biblical figure), 96
Hara: divisions of, 29, 30, 32;
  schools and synagogues in, 103,
  104, 124, 152–53 n. 12; secluded
  from Muslims, 16, 100–101, 107,
  111, 151 n. 30; symbol of
  foreigners, 34, 131. *See also* New
  City; Tripoli
Harem, 25–26
Hazzan, Eliyahu Bekhor, 96, 144 n.
  14
Hebrew, 53, 103, 127, 152 n. 10;
  script, 6, 107, 140 n. 8, 153 n. 18
Henna, 56, 60, 63. *See also*
  Cosmetics
Higgid Mordecaï. See Ha-Cohen,
  Mordechai
High Holidays, 125, 149 n. 18. *See
  also* Rosh ha-Shanah; Yom Kippur
Hizb el-Watani, 114–15, 117–18
Honor and shame, 30, 39, 62, 64, 77,
  80–81, 82, 132, 147 n. 13
Hosha'nah Rabbah, 150 n. 19
Hospitality, 76–78, 80, 81, 120

Housing and lodging, 76, 77, 124.
  See also Tripoli: ethnic residence
  patterns under Italians
Humor, 128, 155n. *See also* Arabic:
  Hebrew word play related to
Husni Pasha. *See* Ahsan Husni
  Pasha

Ibadi, 127
Ibn-Ghalbun, 27
'Id al-adḥa. See Great Festival
Infidels, 17, 32, 108, 112, 118, 134,
  135. *See also* Christians;
  Dhimmi; Non-Muslims
Inheritance, 38, 46–47
Iran, 52
Isaac (biblical figure), 92, 120
'Isawiyya, 28, 43, 44, 105
Ishmael (biblical figure), 92–93, 120,
  151 n. 31
Ishmaelites: meaning Arabs, 12, 39–
  40, 92–93; meaning Bedouin, 87
Israel, 2, 3, 117; migration to, 3, 97,
  98, 122, 150 n. 25, 156 n. 37
Istanbul, 40, 41, 42–43, 44. *See also*
  Ottoman; Porte; Sultan
Italian language, Jews' knowledge of,
  15, 16, 105
Italy: conquest of Libya and Arab
  resistance to, 15, 104, 105, 106,
  133; policy toward Jews, 99, 106,
  108, 109, 133; racial laws, 16, 99,
  103, 104, 108, 110; rule in Libya,
  75, 96, 97–110, 117; settlers in
  Tripoli, 100–101, 115, 124. *See
  also* European influence

Jacob and Esau (biblical figures), 88,
  90, 128, 149 n. 9
Jado, 110
Jarmon, Yehudah, 148–49 n. 7
Jebel Nefusa, 9, 11, 40, 55–57, 60,
  65, 70, 72, 76–78
Jerba, 1, 9, 126
Jerusalem, 65, 93

Jesus (biblical figure), 85, 107
Jewelry, 73, 74
Jewish Agency, 122, 156 n. 37
Jewish Quarter. See *Hara*
el-Jezairli, Ali, 23, 25, 26
Jihad, 156 n. 33. *See also* Riots, anti-
  Jewish
Joseph (biblical figure), 121, 128, 156
  n. 36

Kabbalah, 53, 156 n. 8
Kashrut, 8, 45, 77. *See also* Food and
  drink; Passover; Sabbath: food
  practices on the; Slaughtering
el-Kehya, 30, 31, 142–43 n. 11
Kerkeni, Ali Effendi, 42–43
Kettubah. See Marriage: contract
Khalfon, Avraham, 23–24, 148–49
  n. 7
Khalfon, David, 24
Khoms, 41
Kuffar. See Infidels
Kuloghlis, 19
Kuskus, 87. *See also* Food and drink

Lavi, Rabbi Shim'on, 106, 142 n. 1,
  153 n. 16
Leghorn, 142 n. 3

Ma'aruf, 78. See also *Ṣaḥbi*
Maccabee club, 104, 115, 121, 126
Maghrib. *See* North Africa
Magic, 53, 77
Mahmud Nedim Pasha, 42
Mahr. See Marriage: and betrothal
  payments
Mahzor. See Prayer: Jewish
Maimonides, 149 n. 12
Malta, Knights of, 18, 153 n. 16
Maltese, 19, 96, 100
Marabouts, 9, 12, 27–28, 126, 141 n.
  12
Marriage, 2, 29, 145 nn. 2, 3; and
  betrothal payments, 55, 58, 63;

contract, 55–56, 58–59, 62, 145 n.
  4. *See also* Wedding ceremonies
  and betrothal customs
Martyrdom, 94
Mecca, 93, 116
Mediterranean, 6, 64, 74, 80, 130
Mehmed Emin Pasha, 41
Mellah, 34. See also *Hara*; Morocco
Mesallata, 41, 69, 71, 72, 90, 91, 112
Middle Ages, 4, 5, 27, 34, 46, 94, 95,
  101, 130; late medieval Mamluke,
  143 n. 16; late medieval Tripoli,
  13, 130
Middle Eastern Jews, 1, 7, 42, 88, 122
Midrash, 92, 149 n. 9, 150 n. 28
Mimun, Ya'aqov, 41–42, 144–45 n. 15
Mishnah, 59, 62, 63, 65, 146 nn. 9,
  14, 18, 21
Misurata, 27, 106
Mitzvah, 22. *See also* Religious rules
  and laws
Mizrahi, Mordechai, 26
Mohar. See Marriage: and betrothal
  payments
Morocco, 38, 39, 117, 126, 131, 139
  n. 2, 140 n. 5, 147 n. 4, 158 n. 9;
  Jewish ritual and Muslims, 34, 57,
  76, 147 n. 8, 148 n. 14, 150 n. 23.
  See also Fez; Sefrou
Mosques, 15; Aqsa (in Jerusalem),
  111; Jam 'a Mahmud, 103. *See also*
  Prayer: Muslim
Muezzin. See Prayer: Muslim
Mufti, 156 n. 34
Muhammad, 4, 5, 12, 83, 85. See
  also *Mulid*
Muhammad Ali, 35
Muhammad Bey, 41, 51, 141 n. 15,
  144 n. 8
Muhammad Pasha Sha'ib al-'Ain, 87
Mulid, 28, 103
Music: Hasidic, 156 n. 1; Jews
  specialists in, 26; and weddings,
  56, 60, 85. See also *Qaṣṣa*
Mussolini, 108, 109. See also
  Fascism
Mzab, 1, 34

Names, 40, 107, 127, 144 n. 7
Nationalism, Libyan Arab, 3, 97,
    113, 114, 115, 118, 126–27, 133–
    35. *See also* Hizb el-Watani;
    Palestine; Riots, anti-Jewish;
    Zionism
Nazis. *See* Fascism; Germany; Italy:
    racial laws
New City: Jews moving into, 16,
    101–2, 111; and riots, 111, 114;
    school and synagogue attendance
    in, 103, 104, 152–53 n. 12. See
    also *Hara*; Tripoli
Newspapers, 45, 112, 113, 144 n. 4,
    152 n. 3, 154 n. 26, 155 n. 31
New Year. *See* Rosh ha-Shanah
Noah, Mordechai, 19, 25, 33
Non-Muslims, 25, 37, 127, 145 nn.
    16, 17. *See also* Christians;
    Dhimmi; Infidels
North Africa, 1, 21, 53, 67

Ottoman: Empire and direct rule in
    Libya, 13, 23–24, 36; governors of
    Libya, 13–14, 35–38, 41–50, 119,
    144 nn. 2, 10; reforms in Libya,
    11, 13, 34, 35–38, 41–50, 95, 132,
    152 n. 4; rule in Tripoli, 12, 34, 70,
    75, 96, 98, 100–101, 119. *See also*
    Army; Qaramanli period; Taxes;
    Turks; Tribes: resistance to
    government; Young Turks

Pact of 'Omar, 157 n. 3
Palestine, 18, 111, 113, 142 n. 7, 155
    n. 31
Palestine brigade, 110
Paris, 42. *See also* France
Pashas: Qaramanli, 19, 22–27, 30–
    32, 142 n. 11. *See also* Ottoman:
    governors of Libya; *and names of
    individual governors*
Passover, 86–87
Patron-client relations. *See*
    Protection

Peddlers: Jewish, 14–15, 68–81,
    124; Muslim, 73, 79
Pentecost. *See* Shavu'ot
Phylacteries, 77
Pilgrimages, 93, 126, 135
Piracy. *See* Corsairs
Pogrom. *See* Riots, anti-Jewish
Poland. *See* Europe: eastern
Polemics. *See* Religious disputes
Polygamy, 21
Population, 68, 140 n. 6, 156 n. 37;
    of Jews in the Middle East, 3, 7.
    See also Israel: migration to;
    Tripoli: population of
Porte, 18, 24, 36. *See also* Istanbul;
    Ottoman; Sultan
Prayer: Jewish, 10, 56–57, 77, 146 n.
    8, 157 n. 4; Muslim, 44, 105, 125,
    157 n. 4. *See also* 'Isawiyya;
    Synagogues
Proselytization. *See* Conversion
Prostitution, 101
Protection: in countryside, 38–41,
    77; logic of, 38, 40, 41, 48–51,
    106, 119, 133; during riots, 112,
    119, 158 n. 11. *See also* Honor and
    shame; Qaramanli period
Purim, 96; special holiday of Tripoli,
    24

Qadi, 107, 111, 126
Qaid, 21, 25, 30
Qaramanli period, 13, 70;
    administration, 142–43 n. 11;
    dynasty, 18–34, 35, 130, 131, 135;
    Jews connected to court, 21–26,
    30. *See also* Economy; Pashas;
    Taxes; *names of individual
    Pashas and Beys*
Qaṣṣa, 83, 148 n. 6
Qiddushin. *See* Marriage: and
    betrothal payments
Qur'an, 8, 47, 61, 91, 122, 127, 140
    n. 8
Qusabat. *See* Mesallata

Rabbi, 56, 126, 140 n. 5. *See also* Hakham Bashi; *and names of individual rabbis*
Rabbinic courts and authority, 11, 21, 30, 39, 46, 86, 87, 144 n. 14, 144–45 n. 15
Raccah, Saul, 42
Rajab Pasha, 44, 50
Ramadan, 125–26
Ransom of captives, 19, 22, 29, 32
Raqah, Ya'aqov, 148–49 n. 7
Religious disputes, 5–6, 11, 82–83, 88–90, 92; expressed in customs, 15, 83–84, 89–95. *See also* Sabbath
Religious rules and law, 2, 15, 21, 22, 94, 98, 127, 140 n. 8, 157 n. 3; overlapping Muslim and Jewish concepts, 8–9, 58–59, 146 n. 12, 150–51 n. 29; relation between laws and customs, 10, 54, 63–65. See also *Bar-mitzvah;* Circumcision; Conversion; Food and drink; *Kashrut;* Passover; Phylacteries; Rabbinic courts and authority; Sabbath; Slaughtering; Texts
Riots, anti-Jewish, 16–17, 93, 97–98, 109–22, 133–37, 151 n. 1, 154 n. 24. *See also* Protection; Ritual
Ritual: and cultural processes, 128–30; of daily contact, 2, 81, 93, 99, 107, 133; immersion, 86; and politics, 135–37, 158 nn. 9, 14; aspects of riots, 17, 115–21, 154–55 n. 28; 155 n. 29, 158 n. 14; sexuality in, 61–64, 66. *See also* Folklore; Magic; Religious rules and law; Social drama; Symbols, Jews as
Rosh ha-Shanah, 9, 125, 149 n. 18

Sabbatai Zvi, 18
Sabbath, 45, 87, 143 n. 17, 144 n. 15, 150 n. 25; food practices on the, 84–85, 88, 90–91, 149 nn. 8, 10; Italian policies concerning, 99, 108, 109; Jewish games on the, 29, 31, 33, 131, 135; religious disputes and differences concerning, 84–91, 94; synagogue worship, 57, 104, 128, 153 n. 13. *See also* Religious rules and law
Safed, 142 n. 7
Ṣaḥbi, 76, 78–79
Sanusi, 113, 115
Sefrou, 1, 69, 117, 147 n. 6
Seliḥot, 125–26, 127
Sephardi tradition, 10, 21, 125. *See also* Hakham Bashi; Spanish Jews
Servants. *See* Slaves and servants
Shabbetai, Hizqiya, 50, 145 n. 18
Shame and modesty, 24, 30, 55, 70, 75–76. *See also* Honor and shame
Sharṭ. See Marriage: and betrothal payments
Shavu'ot, 33–34
Shaykh el beled, 42
Sheikh, Jewish, 120
Shiism, 52, 136
Shulḥan 'Arukh, 10, 141 n. 13. *See also* Texts
Sidi, 84–85, 107. *See also* Ritual of daily contact
Silver, Torah-scroll ornament, 86. *See also* Jewelry
Slaughtering, 83, 87, 89, 92–94, 96, 150 n. 19, 151 n. 30. *See also* Food and drink
Slaves and servants, 24, 39, 40, 145 n. 17. *See also* Ransom of captives
Social drama, 17, 119, 120, 121, 133
Spanish Jews, 7, 18, 53
Sports, 13, 29–34, 104, 131, 143 n. 18
Structural analysis, 87–89, 93–94, 116, 147 n. 8, 148 n. 14; linking Jewish and Muslim society, 9, 23, 53, 123. *See also* Rituals; Symbols, Jews as
Sudan, 19, 24, 69

Sufi. *See* 'Isawiyya

Sukkot, 56, 57. *See also* Hosha'nah Rabbah

Sultan, 23, 24. *See also* 'Abd al-Hamid; Istanbul; Porte; Ottoman

Symbols, Jews as, 32–34, 76, 77, 118–19, 134–37, 156 n. 33, 158 n. 13. *See also* Protection: logic of; Ritual; Women

Synagogues, 15, 57, 100, 103–4, 152 n. 11, 152–53 n. 12; destroyed, 112, 142 n. 7; Muslim opposition to building of, 25, 27; sermons in, 67, 128; social aspects of, 27, 49. *See also* Prayer: Jewish; *Seliḥot*

Tabernacles. *See* Sukkot

Tajura, 69, 73, 112

Talmud, 10, 55, 63, 77, 86, 141 n. 13, 145 n. 4, 147 n. 10, 149 nn. 8, 10, 11, 14

Tanzimat. See Ottoman: reforms in Libya

Tawwaf. See Peddlers

Taxes: during Ottoman period, 48–50, 145 n. 17; during Qaramanli period, 21, 23, 25. *See also* Army

Tel Aviv, 101, 152 n. 9

Temple, destruction of, 56, 65–66

Tena'im. See Marriage: and betrothal payments

Ten Commandments, 90

Texts: as a factor in social life, 2, 124, 127–28; Jews more literate than Muslims, 52, 147 n. 8, 148 n. 14; and non-literate members of society, 7, 9, 15; related to wedding customs, 54–55, 59, 65. *See also* Folklore: linked to literate culture and tradition; Hebrew; Midrash; Mishnah; Religious rules and laws; Talmud

Theology. *See* Religious disputes

Tighrinna, 120

Tishri, 56, 87, 149 n. 18, 150 n. 19. *See also* High Holidays

Torah, 85, 87, 88, 92, 140 n. 8, 156 n. 38, 157 n. 4

Torah scroll, 57, 86, 88, 112, 152–53 n. 12

Travel and transportation, 72–74

Tribes: in Jebel Nefusa, 11, 12, 39–40; resistance to government, 19, 24, 40–41

Tripoli: administration under Ottomans, 42, 47; city gates during Ottoman and Italian periods, 34, 36, 100, 108, 143 n. 17; ethnic residence patterns under Italians, 16, 100–101, 108; population of, 20–21, 29, 36, 100; walls of during Qaramanli period, 20, 29–30, 32; *See also* Ethnicity; *Hara*; New City

Tripolitania. *See names of individual towns*

Tully, Miss, 18, 21, 26, 142 n. 3

Tully, Richard, 142 n. 3

Tunis, 33, 90, 148–49 n. 7

Tunisia, 24, 83, 126, 144 n. 15. *See also* Jerba; Tunis

Turks: cede Libya to Italians, 15, 139 n. 3; distinct from Arabs, 12, 19, 106. *See also* Army; Ottoman; Young Turks

Ukraine. *See* Europe: eastern

'Ulema, 27

Umma, 130

United States Marines, 24

Wadai, 12, 27

Wali. See Ottoman: governors of Libya

Watan, 130, 134. *See also* Nationalism, Libyan Arab

Wedding ceremonies and betrothal customs, 53–67

Widowhood, 59, 60

Women, 74, 82, 84, 91, 102, 103, 152 n. 10; Jews likened to, 13, 14, 38,

68, 79–81, 133; in Muslim villages, 70, 71, 74; traditional work and roles, 59, 73–74. *See also* Marriage; Ritual; Structural analysis
World War I, 15
World War II, 15, 16, 97–98, 102, 103, 104, 109–11, 135

Yahudi, 79, 107
Yefren, 40, 69, 90, 157 n. 4
Yiddish, 10, 67, 141 n. 13. *See also* Ashkenazim
Yom Kippur, 56, 65, 125, 143 n. 12, 149 n. 18

Young Turks, 15, 36, 45, 46, 50, 95
Yusef Pasha Qaramanli, 12, 21, 23–26, 29, 33, 34, 35, 41

Zanzur, 112
Zawia, 25, 112, 133, 155 n. 29
Zgharit, 60, 66, 112, 118
Zionism, 7, 97, 104, 110, 114, 118, 126–27, 155 n. 31, 156 n. 36. *See also* Hebrew; Israel; Jewish Agency; Maccabee club
Zliten, 41
Zoroastrians, 4
Zuara, 122